"Simple, uncluttered, apostolic, organic, and eminently doable. I heartily recommend this book to you."

—From the foreword by **Alan Hirsch**, author, *The Forgotten Ways*

"Neil has written a much-needed book. More than raising up pastors and church leaders, the key issue today is raising up disciples if we want to see lives changed and radical transformations take place in our society. Not only is the book good; what Neil recommends makes a difference. I speak from experience. We have used Neil's LTGs for years at NorthWood and have found them core to making disciples. I am convinced that what is needed today is more writing and teaching on discipleship, but resulting in a different kind of disciple. Neil understands that and writes about it."

—**Bob Roberts**, pastor, NorthWood Church; author, *Transformation*, *Glocalization*, and *The Multiplying Church*

"Neil Cole has discovered a startling new style of Christian living, one that's 100 percent free from the standard hassling, coercion, and constant sermonizing that drives people away from church.

"Pastors love it! After centuries of bashing the guy in the pew, pastors can now be free from the futile effort to browbeat people into being 'good Christians.' In fact, they can relax and let God do the heavy lifting!

"Best of all, *Search & Rescue* actually works. Neil Cole's network of friends and co-workers is the fastest-growing informal fellowship of believers in the Western world. Why? Because it instantly attracts every person who desires an exciting role as a genuine hero in the greatest adventure of our time."

—**James Rutz**, author, *Megashift*

"Neil Cole evidences all the fire and intensity of a lifeguard in *Search & Rescue*. He brings to his job of discipling people the same or greater determination than he brought to his job on the beach. In this practical book, Neil gives you everything you need to start patrolling your own beach if you want to get serious about lifesaving efforts."

—**Reggie McNeal**, author, *The Present Future*

"I love it! I will recommend this book to every person on our staff and every leader in our network. No one knows more about how to make and multiply disciples than Neil Cole, and in *Search & Rescue* he shares it with all of us."

—**Dave Ferguson**, Community Christian Church/New Thing;
author, *The Big Idea*

"Everyone dreams about being a hero; not many are willing to do what it takes to be one. Inside every one of us is a desire to live a life of significance. In order to do that, we must live for a purpose bigger than ourselves. In *Search & Rescue*, Neil Cole clearly defines what it means to be a person of significance, what it takes to be a hero in our day, and how to pursue a life worthy of the name Jesus Christ. Warning! This is not another self-help book; it will challenge you to save others' lives. If you read it, believe it, and do it, God will use your life to change the world. Seek not to be a person of success, but seek to be a person of value, because God is looking for ordinary people who will live by his Word and do extraordinary things. This generation needs true heroes. Will you seek to be one? If so, you must read this book."

—**Jaeson Ma**, lead director, Campus Church Networks;
author, *The Blueprint*

"Using his experience as a lifeguard to illustrate, Neil Cole makes Christian disciple making come alive. A captivating story that is solidly biblical and down to earth, with practical application. Right on target!"

—**Robert E. Coleman**, distinguished professor of evangelism and discipleship,
Gordon-Conwell Theological Seminary

SEARCH & RESCUE

BECOMING A DISCIPLE WHO MAKES A DIFFERENCE

NEIL COLE

BakerBooks

Grand Rapids, Michigan

© 2008 by Neil Cole

Published by Baker Books
a division of Baker Publishing Group
P.O. Box 6287, Grand Rapids, MI 49516-6287
www.bakerbooks.com

Printed in the United States of America

Library of Congress Cataloging-in-Publication Data
Cole, Neil, 1960–
     Search & rescue : becoming a disciple who makes a difference / Neil Cole.
        p.   cm.
     Includes bibliographical references.
     ISBN 978-0-8010-1309-6 (cloth : alk. paper)
     1. Discipling (Christianity) 2. Missions—Cross-cultural studies. 3. Christianity and cul-
ture. I. Title. II. Title: Search and rescue.
     BV4520.C62 2008
     269'.2—dc22   2007047379

Published in association with the literary and marketing agency of C. Grant and Company.

This book is dedicated to those heroes who are willing to blaze new trails for the sake of God's kingdom, those who have sacrificed security and salaries to show people the way. Your tribe is increasing and the world will soon show it.

So Others May Live

Motto of the U.S. Coast Guard Rescue Swimmers

Contents

Part 2   A System for Making and Multiplying Disciples

Foreword

It was Oliver Wendell Holmes who said, "I would not give a fig for the simplicity this side of complexity, but I would give my life for the simplicity on the other side of complexity." Simple answers, offered without taking into account the vast intricacies of human life in an infinite universe, are close to being outright worthless to any human being in need of real truth that addresses real, live situations. Simplicity this side of complexity simply doesn't fit or resonate with our condition and is not worth a dime. However, when simplicity presents itself beyond the complexities that we all face, and it takes into account the nuanced and often perplexing situation we find ourselves in, then these truths are worth all that we own. I think this is partly what Jesus was alluding to in his parables of the pearl of great price and the hidden treasure. Some truths are worth serious personal investment. Neil Cole's writings are of this order. Sell everything and buy in!

Search and Rescue brings to light a suspicion that I have long held about Neil—that behind the catchy slogans and folksy narratives that lace his teaching lies authentic spiritual genius. Neil's genius (and it is that) confers upon the reader genuine, and all too easily lost, insights into the organic nature and workings of the kingdom of God. He just seems to have a real gift in putting his apostolic index finger on things that are essential to the ongoing life of the church, and he does it in his characteristically generous and disarming way. *Organic Church* is a case in point, but *Search and Rescue* is no exception. Make no mistake, in this book Neil is subversively reworking your, and by extension your church's, priorities around what is most essential in our day—the lost art of disciple making.

And it is hard to find someone more qualified for the job. You see, Neil is a real, live hero. He is a Californian lifeguard who has been involved in actually saving many people from drowning. He has also pioneered a missionary movement across the world. He knows heroism from the inside. He knows the real meaning of "search and rescue" even at risk of his own life. He is someone we can trust to guide us here. And the metaphor of lifesaving, from which the book derives its name, extends far beyond individual heroic acts in which one risks his or her life in the waters. Neil uses it to describe the kind of quality that should infuse any authentic following of Jesus. This book is deliberately designed to awaken the heroic potential in and among Jesus's people. In effect, *Search and Rescue* is an agenda for invoking spiritual heroism in our day.

This agenda goes beyond merely giving a deeper meaning and character to our following of Jesus in the twenty-first century. Neil suggests a whole lot of ways in which we can actually activate spiritual heroism. Neil's previous revolutionary work, *Cultivating a Life for God*, literally launched a movement. Not only did it give rise to the Church Multiplication Associates (CMA), but the Life Transformation Group (LTG) concept introduced therein became a worldwide phenomenon as people from all walks of life and denominations began using it as a means of loving God, following Jesus, and doing kingdom mission. So in this new work, Neil seriously enhances the previous insights of *Cultivating a Life for God* by adding hard-won insights gained from six years of application and development in the white heat of grassroots mission among the lost.

This book is simple, uncluttered, apostolic, organic, and eminently doable. I heartily recommend it to you.

Neil, you are not only a hero, you are *my* hero.

Alan Hirsch, author of *The Forgotten Ways*;
coauthor of *The Shaping of Things to Come*;
founding director of the innovative
Forge Mission Training Network

Preface

At the end of my previous book, *Organic Church*, I wrote the words of the Hobbit Samwise Gamgee, the trusted friend of Frodo Baggins, from the second film of *The Lord of the Rings*. After narrowly escaping complete devastation, Sam's companion, Frodo, has just said in exhaustion and exasperation from having to bear the responsibility of saving the world, "I can't do this." Sam inspires Frodo to carry on once more.

Sam says, "It's like the great stories, Mr. Frodo, the ones that really mattered. Full of darkness and danger they were. And sometimes you didn't want to know the end, because how could the end be happy? How could the world go back to the way it was when so much bad had happened? But in the end it's only a passing thing, this shadow. Even darkness must pass. A new day will come. And when the sun shines, it will shine out the clearer. Those were the stories that stayed with you, that meant something. Even if you were too small to understand why. But I think, Mr. Frodo, I do understand. I know now. Folks in those stories had lots of chances of turning back, only they didn't. They kept going because they were holding on to something."

"What are we holding on to, Sam?" Frodo sighs, still overcome by the near defeat of the previous moment.

In determination to help his brother for whom he would gladly die, Sam lifts Frodo to his feet, looks him sternly in the eye, and says, "That there's some good in this world, Mr. Frodo, and it's worth fighting for."

We all need a friend like Sam when we face the overwhelming odds of this battle we are in. We also need to be a friend like Sam. The struggle against the evil that dominates the world is bad enough; to go through this fight alone is too much. We must have a small band of brothers and sisters who would give their lives for us, for the cause, for Jesus.

Yes, there is conflict. Yes, there is evil that wants only to destroy you. Yes, there will be pain and loss. But the struggle is worth it. Any great story has conflict; this is what makes the story worth telling. There would not be three major motion pictures, dozens of Oscars, and a billion dollars in revenue if there were no struggle involved with the *Lord of the Rings* tales. If the Hobbits never left home but stayed in the Shire, under the party tree smoking pipe weed, we would not really be all that interested in their stories. The conflict makes the struggle compelling.

If we can stick together and pull each other through, much like Sam and Frodo, I believe we can defeat the enemy and win this war. There will be great stories to tell our children's children. These are the days when grocers, high school kids, nurses, and simple gardeners, like Sam, overcome incredible evil to bring change and hope back to humanity.

This is what you were born to be: a hero. You were created for good works that have been foreordained by God to destroy evil strongholds and set captives free. Do not settle for rusting in the harbor over the decades. Set sail on the oceans of risk, and let God lead you to stories that are worthy of being told.[1]

This book is about being the hero you were born to become.

We do not need men in tights with capes and mutant powers. Wizard wunderkinds with magic wands and flying broomsticks cannot help us. Fictional heroes fail to fill the void of the real thing. We need accountant heroes, store clerks who will save a life, or grade school teachers who sacrifice themselves for their students—real-life people who rise to an occasion because deep in their hearts is something noble and true. That is what we need today.

Jesus said his prime directive was to search for and rescue the lost. He also said, "As the Father has sent me, so I send you" (John 20:21 NRSV). Christians are called to the greatest mission in human history—the freedom and salvation of those who are drowning in the bondage of evil. In a very real sense, we are on a search and rescue team sent to find those who are drowning and to bring them hope and life, the same hope and life that we have received. We are all called to be kingdom heroes to this generation.

Occasionally we see true heroism rise out of our people, and I will share many stories throughout this book. Take, for example, the passengers aboard United Flight 93, which was about to become another explosive weapon dropping out of the sky onto our nation's capital. With courage and conviction these passengers yelled, "Let's roll," and took on their captors. When their plane went down in the fields of Pennsylvania, they saved many lives by sacrificing their own. Mission accomplished.

My eyes water when I hear stories like that. They call out to some place deep in my heart. I want to be like those heroes. How about you?

In this book we will learn from a hero who is near the end of his life as he passes on to his younger apprentice what it takes to be heroic. In a dark, damp, and lonely place, the apostle Paul challenges his young apprentice Timothy to become the next hero by creating more heroes for succeeding generations. Though I tell stories of many heroes in this book, the true hero is Paul; we will learn from his example more than any other.

In the eighties I worked as a lifeguard. I saved lives. A few times I had to risk my own life in the process. In hindsight those experiences turned out to be more than just a summer job to get me through college and seminary; they were foundational for my future.

Often, after I share a few stories of my working nearly a decade as a lifeguard on the beaches of Los Angeles, people tell me that I am still a lifeguard, but in a different ocean. I fully understand what they mean. I am not trying to say that I'm a hero, though I hope to be one when the occasion arises. I have learned something, however, about saving lives that I believe is pertinent to this important subject of heroism.

For many years I shared most of these stories only with my kids and an occasional youth group. As I studied the New Testament, with some distance from my lifeguarding days and in hindsight, I began to see how lessons learned more than twenty years ago are relevant today. Weaving together lessons from lifesaving and Paul's last letter written to Timothy, I will expand on how ordinary people can become heroes and save lives.

In this book I present principles and a simple tool that can be used to rescue thousands of victims who are drowning. I wrote this book with the hope that it may capture your imagination and cause you to dream of what your life can and should be. Jesus paid a steep price to call you out of darkness and into his light—not so you can be safe and comfortable, but so that your life can ignite others to live the same sort of life.

One thing I have learned is that regular people can be the greatest heroes, and in fact they represent the type of hero we need most today. Will you be a hero? Will you engage in the self-sacrificial work of search and rescue? This is my prayer, which bathes the pages of this book. Join us in changing the world again.

Acknowledgments

To the heroes I am privileged to work with as we take God's kingdom into dark places.

First, I want to acknowledge my spiritual family that is Awakening Chapel and especially my LTG brothers, Josh Wilshusen, Chris Wright, Gary Parker, and Scott Hughes. You have walked with me as brothers in Christ through thick and thin. I see Jesus in you more each week and that is a great encouragement to me.

I also want to thank Jaeson Ma, Caleb Lin, Sam Kim, Alyson Hsiao, Anita Lee, Mike Han, and all the passionate students (too many to mention by name) at UCLA who are some of the boldest and most motivated heroes I have ever worked with. What a privilege to labor alongside these heroes for the next generation! You are the seedlings of what is to come.

Phil Helfer, Ed Waken, Paul Kaak, Dezi Baker, Brad Fieldhouse, Mike Jentes, Angela Bokkes, and my associates at CMA who watch my back and lift me up in the midst of the battle, you are the people who make me a better person, and I sincerely hope I can do the same for you.

Thom Wolf, Tom Julien, George Patterson, and David Black are the men who invested in my own understanding of what it means to be a follower of Christ and to make disciples. I carry in me your spiritual DNA and have passed it on to others. I am your Timothy, and you have each been a spiritual father to me.

Finally, I wish to acknowledge my wife and best friend on earth, Dana, for her always practical voice of wisdom. The more I know you, the more I love you. Walking through life beside you is a grand and glorious journey. Thank you.

Between a Rock and a Hard Place

The Need for True Heroes

It was another warm, sunny weekend with large crowds at Venice Beach. Venice is world renowned for drawing large crowds of crazy people. This day was no exception. The surf was big and the crowds bigger. On a day like this I expected to make rescues, but I never expected what was about to happen.

Supervisory tower of Venice North with the breakwater in the background.

This rescue should not have taken place. I deserved no glory. I did not do everything the way I should have. My boss wasn't sure whether to write a commendation or write me up for being foolish and breaking the rules. It wasn't even my area, and in fact I didn't do much. I just showed up and was trying to do what was needed in a harrowing circumstance.

The Venice section of beaches is divided into two areas: Venice North and Venice South, each with a supervisory tower as well as other towers. I was working at a tower next to the supervisory tower in the Venice North area. The supervisory station is at a beach point at the end of which is a man-made breakwater—a row of large rocks running parallel to shore providing some break from the surf. More than one lifeguard always mans the supervisory towers, they have a rescue vehicle assigned to them, and they always have a higher ranking and more experienced personnel than the other towers. At the time, I was a third-year guard who didn't have much seniority.

Our lieutenant, Don "Rosie" Rosenthal, who supervised the whole area of Venice, didn't have a tower. He cruised the beach in a truck and stayed at head-quarters when not on patrol. I chose to work the Venice area because of Rosie's reputation as a good lieutenant. He was also an old friend of my dad and uncle. They lifeguarded and competed with each other when they were younger. Rosie's son and I were in the same rookie lifeguard class, much like our fathers.

On this particular day there was another guard in the tower with me be-cause it was a busy summer weekend. He was older and more experienced than I, but this was my assigned tower, so he gave me a lot of respect, prob-ably more than I deserved. That day we both noticed two things: a boat was getting dangerously close to the rocks in front of the Venice North station and was rocking up and down on some pretty big waves, and the lifeguards in the main tower were not doing anything about it. We assumed this because a lifeguard never goes anywhere without his or her floatation device, which is known as a rescue can. When a guard is in the tower, the bright red plastic can hangs from the roof at the front of the tower to let the other guards know that he or she is inside (see the picture on p. 17). In this case, the can was still hanging from the tower, and the rescue truck remained parked alongside the tower. We could not see that the guards in the tower were moving, even though they were right in front of the impending shipwreck.

The impending crisis was causing a crisis in our tower. We weren't sure what to do. It is one thing to respond to an urgent situation that is occurring in front of a tower next to you; it is quite another to do so when that tower belongs to the boss. Besides, how could anyone miss such an obvious emergency?

Suddenly the boat surrendered to the power of the ocean and crashed up against the rocks. The boat's mast was flying up and down on the rocks like

The Venice North tower.

The rescue can hanging in Venice North tower, with the breakwater off in the distance.

a fly swatter desperately trying to kill a fly. Yet neither my supervisor nor his comrades responded. That's enough, I decided; I no longer cared about the reputation of my boss. I ran down the beach at full speed, leaving my area under the watchful care of the other guard.

White water was spewing high above the jetty, and the mist, carried by the wind, fell all around like raindrops. The boat was lodged in the rocks and still bowing continuously to the lordship of the sea and the unforgiving judgment of the rock jetty. I ran out to the point and started to climb up over the rocks, timing my entrance between the waves. When I got close to the boat, I saw three middle-aged men full of panic, gripping the rails of the boat with knuckles as white as their huge eyeballs.

Climbing over the wet rocks, I got down to the boat and took hold of the rail high on the tip of the bow. I reached out to the closest passenger, who quickly took my hand and climbed off the boat, over me and onto the rocks. As I was reaching the next boater, I yelled to them, asking how many were on board. Then I told them all to climb back over the rocks to the other side as quickly as possible before the next wave came.

Soon I discovered the location of the other lifeguards. Three or four were stroking as hard as they could through the surf to get to the boat. I also noticed that the Santa Monica rescue boat, called Baywatch, was arriving. In their hurry to reach the boaters, the lifeguards had left the rescue can on its hook in front of the tower. They had chosen to swim all the way around the breakwater from the south side because it was too risky to climb up on the rocks with such high waves hitting them. I was soon to realize the wisdom of their decision and the recklessness of my own.

While assisting the third and final victim off the boat, the lull in the swells ended and a wave picked up the ship. With one hand I was holding on to the man who was halfway off the boat; with the other hand I was holding the bow rail. So when the surge of water lifted the ship over the rocks, I was lifted off my feet. My life hung literally between a rock and a hard place. My supervisor, swimming hard for the boat, said to me later that he was certain I would be crushed under the weight of the boat. But for the grace of God, I am sure I would have. Instead, the surge lifted me off the rocks, and I hung in the air a few seconds, holding both boat and boater. The surge subsided, and I was gently let down to the rock I had been on.

With speed and efficiency I managed to get the man off the boat just as another lifeguard handed me the hook from the rescue boat. I tried to attach it to the same rail I had been clinging to but was in too much of a hurry to do it right. My ride in the sky over the rocks shook me up. Fortunately, the other lifeguard helped me attach it. Immediately the boat was towed off the rocks, through a few waves and out to safer water.

Just as I was climbing back off the rocks and the other lifeguard was trying to swim back out, I noticed the largest wave yet building fast to crash on the rocks. I hesitated, watching my fellow lifeguard to make sure he made it out. He did, but my hesitation was a mistake. When the wave struck I was blown completely off the rocks. I remember flying through the air with white water all around me and landing on my back on rocks about six feet below. The amazing thing is that I came down gently without a broken bone or even a bruise. I did have a slight abrasion on my left shoulder, just enough to have some blood trickle down for dramatic effect as I rose up out of the wet rocks fully intact. When I stood up, I noticed that Rosie's truck was there and he was watching, along with dozens of bystanders and three shaken boaters. They broke into spontaneous applause as I emerged from the water.

The rocks where I was thrown into the air while rescuing the shipwreck in big surf.

Later that week I received calls in my tower from other lifeguards to congratulate me on such a dramatic rescue. I had many chances to tell them that it was God who set everything in motion and protected me in this dangerous endeavor. A letter of commendation was placed in my file. As a result of

The same rocks in big surf.

that one rescue, I was known as a gutsy lifeguard.

Rarely in my life have I felt God's grace exhibited more blatantly. I was set up. From the beginning, every piece was put in place for me to come and make a difference. God did the rest. In all the rescues we have to make, he orchestrates the situation and choreographs our moves. We are privileged to play a part, but he is the one who does all the heavy lifting.

Glories await those who are willing to follow God into the dangerous places to rescue the lost and shipwrecked. Granted, none of us deserves the glory, but God delights in sharing his glory with us. It is his nature, his way. But we will never know the glory if we play it safe. If we count our own lives too valuable, we will never know the great things God has in store for us.

Being Proactive and Preventive

The Los Angeles County Ocean Lifeguards used to be its own department. A few years ago the department became a division of the LA County Fire Department. In many ways this has been an appropriate marriage. There are some important distinctions, however, in the way a lifeguard operates and the way a firefighter operates that could cause tension.

Both the lifeguard and the firefighter save lives and respond to emergencies with dedication, heroism, and quick action. Both are servants to the community. Both are well trained for emergencies. Both deal with life-or-death situations and, at times, can put their own lives on the line (though the firefighter is more often in greater danger than the lifeguard). Both need to be in good physical shape.

One of the biggest differences in the way a firefighter functions and the way a lifeguard functions is in how each responds to emergencies. A firefighter's response, by necessity, is a reactionary response to a problem. Firefighters wait in the firehouse until a problem is already in process and they respond. In fact we have a colloquialism that refers to this. When someone is functioning in a reactionary way to a chaotic set of problems, we say they are running around "putting out fires."

Lifeguards, however, are more proactive and preventive than firefighters. A lifeguard is trained to spot problems before they happen and work to prevent situations that could cause serious injury or loss of life. The best lifeguards are not the ones who make the most rescues, but the ones who prevent the need for rescues.

A lifeguard is assigned to more than a tower; he or she is to cover the entire beach in front of the tower and extending as far as the next tower on either side. That way there is constant overlap of coverage.

Lifeguards are trained to read the ocean, identify dangerous currents, and relocate patrons before they become victims. Some of the daily activities a lifeguard does that are proactive and preventive include picking up broken glass in the sand; assigning safe places and times for surfing, so that surfers do not strike swimmers with their surfboards; waving people away from rip currents or riptides; keeping unsafe floatation devices out of the water; keeping people off rock jetties; waving boats away from shore before they get too close; not allowing fires or charcoal barbeques on the beach. The list goes on; even keeping dogs off the beach is a form of preventive lifeguarding. Lifeguards do a whole lot more than soak up the sun and flirt with sunbathers on the beach.

Unlike lifeguards, though, firefighters can react only to existing problems. Like Smokey the Bear says, "Only *you* can prevent forest fires." Firefighters cannot. They react to whatever emergency occurs and strive to put out the fires.

In the spiritual climate of today's world, we need both types of response. There is little doubt that the world is already in crisis, and hell is already consuming lives all around us. Followers of Christ must take the initiative and go about bringing change before the crisis gets out of control. We are called to watch for the signs and do whatever we can to bring hope, peace, and health to the society in which we live—being salt to the world.

Each church should cooperate with other churches in a community to "watch the water" and take preventive measures to make sure that danger and darkness are kept to a minimum. If Christians started to take responsibility for our communities and cities, began being more proactive in prayer, and established a real presence of grace and truth, we could have a huge impact.

Between a Rock and a Soft Place: Paul's Letter to Timothy

In this book we will be learning from a letter written almost two thousand years ago by a man in a dark, damp hole carved out of stone with bars over the hole. From this place in Rome, Paul wrote his last letter to Timothy, his son in the faith.

This is one of my favorite books in the Bible because it is written by a man who, while he is awaiting his own execution, not only changed the world in his day, but changed all of human history. It is one of the more personal of Paul's letters, and it gives us a glimpse into the psyche of a real hero, a man who is willing to die for what he believes.

My oldest daughter, Heather, and I visited the Mamertine Prison a few years ago, where it is commonly believed that Paul wrote 2 Timothy. Hidden among some of the most famous ruins in the world, it was the first thing in Rome I wanted to see. In preparation, we decided to read 2 Timothy every day while on the trip, which made the experience and the Scriptures come alive for us.

We descended into the Mamertine Prison, also called Paul's prison.[1] At one point, my head could touch the ceiling. I am just a little taller than six foot one. It is in places like these that real heroes are found.

Inside the Mamertine prison.

Paul's view from prison, looking up through the only entrance and exit at the time.

Ironically, we visited the Vatican later that same day. Wow, what a difference a few hundred years can make for Christian leaders! Great riches of history adorn this palace, this religious city. The ceilings were way too high to touch. You wouldn't be allowed to touch them anyway—as one is even an original Michelangelo masterpiece.

Both sites are impressive. My art background drew me to the Vatican, but my heart never left the cave. Being there and trying to imagine Paul in this place at the end of such a heroic life changed me forever.

Heather and I looked at each other in the dim light with the smell of mildew and realized that this is the very rock where God inspired one of my favorite books of the Bible. It was in this tiny place that Paul agonized over his few remaining days and the lasting impact of his life. He was in this place just a few moments before his head was separated from his body, and his soul was transferred into the light of God's eternal presence.

Some of the books of the Bible were written from palaces like the Vatican, but not as many as were written from dungeons and on the run in the wilderness with a posse breathing down the author's neck.

I couldn't help but ask myself, *Neil, which place would you prefer as a Christian leader?* I am afraid too many of us would choose the elegance of privilege before the cold, hard, and unforgiving stone of Mamertine. But as I think of real heroes throughout history, most have lived their days in dark, marginalized places. In our society, however, we tend to exalt those who make the most money and are the most famous, whether actors, musicians, or athletes, regardless of their character. Real heroes do not emerge from places of comfort, elegance, and privilege, but from pain, hardship, and trouble. It is under the pressure of great diversity, conviction, and challenge that heroes are forged.

We are called to make a difference in this world. More to the point, we are called to make this world different. May we all choose the dark cave of obscurity over the posh privilege of the Vatican.

The Power and the Calling

This book will give you what you need to take the initiative and begin to make a difference in the lives of people around you. Some of the concepts here are developed from ideas I have shared in previous works. I have felt the need to recast the message so that more people will understand and real change will take place. The second section of the book is a refashioning of some chapters from *Cultivating a Life for God*.[2] The material has been revised dramatically and many chapters are completely new, making it a worthwhile read even for those who have read my previous works. This latter section presents a discipleship model and explains some very practical ways to be a disciple maker who reproduces healthy disciple makers. But this is not just a how-to book of discipleship methodology. I have found that implementation of the model without a grasp of the underlying principles often leads to frustration and failure. Granted, most of us like to receive practical how-to methods that can be immediately and effectively applied. The truth is, without the framework of the principles and values described in this book, the methodology lacks a healthy environment in which to thrive.

Hear me when I say it is not the methodology that transforms lives, it is only the power of the gospel of Jesus Christ applied to a needy soul by the Holy Spirit. The methodology is only helpful in that it brings the desperate sinner into prolonged contact with God and his Word in the context of a community of others who are also pursuing the Lord.

The power to change lives is within each of us, and the call to do so is on us all. Take the initiative and join Jesus as he searches and saves those who are lost and drowning.

PART 1

LAST WORDS FROM A DYING HERO

Paul's Second Letter to Timothy

Revealing a Secret Identity

What Is a Real Hero in God's Kingdom?

On the morning of January 2, 2007, Wesley Autrey did not wake up thinking of himself as a hero. He doesn't wear spandex under his clothes and have a red *S* on his chest. The people he spoke to that morning did not think him an extraordinary man. Perhaps the only ones who did think he was larger than life were his two daughters, four-year-old Syshe and six-year-old Shuqui—most little girls think their dad is a hero. Soon, however, much of the Western world would know that Wesley Autrey had done something heroic.

Just before 1 p.m. that day, this fifty-year-old construction worker and his daughters were waiting for the downtown local subway at 137th Street and Broadway when Cameron Hollopeter fell into a convulsion and collapsed on the tracks just as an incoming train appeared.

Wesley Autrey with Syshe and Shuqui.

27

Wesley was not thinking about heroic things at that moment. Instead he remembers thinking, *Someone should help that guy.* His next thought was, I *should help that guy.*

Without a whole lot more thinking, he took action. With the increasing roar and the light of the oncoming train swallowing up the whole scene, and as his two little girls watched in horror, Wesley jumped between the tracks, lay down on top of Cameron, and held him down while the train ran over the two of them.

Five cars rolled overhead before the train came to a stop. Hearing shrieks from the train and cries from onlookers, Wesley called out, "We're okay down here, but I've got two daughters up there. Let them know their father is okay."

That was one heroic leap. And Wesley did it, not for a great man or a friend, but for a complete stranger, just one of millions of commuters in New York City whom he passes each day without a second thought.

There are about twenty-two inches of space in the gutter under the train. The two men took up twenty-one. Wesley's cap was smudged with grease from the undercarriage of the train. When Cameron awakened with a stranger lying on top of him in very tight quarters, he started to fight. Wesley tried to hold him down and explained in as calm a tone as possible where they were and why he was lying on top of him just inches from the high-powered electrical current.

Superman would have jumped in front of the train and held it to a stop. The Flash would have had time to run down, pick up the victim, and take him to the safety of a hospital before the train even arrived. Spider-Man would have spun a web to catch the train and bring it to a stop. While all those rescues would have been dramatic and awesome, what Wesley did is far more heroic. It is impressive to leap tall buildings in a single bound, but the leap Wesley made that afternoon is even more amazing. He demonstrated that it's not special powers that make a real hero; it's courage and the willingness to be self-sacrificing to help a desperate person.

Could it be that the very average and everyday nature of who you are makes you a more impressive hero? When ordinary people rise to do extraordinary things, we find a true hero, one whom we can understand and follow. When someone like Wesley Autrey takes a risk for someone else, we are inspired to do the same.

That's why I have always liked Daredevil as a hero (the comics more than the movie). He bleeds and can die like everyone else and he is also blind. Granted, he has some special powers that enable him to see with sonar, but if he falls from the top of a building, he will die. In fact it is his weakness that becomes his strength. There is something spiritual and powerful about that. You have weaknesses as well. For most people, their weaknesses keep them from doing special things. But in God's kingdom, you have a chance to turn your weakness into strength.

As a child, I read comic books and dreamed of having super powers. Now that I have grown up, I have realized that real heroes do not wear tights, capes, or masks to hide their true identity. Like Wesley, their inner hero may be hidden, but not behind masks. The true heroic nature of a man or woman is lying in wait for a moment when it can reveal itself, a moment of crisis when the hero can come out to show the world who he or she really is.

Dr. Liviu Librescu

The late Dr. Liviu Librescu, former head of the Engineering Science and Mechanics department at Virginia Tech University, is such a hero. There were moments in his life when his heroic nature was unmasked. While living in Romania he survived internment as a Jew under the Nazi holocaust. He survived the cruelty of Communism and the dictator Nicolae Ceausescu in Romania in the seventies. But perhaps his most heroic moment came on what started as a quiet morning at Virginia Tech University, where he was teaching his engineering class.

Students and faculty heard gunshots, as Seung-Hui Cho started entering classrooms and shooting. Dr. Librescu had all of his students climb out of the windows as he went to the door to slow the killer with his own body. He sacrificed his own life to save his students. One of his students was wounded, but Dr. Librescu was the only one from his class to be killed. He was a true hero who finished his life with his most heroic moment.

Heroes may be found in a moment, but they are not made in a moment; it takes years. If we simply wait for a big crisis and hope we will respond right in that crucible, we are hanging a heavy weight on a very thin wire. Heroes are not made by dangerous circumstances,

Dr. Liviu Librescu.

but they are recognized in them. Heroes are made in the simple decisions made each day in ordinary life. Those decisions may not seem heroic at the time because the stakes do not appear to be high, and few take notice, but in reality they are heroic, for they make up the strength of the man or woman who will step into the dangerous crisis in the future. You cannot be selfish in all the little choices of life and expect to be self-sacrificing in the moment when it counts.

A Superhero

As a kid, I used to talk with my friends about who our favorite superheroes were. My heroes have changed now that I am an adult. One of my all-time favorites in human history is the apostle Paul. In this chapter we will examine seven characteristics of Paul, found in the first chapter of 2 Timothy, that demonstrate the qualities of a kingdom hero. The first chapter of this epistle summarizes all that Paul speaks to throughout the body of his letter.

Internal Conviction

A hero has internal conviction that is not swayed by external pressures (2 Tim. 1:8–14).

Paul faced much external pressure to end his spiritual influence. But he was convinced of who he was and what he was about, so he continued his ministry. So many live their lives wondering *why?* Not Paul. He knew what he was here for, and he never let the pressure of others sway him. He said, "For this reason I also suffer these things, but I am not ashamed; for I know whom I have believed and I am convinced that He is able to guard what I have entrusted to Him until that day" (2 Tim. 1:12).

Strength comes from an internal confidence in who you are and why you are here. Add to that faith in an omnipotent and loving God who cares for you, and you have a remarkable person. This is what characterized Paul.

Self-Sacrificing

A hero will sacrifice himself for the sake of others (2 Tim. 1:8).

The opening lines under the heading "Hero" in Wikipedia read: "From the Greek ἥρως, in mythology and folklore, a *hero* (male) or *heroine* (female) usually fulfills the definitions of what is considered good and noble in the originating culture. Typically the willingness to sacrifice the self for the greater good is seen as the most important defining characteristic of a hero."[1]

Paul constantly laid his life on the line so that others could live. This quality, more than any other, is what separates the heroes from the zeroes. To give your life *for a friend* is indeed noble and heroic. Jesus said, "Greater love has no one than this, that one lay down his life for his friends" (John 15:13).

To lay your life down *for a stranger* is even more heroic. Paul was constantly giving his reputation, his body, and even his life away to bring the Good News to people whom he did not even know. He writes to Timothy: "Remember Jesus Christ, risen from the dead, . . . according to my gospel, for which I suffer hardship even to imprisonment as a criminal. . . . For this reason I endure all things for the sake of those who are chosen, so that they also may obtain the salvation which is in Christ Jesus and with it eternal glory" (2:8–10).

Romans 5:8 says, "But God demonstrates His own love toward us, in that while we were yet sinners, Christ died for us." To give your life *for those who hate you* is beyond belief. Jesus did so without hesitation. Paul connects on a personal level with this particular love, because he was one who persecuted and attacked Jesus. He carries a love like this for others. If it were possible, he would even be willing to give his own soul to bring salvation to the people who hated him the most (see Rom. 9:1–5).

Paul says near the end of this epistle, "For I am already being poured out as a drink offering, and the time of my departure has come" (2 Tim. 4:6). He made the ultimate sacrifice for others. He is a hero to the utmost.

A Clear Conscience

A hero has a clear conscience because he or she does what is right (2 Tim. 1:3).

We all would agree that Wesley was a true hero when he saved Cameron. Part of his story is the gifts and accolades he received from many famous celebrities when they heard what he had done. But Wesley did not do this brave thing for accolades. True heroes do not risk their life for attention or a decent paycheck. Usually they don't seem to comprehend the immensity of their actions. "I don't feel like I did something spectacular; I just saw someone who needed help," Wesley said. "I did what I thought was right."

That is a part of what a true hero is all about. The hero does not think of him- or herself as someone who did anything unusual. The hero wants to be able to sleep well at night because he or she has done the right thing throughout the day. Most days a hero sleeps well because he or she did little things and made right decisions that may go unnoticed and do not have huge implications. But because the hero lives in this manner, there are a few other days, like January 2, 2007, when that thought process results in a dramatic, death-defying leap of heroism.

Paul writes to Timothy, "I thank God, whom I serve with a clear conscience the way my forefathers did, as I constantly remember you in my prayers night and day" (2 Tim. 1:3). Heroes in God's kingdom live each day in such a way that they are not ashamed of their actions. They follow the example set before them by others they admire, and they bear responsibility for those who follow them. My friend and co-worker Dezi Baker often talks of "Sleeping the sleep of innocence upon the bed of no regrets." To live each day without regrets because you choose to live by your own convictions is a great gift and its reward is often a night of sound sleep. As a result, one day you may be in a moment of crisis and find that you too are a hero.

Perhaps one of the most moving examples in our lifetime of someone who lived and died by her convictions is Rachel Scott, who died in the Columbine tragedy in 1999. She exhibited her faith to the killers in the days leading up to the rampage. When they committed their murderous spree, they targeted people of color, athletes, and Christians. One of the boys shot Rachel in the legs and torso. As she lay on the ground, he came to her, grabbed her by the hair, and asked, "Do you still believe in your God?"

She said to his face, "You know I do."

"Then go be with him" was the response before Eric Harris fatally shot Rachel.

A true modern-day martyr for her faith, Rachel Scott is a strong example to her generation of a person who lived and died for her convictions. We can learn much from this little girl. She is a hero.[2]

Taking Initiative

A hero takes initiative rather than waiting for others to fill the gap (2 Tim. 1:6–7).

Paul sets an example for Timothy and then challenges him to rise to the same standard as a leader. He writes: "I remind you to kindle afresh the gift of God which is in you through the laying on of my hands. For God has not given us a spirit of timidity, but of power and love and discipline" (vv. 6–7).

So many leaders, especially men, wait on others to take the initiative in life. One could argue we have been suffering from passivity ever since the fall when Adam followed his wife into sin rather than taking the initiative to lead into righteousness. I believe that this is so important that in training my own son to be a real man, *initiative* was one of the five principles I taught him.[3] Women, of course, can take initiative, lead, and become heroes as well.

I am not suggesting otherwise. I am merely stating that too often men do not take the lead, especially as it relates to raising their children. I believe this is perhaps the greatest threat to our society today. I long for a time when the kingdom of God is so real to our people that the hearts of the fathers are turned back once more to their children (Mal. 4:6).

Paul was a real man and a spiritual father to Timothy. He went to Timothy and initiated a whole new level of spiritual leadership with him, and then challenged him not to be passive or timid or to go on retreat. Instead, he reminded him to demonstrate the power, love, and discipline of a true hero.

Paul goes on to raise this challenge higher with Timothy when he writes, "I solemnly charge you in the presence of God and of Christ Jesus . . . preach the word; be ready in season and out of season; reprove, rebuke, exhort, with great patience and instruction" (4:1–2). He finishes this thought with, "Be sober in all things, endure hardship, do the work of an evangelist [telling others the Good News of Jesus], fulfill your ministry" (v. 5). We must all fulfill the call of God on our lives by taking initiative when it is convenient and when it is not.

Transformed Within by the Voice of God

A hero of God's kingdom is transformed within by the present voice of God (2 Tim. 1:13–14).

While it is true that we are all, for the most part, ordinary people who can be extraordinary heroes, we do have something special in us if we are Christians. Paul writes to Timothy, "Guard, through the Holy Spirit who dwells in us, the treasure which has been entrusted to you" (v. 14). I guess we actually do have some super powers, but they are not inherent in us as much as imported into our lives by the Holy Spirit. He dwells in us. That means that he lives within us and has a positive influence on our internal lives.

It is hard to imagine what the "treasure" is if not the presence of the Holy Spirit, but as Paul says, it is his presence that we use to guard the actual treasure. "Wow, you mean there is more than the indwelling of the Holy Spirit?" Yes! There is the fruit of his presence in our inner life: love, salvation, power, hope, strength to endure, and an intimacy with God in all things at all times. We can hear from God about anything in life and have the freedom and power from within to fulfill anything he asks of us.

In the heading I use the phrase "voice of God" intentionally. There are, of course, many other terms I could use that may actually have a wider appeal in the kingdom of God. I could have easily said "word of God." This would have the broadest acceptance, but it would probably limit our thinking to just the written Scriptures and not include the very present Holy Spirit within.

I could have used the term "message of God," but this could easily imply that simply knowing and passing on some relayed facts is enough. The word and the message are powerful and true, no doubt, but they are so because they come from the mind and mouth of God. I choose the phrase "voice of God" because it connotes something active, intimate, and ongoing. It also encompasses the other terms.

Paul does go on throughout the letter to highlight the transformative presence of God's Word in our lives and how we are to live according to it (2:15; 3:16–17; 4:2). Some would argue that the "treasure" mentioned in verse 14 is the Word of God written on our hearts, which is very plausible. But we must understand that having the Holy Spirit dwelling within us is indeed more than simply being able to know the Bible and obey it. There is an intimacy factor that is infinite and powerful for the transformation of our lives.

Knowing Bible verses is valuable, but it is the voice in the words that holds the power. This is so important that Jesus says that hearing his voice is a test of whether or not we are even his followers. He said, "My sheep hear My voice, and I know them [intimacy], and they follow Me [lordship]" (John 10:27). Hearing the voice of God is essential, not just a bonus for the Christian life. And this is not just for important Christian leaders who will then pass information on to the rest of us. It is essential for any and all who follow Christ.

A Link in the Chain of Heroes

A hero is usually a link in the great chain of heroes (2 Tim. 1:3–7, 13).

Often in the early verses of a letter, Paul brings up the main reason he is writing the letter, and 2 Timothy is no exception. From the start, he is writing this letter to challenge Timothy to keep the faith and pass it on to succeeding generations. He even begins by addressing Timothy as his "beloved son." Paul responds to Timothy as Timothy's spiritual father. He is passing on a legacy from one generation to another. As the letter unfolds, Paul will elaborate with more depth on the idea of passing on the work to the next generation (2:1–2; 3:10–14), and we will look at this idea in depth in later chapters.

Paul begins this epistle to his apprentice by saying they both are responsible to the ones who came before and invested in them. Paul serves with a clear conscience, keeping in mind his own forefathers (1:3). He reminds Timothy of the sincere faith that was first in his grandmother Lois, then his mother, Eunice, and is now in Timothy (v. 5). He also ties both lineages together

when he tells Timothy to "retain the standard of sound words which you
have heard from me" (v. 13).

Heroes are not accidental; they are raised that way. There is a long chain of
heroes who pass through history, and each of us is merely another link. We
must pass on the stuff that makes a hero to our children and our disciples. If
we don't, we have not only been irresponsible, but have failed all who have
come before us and certainly all those who will come after. *Legacy*

Paul goes so far as to mention others who have dropped the baton. Demas,
who is mentioned positively in other epistles (Col. 4:14 and Philem. 24), has
loved the world more than Christ and deserted Paul and all he stands for
(2 Tim. 4:10).[4]

While we carry the responsibility of passing on the faith to the next generation, we cannot make decisions for them. Every parent must learn this.
We must let go and allow others to rise up on their own, and some will dis-
appoint us. This only adds to the passion Paul must have felt when he wrote
these words to Timothy.

After all his influence in Asia, many turned away from Paul (1:15). This
may not mean that they turned away from Jesus, but merely lost trust in Paul
who is publicly condemned as a criminal of the worst sort.

Being a hero can be a lonely life. Perhaps I should have included that as
one of the seven characteristics in this chapter. The words "Only Luke is
with me" (4:11) haunt me as a disciple maker. I have seen my own disciples
turn on me, abuse me, and go back into the world to pursue the lure of sin,
and it hurts.

At a recent conference for the leaders in our movement, Church Multiplication Associates, I began in an unusual way. I used a reference from the
movie *The Matrix*. In this movie a red pill and a blue pill are offered to those
who are sought out in order to be set free from the bondage of the Matrix.

In the movie Morpheus explains to Neo: "You take the blue pill, the story
ends. You wake up in your bed and believe whatever you want to believe.
You take the red pill, you stay in wonderland, and I show you how deep the
rabbit hole goes."

We often show this clip in our training events and have adopted the language of "the red pill" in our movement.[5] When someone comes to understand the kingdom of God in a real, organic, and dynamic way, we refer to
that as "taking the red pill." Often such a transformative awakening leads to
a change in lifestyle.

The opening message (the only one I presented) at our conference was
titled: "Why, Oh Why, Didn't I Take the Blue Pill? The Dark Side of Organic
Church." The bottom line is that approaching the Christian life relationally

is the best choice. It is the most rewarding choice but also a painful choice. When you lead people into the kingdom, invest all you have in them, and cheer for their success like your own children, it hurts deeply when they fall away. In a typical church setting, when someone falls away, you may see an empty seat for a few weeks, but it doesn't hurt as much. Even if you are personally invested in the person, if you haven't been the spiritual parent in his or her life, it still doesn't hurt as much.

The apostle John writes, "I was very glad to find some of your children walking in truth" (2 John 4). This is the greatest joy, and it makes all the effort worthwhile, but hearing how our "children" fall away can be the source of the greatest pain also. There is a cost to being a hero, a lonely one. Though it is painful to invest our lives in people who fall away, still God has called us to be links in the chain of faith, and it is worth the cost.

Leaving a Lasting Impact

A hero finishes strong and leaves a lasting impact after he or she is gone (2 Tim. 1:12).

There is one quality of a hero that is the ultimate test of a heroic life. How you finish at the end, and what you leave behind, is the final exam of a hero's life.

I used to compete in triathlons; well, I used to *participate* in triathlons. There is a big difference. All of the participants would line up at the same starting line. When the gun went off, we would start running at the same time to cheers from the crowds. We all felt the rush of adrenalin and the hope of a successful race.

The starting line and the finish line produce very different feelings for the people in a race. A few receive even more applause at the finish line than at the starting line. For the participants like me, the finish line is a welcome end, but there is only a trickle of applause from a few remaining relatives anxious to get home. The applause at the beginning feels great, but I have come to realize that it is only the applause at the finish line that really matters.

Paul writes to Timothy, "For this reason I also suffer these things, but I am not ashamed; for I know whom I have believed and I am convinced that He is able to guard what I have entrusted to Him until that day" (1:12). Paul put his trust in God to keep him during all the suffering until the day when his race was over.

As he wrote to Timothy, he was close to the end. He could even see the banner overhead that read "finish" in bold letters. He was kicking harder with strength he didn't even know he had as his heart soared with the hope

REVEALING A SECRET IDENTITY

that the end was so close. At this point he held nothing back but gave every ounce of strength, knowing he would soon be able to rest. Paul would leave everything on the course and have nothing left when the race was over. Near the end of this letter he wrote of his hope:

> For I am already being poured out as a drink offering, and the time of my departure has come. I have fought the good fight, I have finished the course, I have kept the faith; in the future there is laid up for me the crown of righteousness, which the Lord, the righteous Judge, will award to me on that day; and not only to me, but also to all who have loved His appearing.
>
> 2 Timothy 4:6–8

Like any competition, the number of people who start the race is greater than the number of those who finish. And of course the number of those who win the race is much smaller—only one per race. Paul was a winner, not only in how he lived his life, but in how he anticipated his death. Others would knock his reputation and spread lies about him. He would suffer imprisonment and execution as a criminal, but he knew that he would face a righteous Judge who would ultimately crown him with glory. He always kept this in mind and encouraged others, like Timothy and us, to have the same hope. It is fine to merely participate in triathlons, but when it comes to your spiritual life, anything shy of winning the race is a failure.

What Is a Disciple?

It may sound a little grandiose to use the word *hero* when I am speaking about being a disciple. But, you see, I think that being a disciple in God's kingdom is indeed grandiose. The word *disciple*, however, has been used and abused so much that its meaning is no longer clear. It no longer has the romantic, larger than life connotation it should have. Because the Greek word can mean "pupil," we have turned discipleship into a lesson in cognitive learning—the more you know, the more advanced you are in following the Master. But that connotation is just not sufficient. Moving from workbook five to workbook six is not an adequate understanding of discipleship.

Follower of Christ is in some ways a better term than *disciple*, and I use it frequently. It is too easy these days to be called a disciple, easier still to be called Christian. One is called a follower of Christ or a hero, however, because one has earned the title and proven he or she is worthy of it. I intentionally use the term *hero* in this book, because of the following:

1. *It is an action word. Disciple* is a thinking word. It connotes learning, which is very important, but *hero* goes further.
2. *Many consider themselves disciples, but to be a hero is something special.* When we hear the word *disciple*, we think of a spiritual understudy or apprentice. If we're called a hero, our heart soars. Who doesn't want to be considered a hero?
3. *It speaks to a dire need in all of us, and especially in our culture today.* Our nation needs heroes. There is a void in this category, and it cannot be filled by religious students. A follower of Christ should be a hero, not just a spiritual understudy.
4. *It accurately captures the idea of someone who is called to search for and rescue the life of another, even at his or her own expense.* This is what being a disciple is all about: search and rescue no matter what it costs us. Jesus said that the world would hate us because it hated him. We are called to do more than learn information. Discipleship is a call to a lifestyle that sacrifices itself on the cross for the betterment of others.
5. *People want to be heroes, and why not?* What makes a person memorable is the life he or she leads. The reason comic books sell so well, and movies about their superheroes sell even more, is that deep in all of us is a voice crying out to be significant—to be a hero.

Why do we make heroes out of celebrities today? Are we so lacking in real heroes that we applaud the pretend ones and grant them the respect that true heroes deserve? We take an actor who plays someone of importance and grant him that same importance. Actors may feel a little insecure with such power, knowing that in fact they were just pretending to be someone great, rather than actually being someone great. For this reason, perhaps, they begin to feel the need to live up to expectations, and that's when we get actors speaking out about issues of the day, as if they deserve to be heard. But in reality they are just good pretenders. So why do we listen to them?

Of course there are always exceptions. Ronald Reagan was an actor who became a politician and did some rather incredible things. We do not remember him as an actor but as a president. All people have the opportunity in life to do something of significance, even actors, but only a few seem up to the task. Simply spouting an opinion as if it merits more consideration than the opinion of others is not being heroic. It is just being arrogant and opinionated. The real issue is not what you think, but what you do about it.

I think, because we know that people like Britney Spears, Barry Bonds, and Tom Cruise will ultimately let us down, we end up manufacturing fictional heroes with super powers that can never let us down because they are not real. Spider-Man, Superman, the new characters on the NBC show aptly named *Heroes* all point to our crying need for heroes. They are extraordinary people who are vastly different from the rest of us because they have special powers.

We need real heroes not pretend ones. I admire Tiger Woods's golf swing, but I can't say this makes him a hero. I have no interest in taking anything away from Mr. Woods, but heroes are people of substance and character who will sacrifice themselves for a greater cause, not just birdie on the ninth hole to take a lead in the Masters.

On that memorable January day, Wesley Autrey, on his way to his night shift, stopped by the hospital to visit Cameron Hollopeter. Cameron had only some slight bumps and bruises, and Wesley did not have any injury at all. Until that day these two men were complete strangers, but then they had an experience that they will never forget. We all learned a lot about the man named Wesley Autrey that day.

"I don't think I did anything heroic," Autrey later commented. "I just saved a life. I don't call myself a hero, because the real heroes are overseas dying for you and me." He may not think what he did was heroic, but we do.

My hope is that after reading this book you will go through the same quick thought process that Wesley did while standing in a safe place on the platform. When you see a person in need, you'll think, *Someone should help that person.* And then you will think, I *should help that person.* I hope you will take a risky leap to rescue someone in need, because you think it is the right thing to do. You too can be a hero. And there is a super power that is available to you. The next chapter will unlock that power for you.

2

Good News Worth Sharing

The Gospel of the Kingdom

In all my years of lifeguarding, only two people whom I had helped came back later to see me. The first was a man I pulled out of a rip current. He was desperate and panicky, and I was just in time to bring him back to shore. He was so grateful. He came back and said it gave him a new lease on life. I could see that even after several weeks, the sense of freedom and the value of living each day was still fresh for him. He was determined not to let life become something that he took for granted. He hoped that every day he would remember that he could have been killed and instead was given a second opportunity to live well.

The other person who came back to visit is an entirely different story. He had been bodysurfing in front of my tower in some very strong shore break (waves that were crashing directly on the beach). One time he hit the sand and came up a little wobbly. I asked how he felt, and he told me he had a headache. I looked at his eyes and asked him to press his hands and feet against some resistance I was providing. He was able to move and press hard enough and his pupils looked clear and responsive. Nevertheless, having seen a series of broken necks on this beach due to the shore break, I decided to play it safe and I told him to go to the local hospital for an X-ray. He was resistant. I told him it could be nothing at all or it could be very serious and even life threatening, so he gave in and left for the hospital. I never expected to see him again and, frankly, I thought he would be fine.

Two weeks later he was back at the beach—with a halo attached to his skull! A halo is a metal crown that is surgically attached to your skull and shoulders to keep you from turning your head so your vertebrae can heal. It turns out that he did break his neck, and his condition was more serious than either of us thought. I was glad that I had the sense to send him to the hospital and not let him resist. Unfortunately, he was not grateful. He informed me that he was suing the lifeguards and the county of Los Angeles because of his broken neck.

I couldn't believe it. He broke his own neck, not us, and we were the ones who responded intelligently and kept him from doing worse damage to himself. I told him that he is very fortunate that his break was caught right away and that he was able to walk. He started ranting about no warning signs and how negligent we were for not preventing him from hurting himself.

I felt a little like Jesus when he healed the ten lepers and only one returned, except that in this case a second leper returned with a lawsuit because the healing caused him to lose his excuse to beg, and now he was out of a job.

There are two reactions to the grace of God's kingdom. Some will receive the grace but hold on to pride and arrogance. They will make excuses for their lives, all the while blaming everyone else and ultimately God for the mess they're in. The other response, which comes far less frequently, will be that they are changed forever. There will be some, like the one leper who returned to Jesus post-healing, who will never look back. These are world changers. In an instant they go from being changed to becoming change agents. Such is the way of God's kingdom message—it will either transform you forever or be ignored and rejected.

The Super Power within You

In writing his last words to his spiritual son, Paul was looking for something that would inspire Timothy to fight the good fight and finish the race as a hero, just as Paul was doing. He knew that continuing on in life without transformation is not success but failure. Sometimes I fear that parents and pastors alike will be content if their children and parishioners just hold on and do not fall away. I can understand this fear, but simply holding on is not godly faith. Jesus didn't die and rise again so that we can stay the same, and for Paul, this was abject failure. We are to be more than mere survivors; we are to be victors in Christ.

Many assume that Timothy, by nature, was a timid and quiet type, perhaps even shy. This assumption comes from the many times Paul exhorts him not to be ashamed and timid but bold. Whether or not Timothy was shy, most of us in the Western church are either one of two things: obnoxiously loud or shamefully shy.

Paul inspired Timothy to boldness by reminding him of the power already within him. He wrote:

> God has not given us a spirit of timidity, but of power and love and discipline. Therefore do not be ashamed of the testimony of our Lord or of me His prisoner, but join with me in suffering for the gospel according to the power of God, who has saved us and called us with a holy calling, not according to our works, but according to His own purpose and grace which was granted to us in Christ Jesus from all eternity.
>
> 2 Timothy 1:7–9

Paul goes on to say this God of power has now "been revealed by the appearing of our Savior Christ Jesus, who abolished death and brought life and immortality to light through the gospel" (v. 10). Yes, the coming of Christ and his atoning work on the cross are essential parts of the transforming power of the gospel, but this power is current, immediate; it changes us in this life. It is not just a promise or future hope.

The gospel powerfully transforms us from what we once were into what we can and should be. "I will do the best I can" is just not enough. We are not to do what we can, because it is not what we do that makes a difference. We must step out in faith and attempt to do the impossible, even at great risk, if we are to be the heroes God has called us to be. Jesus's sacrifice deserves nothing less. The power of God comes when our own power is either exhausted or set aside. Of course God's power and ours are, well, not even comparable. When the world sees the best we have to offer, they yawn. When they see God at work among us, there can be a chain reaction of power that sets a whole nation or world on fire with his gospel.

Paul comments on the difference between the power of human religious ingenuity and the true power of the gospel when he describes the futility of religious leaders who espouse a religion that is man-centered. He describes them at one point as "holding to a form of godliness, although they have denied its power" (3:5). Through manipulation, guilt, and shame they use and abuse the weaker ones in the kingdom (v. 6). These are men who are "always learning and never able to come to the knowledge of the truth" (v. 7).

To know the true power of God's kingdom, we must let go of any other source of power—or supposed power. Whatever it is that you use to feel important and influential in the church, if it is not the true gospel, then you must abandon it in favor of the one thing that truly can change a life from within.

We tend to think that knowing sound doctrine is all that is needed for godliness. I would argue that sound doctrine is not mere knowledge but practical and radical obedience from a heart of love (see Titus 2). Unfortunately, in much of the Western church we have come to think that having knowledge is enough.

Knowledge does not change a life in any way other than puffing up one's ego (see 1 Cor. 8:1–3). It is love that transforms. When Paul was planning on coming back to Corinth to put things in order, he said with a bit of sarcasm, "But I will come to you soon, if the Lord wills, and I shall find out, not the words of those who are arrogant but their power [or lack thereof]. For the kingdom of God does not consist in words but in power" (4:19–20).

Paul writes in that same Corinthian letter: "I determined to know nothing among you except Jesus Christ, and Him crucified" (2:2). Paul knows well the source of his true power. Power, love, and discipline come from knowing Jesus Christ in all his weakness, demonstrated on the cross, and in all of your own weakness. We should never be so sophisticated in our ministry that we lose sight of this very simple and powerful reality.

The Gospel of the Kingdom

One thing that the evangelical Protestant church thinks it knows well is the gospel. After all, it is part of their name. "Evangelical" comes from the very word for good news, which is really what *gospel* means. I wonder if any in our world would consider evangelicals to be good news.

Sometimes, however, familiarity breeds contempt. We are so close to the facts inherent in the gospel that we have lost sight of the true nature and power that are intrinsic to it. We actually have a reduced view of what the gospel is. In much of Christendom, I fear the gospel has become a small statement of facts that one must agree to intellectually to be welcomed into the "club." In most cases, if you believe that Jesus died for your sins and rose from the dead, you're in—you now have eternal fire insurance and are a Christian. But is that truly what it means to be a Christian? Is that all that the gospel is? Is the gospel some sort of litmus test of who is in and who is not?

The world is not enticed by a list of historical facts. They need real good news, and that is something far more dynamic and holistic than just "Four Spiritual Laws."[1] Others have written about this, and I am forever indebted to them.[2] I will merely challenge us to see the gospel as more than a few facts (as sacred as those facts are) and see it as a living and powerful presence that does more than grant us a "Get out of hell free card."

For most of my life the gospel was clear and compelling. As the apostle Paul put it so well: "Now I make known to you, brethren, the gospel which I preached to you. . . . that Christ died for our sins according to the Scriptures, and that He was buried, and that He was raised on the third day according to the Scriptures, and that He appeared to [many]"(1 Cor. 15:1–5).

This is the gospel that Paul preached. This is true and powerful, and it has changed my life forever. I must ask, however, is this all that the gospel is? Is accepting these facts enough, or does the truth need to be deeper, incarnate and revolutionary in one's life? Even for Paul, the gospel became so intense and personal to him that he sometimes referred to it as "my gospel" (2 Tim. 2:8).

Because we have limited the gospel to the four historic facts that Paul states in 1 Corinthians 15:1–5, we have also limited the impact of the very message itself. Do not hear me incorrectly: the redemptive mission of Christ—the sacrificial atonement for sins, the power of the resurrection, and the authenticity of what Christ did for us—is without question powerful and true, and it shapes all of human history. But this is the starting place, not the destination.

We must come to terms with the fact that the gospel was preached by Jesus and his disciples *before* the death, burial, and resurrection of Christ. It is perfectly clear from all the Gospel accounts in the New Testament that the disciples did not understand that Jesus had to die and rise from the dead until after the fact. Nevertheless, they went about the cities and villages preaching the gospel before Jesus's sacrifice. What gospel were they preaching? Is it possible that the gospel is more than just the cross and empty tomb, as incredibly powerful as they are? I think there is more to the gospel.

What would a first-century Jew living in Jerusalem consider good news? I imagine the coming of the promised Messiah who is the true King of the Jews would be good news. The Jews lived under an oppressive Gentile government, so the good news would entail an overthrow of injustice and putting in place a true rule of God on this earth. Well, perhaps the gospel does reflect some of that good news as well. Actually, I can't imagine that the horrific suffering and death of the Messiah would be considered good news to these people, which is one reason why the disciples could not hear what Jesus clearly told them.

Mark writes that Jesus came into Galilee, preaching the gospel of God, and saying, "The time is fulfilled, and the kingdom of God is at hand; repent and believe in the gospel" (Mark 1:15). For Jesus, the gospel was this: the kingdom of God is *here*. It required a change of heart and a response of faith and obedience. It was a change of allegiance that would forever alter the direction of one's life.

The gospel of the kingdom is the good news that the King has come! This was what the disciples (Matt. 10:7) and John the Baptist (Luke 3:18) as well as Jesus himself (Mark 1:14–15) were preaching.

When the King comes, he is not just selling afterlife insurance policies door-to-door. He is bringing the rule and reign of his kingdom wherever he goes. Every person who comes under his rule is empowered to be one of his kingdom agents. This is good news for the here and now not just the hereafter. The good news is that Jesus came, died, rose again, and lives in heaven, and he is interceding for us every day. The good news is also that the King is here now ruling in our lives and bringing a revolution of hearts and lives that will transform neighborhoods and nations. The whole point of the cross and empty tomb directs us to a more profound reality: the continual and abiding acceptance into God's holy presence and power. And that doesn't just happen when you die; it is yours right now.

This understanding of the gospel is bigger than just a few facts regarding our eternal salvation. This good news makes a difference in the way you raise your children, balance your checkbook, treat your neighbors, and give to the poor. This good news can make you love your enemies and pray for those who persecute you. This good news will also make enemies for you and incite persecution, whereas the simplistic view of the gospel with which we have inoculated our culture does not, because it doesn't let loose the flame of a changed life. It is so concerned with life after death—where we actually can make a difference.

We have a saying in our ministry: "Where you go, the King goes, and where the King goes, people bow." The idea is that you bring the rule of Christ with you. Where Christ rules, things change. The gospel is not just a set of facts to believe; it is a change in allegiance and therefore a change in life. Someone who accepts the gospel does not just accept a few facts about Christ, he or she accepts the rule of Christ as King—a King with all authority over heaven and earth (Matt. 28:18–20). Imagine what we could do with such authority filling our sails.

To us there are resources lacking, closed doors, and insurmountable obstacles to fulfilling a global transformation movement. It is too much. But to the King, who has all authority over heaven and earth, there are no limits. The kingdom of heaven is more powerful than any kingdom of the earth. There is not a government, a law, a criminal cartel, a cultural fad, or a religious movement that can withstand the rule of God's kingdom.

When instructing his disciples to go out and preach the gospel of the kingdom in the various cities and villages of Galilee, Jesus told them firmly that even when people reject the message and they leave town without any change left behind, they were to announce, nevertheless, "that the kingdom of God has come near" (Luke 10:11). The kingdom of God is not subject to the whims of man.

While there is no doubt that the gospel brings eternal salvation and escape from death and hell, it is more than that, much more. The gospel of God's kingdom will consume an entire life. There is nothing that is kept from falling in submission to the King. To withhold something from the rule of the King is foolish when one comes to understand who Christ is.

When is the last time you heard someone announce that the kingdom of God is here? I must ask, why haven't we heard this? Jesus instructs us to announce this, whether or not people are willing to accept it (vv. 9–11). In my experience the last couple of years of introducing the kingdom of heaven into dark corners of the world, I have found Jesus's instructions shockingly relevant.

I remember when this truth struck home with me in a profound way. My friend Jaeson Ma and I were driving up the freeway to UCLA to begin a new campus church movement. We both had some experience but also had a sense that there was much more that both of us had to learn.

In the car I asked Jaeson what he felt the Lord was telling us to do that afternoon on campus. Without hesitation Jaeson said we were going to worship and preach out in the center of the campus on Bruin walk.

Having found Christ on a college campus and served as a collegiate pastor for several years, I have seen hundreds of open-air preachers in my day. Memories of obnoxious preachers holding big Bibles and waving American flags flashed through my mind.

With a little concern I tried to ask the next question with my best "poker face." In the tone of a mentor, I asked, "What results do you expect from this preaching?" My experience has taught me that preaching the gospel to strangers, void of relational context, yields minimal results.

Jaeson was not at all slow in his response. He said, "Oh, we're not preaching for evangelism, though people could come to Christ. We're preaching for two reasons. First, it is for spiritual warfare on campus. The enemy has held that ground for years now, and we need to announce that the kingdom of God has come. The second reason I feel the Lord leading us to do this is because I sense some fear and timidity in the few students that want to work with us, and I think this will address that fear head-on."

In my spirit I knew this young man was absolutely right. We have let our fear of other people's opinions prevent us from announcing the imminence of the kingdom of God. I do not think we need to be obnoxious about it, but at the same time we do need to learn to be bold. My first day on campus was already a learning experience, and we hadn't even arrived at the school yet.

We worshiped and preached in the open air in front of all the students passing by. Jaeson was right. In our own hearts fear was replaced with boldness.

We were announcing the coming of the King, and we continued to do so throughout the year. A small team of students willing to make fools of themselves for Jesus became solidified. In that first academic quarter a beachhead for the kingdom was established. In the second quarter the team itself had to go through a season of adjustment, which we have taken to calling detox. This is a period of breaking free of old forms and religious mechanisms that all of us have grown dependent on, so that we can truly rely on Christ's Spirit and Word and listen to him without any human layers or filters.

By the third quarter we began to see incredible results; the gospel was changing lives. A fraternity leader came to Christ, and then another. Some other fraternity men came to Christ in another frat house, and a church was started in both. A chain reaction of transformed lives began to be unleashed on campus. By the end of the school year, thirty or forty people had come to Christ and the students had started eight to ten organic churches. (Organic churches are usually small, simple spiritual families that emerge where people live, work, and play, and they are begun by the planting of the gospel in the soil of people's lives.[3])

The next year the momentum increased even more. The students who had been involved the previous year formed another eight to ten new evangelistic Bible studies, many turning into organic churches. There is a growing cooperation of almost all the campus ministries at UCLA, with periodic weeks of twenty-four-hour prayer.[4]

Decisions to follow Christ came almost exclusively through natural relational connections, not the public preaching of the gospel. But I came to understand that a spiritual climate must be established that can see change happen, and that begins with calling out to God and proclaiming that the kingdom of God has come.

I am not recommending that we all start preaching on campuses. The truth I am trying to unlock is the importance of announcing Christ's present rule and power. We need to learn ways to let people see and experience the presence of the King in their lives. Jesus's explicit instruction was that when we take the gospel into dark places, we announce or proclaim that the kingdom of God has come. What does that mean in today's context? There will be myriad answers to this question, but I have found that when we announce the King's presence, good things happen. Anticipation and expectations are raised and faith is placed in the right place—in the coming King rather than in methodology or personalities.

When you proclaim the coming of the kingdom, there are four sets of ears that hear the message and are affected by it:

1. *The demonic realm hears.* You say to them out loud, "Your days are numbered and the King who has all authority over heaven and earth is coming." This scares the hell into them, if not them into hell.
2. *The people who are a part of that community hear the announcement.* Even if they do not believe and are unwilling to believe, when they hear this they will begin to watch to see what happens. They may think you are foolish, but they will watch to see what happens nonetheless, and that is a good thing.
3. *You hear the message yourself as it comes out of your mouth.* There is something powerful about putting your reputation on the line for Christ. Faith requires that at times you are willing to risk looking like a fool for the sake of the gospel. And of course you pray like a madman to see God come through for both of your sakes! This is faith in action.
4. *God hears the proclamation.* One thing you can count on is that God is reliable and protects his reputation when his name is on the line. When it is his idea to announce his coming, and you, in faith, do what he asks, he will come through. This is God's response to our faith.

I truly believe that one of the ways the enemy has kept the kingdom of God from ruling in this world is to convince Christians to be timid and easily embarrassed. Often, under the guise of spiritual outreach, we convince ourselves that we need to be quiet and respectable, not stirring up people. This just reveals that we don't really believe in the good news the way we say that we do. What other explanation is there? If we truly believed that the good news is what we say it is, we would not be ashamed to tell others about it. We could surmise that, if we really believed in our hearts that the good news is true, we would all be sharing it boldly. If you found a cure for cancer, you would not be shy about letting people know.

This is where the path of disciple making begins—with a changed life. If your own life isn't transformed by the power of Christ's reign, you have no business trying to make other disciples. Once a life is changed by the presence of Christ ruling over his kingdom subjects, each person becomes a change agent.

There is no system, program, or tool that man can fashion that will have the power to change a life. Only the gospel has that power. Only the presence of Christ and all his authority can set captives free and overturn injustice and evil. Now that sounds like good news to me! As we talk about making and multiplying disciples, it all starts with a heart set free from the shackles of evil bondage to sin. Nothing else can change a life. From that point on, a disciple is to give freely to others the same good news he or she received.

Salvation is a lifelong process. It doesn't begin at Spiritual Law One and end with a prayer after Law Four. I like the children's fantasy film *The Never Ending Story*. At the end of the film, just before the credits begin to roll, instead of saying "The End," it says "The Beginning." The adventure has just begun. They released a fourth part to *The Never Ending Story*, so I guess we can take them at their word. It's like marriage. When you say your vows, the engagement is over, but the marriage has just begun. When you choose to commit to Jesus, it's not the culmination of your salvation—*it's the beginning*.

The Transformed Life

The gospel is not just for the unbeliever but for the Christian. It's the "power of God for salvation *to everyone who believes*" (Rom. 1:16). In fact I don't think the non-Christian will take the cross seriously until we Christians take it seriously. It's not enough that we have once tasted the blessing of the cross. To attract the lost to Jesus, we need to have an appetite for the gospel. The more it means to us, the more attractive it will be to the lost. Why should they be interested in something in which we feign interest? If they don't see that the gospel is vital to us, why would they find it compelling?

Salvation is about a transformed life, a becoming. Regeneration is an ongoing process of the Holy Spirit working in our lives, so that each of us should be more like Christ this year than we were the year before. Our lives should reflect more of the grace and truth found in Christ next year than they do this year.

I have as much or more need to take up my cross and follow Jesus today as I did years ago when I first started on this path. My need for freedom remains. My need for being cleansed and renewed is as strong or stronger than ever before.

Theologians refer to this ongoing salvation process as sanctification. It means to be set apart for significance. The idea is that we are in a process of becoming closer to who we are to be in heaven—closer to being like Christ. If we are truly moving closer to God, nearer to holiness, our awareness of our own flesh must become more obvious to us. Our sensitivity to sin and its subtleties should increase as we grow closer to Christ.

Some older Christians have done away with certain obvious sins, and their spiritual life is now placid and, in their own minds, holy. But comparing ourselves with ourselves is foolishness and is not anywhere near what holiness is all about (see 2 Cor. 10:12). For the one who is truly becoming sanctified in Christ is taking on more and more the character of Christ and realizes more and more the distance he or she still has to go to realize the fullness of Christ.

As we come to know God better, we should all experience an ongoing, deep hungering for the things of God, not a dull routine of spiritual and cultural behaviors suitable to be labeled "Christian." There is so much more in Jesus, we have not even come close to the full knowledge of Christ.

Salvation is more than the decision we made to receive Christ. It is a process, a state of being, as well as a destination. It is so much more than what is sold to people today from most pulpits, tracts, and crusades.

Joining the King

All of us can be channels of the lifesaving Good News to others. If we open our hearts to the Savior and our eyes to those who are drowning, we can be used to do some incredible things. God will do the work through us, and he will use us if we are willing to lay ourselves down for others.

Every summer, when I worked as a lifeguard, there were days when the surf was big and the crowds were also big. One particular day I was working at a tower called Venice South, which sits atop the Venice pier. I spent the day on the sand, though, constantly pulling victims out of the freakishly large surf. The Venice pier is very tall, but the waves were so big they were licking its bottom. When the surf gets big, a strong current will sweep right through the tall pilings of the pier.

My fellow guard, Ion, and I saw three kids on a boogie board that got caught outside in the huge surf. As they went up over the top of the mountainous swells, we could see their eyes bulging from fear. We started to swim out through the large surf to help them when I noticed a man actually swimming

The Venice South tower sitting on the pier.

This gives an idea of how tall the pier is.

toward the pier. I signaled to Ion that I would get the guy near the pier, and he could get the kids on the boogie board.

I was about fifty yards away, but the current was so strong that after a few minutes of diving with the current, regrouping, and diving again in waist-deep water, I was able to get to the pier and the man in no time. As if I were walking on a moving sidewalk at an airport, I traveled the distance with an accelerated pace. The man was clinging desperately to a piling covered with mussel shells and barnacles and was bracing for the next big wave. This is the worst thing you can do in this kind of situation. If the man stayed there, his

Large surf at the
Venice pier.

body would be ripped to shreds between the force of the wave on one side
and the razor-sharp barnacles and mussel shells on the other.

I got to the man just seconds after he gripped the piling. The current
brought me right to him. All I had to do was simply pry his white knuckles
off the piling and the current itself swept him out from under the pier where
the next wave washed him right up onto the beach unharmed. On the other
hand I was left under the pier. When that same wave got a hold of me, it threw
me right at another piling headfirst. I didn't have time to think or react. I was
like a little rag doll totally at the mercy of the power that had swallowed me
whole. Then the wave went right past me, and I stopped completely before
hitting the next piling.

God in his mercy and wisdom had sent an angel to wrap the cord of my
rescue can around a second piling while I was releasing the grip of the victim.
The strap around my shoulders, connected to the rescue can, held me back,
preventing me from being crushed against another cement piling.

You see, a rescue can, which a lifeguard always has with him, has a strap
that goes across his shoulder and is attached to the floatation tube by a nylon
cord. Usually, when in the water, the strap is on over his or her shoulder and
the actual can floats behind as the lifeguard swims. The rescue can is then
given to a drowning victim so that they can stay afloat and be pulled to safety
by the lifeguard. In this particular rescue, the can was not needed (at least
I didn't think so), but of course it was still strapped to my shoulder. While I
was working to free the victim from his death grip on the jagged barnacles,

my rescue can floated behind me, wrapped around a piling, and caught on the barnacles.

A lifeguard with a rescue can strapped on behind him.

After the surge of the wave passed, I found myself, now underwater and unable to breathe, still strapped to a piling. I released the strap and with one big kick and the help of the strong current I was on the other side of the pier. Feeling the warmth of the sun away from the shadow of the pier was a welcome relief.

Mike Frasier, the lifeguard two towers down, was there on the beach to see if I was okay. I was shaken up a bit but didn't have a scratch or bruise on my body. I remember Mike telling me, "There was no way I was going in after you on that rescue." As we were talking, my rescue can washed up right at my feet. The angel (sorry, but I have to assume there was angelic assistance on this rescue) was very complete in carrying out his assignment.

Yes, I was a lifeguard during this rescue, but there is no doubt that God saved the other swimmer and me. All I did was surrender my life to the task of saving another. The swift current and a submissive angel did the rest. In a real sense, I happened to be at the right place, at the right time, with a willingness to put myself in harm's way for the salvation of another. God did the rest.

Apparently even lifeguards need to be rescued. Heroes do as well. Paul needed rescuing. Second Timothy has more to do with lifeguarding than one would think. Paul is not just a lifesaver; he is also a victim who needs to be rescued. When recounting all the persecutions and beatings he endured, he says, "and out of them all the Lord rescued me!" (2 Tim. 3:11). When remembering his first stand before the judgment seat of the emperor in Rome, he says again, "I was rescued out of the lion's mouth" (4:17). And even while facing his own execution, he says with a twinge of defiance, "The Lord will rescue me from every evil deed, and will bring me safely to His heavenly kingdom" (v. 18).

That is good news, to be rescued from every evil deed and to enter into the heavenly kingdom. This will, of course, happen in the end, but we can live in that same kingdom's power and influence right now. And we can be a part of bringing that deliverance to others.

When we are willing to lay our life down for the salvation of others, God will do the work. We partner with him in this great work and not only do we find that he brings salvation to others, but we find our own life in the process.

A self-preservationist attitude is perhaps the greatest obstacle to being the powerful agents of God's kingdom that we are meant to be. Jesus said, "Whoever loses his life for My sake and the gospel's will save it" (Mark 8:35). The glory and the credit will go to Jesus, and yet he chooses, in his humble generosity, to share his glory with us. In the next chapter we will look at the type of person the Lord of the harvest chooses to use.

3

Scuba-la Happens

The Raw Material of a Real Hero

One slow afternoon I was working at a tower called Ave 18 in Venice North. It was not a very busy day, so watching a couple guys with their scuba gear going for a beach dive kept my interest. I had no idea just how entertaining this endeavor would actually turn out to be.

There isn't really much a lifeguard can do with scuba divers. They had each other as buddies and a dive flag, so I just watched them go into the water and didn't really give them a second thought—that is, until *one* of them surfaced and the other did not.

That got my attention, so as the one diver started walking up to the water's edge, I confronted him and asked, "Where is your buddy?" It is a law that certified divers always have a buddy with them.

Ave 18 tower (in the foreground) where I encountered some drunken scuba divers.

The diver responded, "He wasn't ready to come up, and I was out of air, so I came up alone."

I asked, "If you're out of air and you both went in together at the same time, why is he still breathing?" The real story, however, was on his breath: a strong smell of alcohol.

I gave the diver a stern lecture about diving and staying with his buddy, but there was little else I could do. I couldn't go looking for the other diver underwater.

Suddenly the second diver popped up about ten yards outside of the surf line and he was flailing around the water in a panic. Immediately I entered the water and swam out to him. He was panicking because he had run out of air. While thrashing about, he also managed to shoot himself in the thigh with his spear gun!

I dropped his weight belt, pulled him to shore, patched up his wound, and sent the two of them to the hospital to have the wound cleaned properly and stitched up. Fortunately, it was not too deep.

It is hard to fathom the many ways these guys were stupid: diving under the influence of alcohol, deserting a buddy, diving until all the air is out of your tank, panicking, rising to the surface in a hurry, shooting yourself in the leg with a spear gun. It's a "hall of shame" list of mistakes.

God's grace saved these guys. I couldn't save them; I couldn't even see them underwater. We don't give breath tests to scuba divers before they enter the water. These two really did not deserve to have survived, but I am glad they did.

For a long time I looked back at these two guys as fools—unlike me. But I am realizing that I am the same type of fool, capable of as many or more screwups. And I am fortunate that I am not fish food at the bottom of the ocean.

All of us need to recognize that without Christ we are lost in a sea of sin and death. Perhaps it is true that those closer to the bottom of the sea are actually more ready to recognize this fact, but this need not always be true. For all of us, our sense of urgency and dependence on our Lifesaver must grow and not diminish with time. Our desperate hold on him is our best asset. Then Christ's presence will become the most noticeable part of our life, and others will begin to see our Savior more than they see us. Christ in us will be our hope of glory (Col. 1:27), rather than our own intelligence, social skills, or appearance.

The raw material for a real hero is a numbskull who should be dead by now. I know that sounds wrong, but bear with me as I pursue this idea a little more.

Two Criteria for Selecting Those We Rescue

There are two very frustrating rescues that every lifeguard experiences. These two types of rescues have something to teach us about the people we try to rescue with salvation as well. They are what I use to test the water before I invest time and energy in a disciple.

Perhaps the most frustrating rescue is when a lifeguard spots a strong rip current pulling a weak swimmer out to sea. The guard dashes out of the tower, rips off his jacket, and straps on the rescue can. He leaps over the first wave, hurdles the second wave, dives under the third, and swims as fast as he can to the victim. As he approaches, he pulls the rescue can over and hands it to the weak swimmer who looks back at him in indignation and says, "What are you doing out here? I don't need your help." When a swimmer is in a dangerous rip current but his pride does not allow him to admit his need for help, it's infuriating.

What can a lifeguard do in such a case? We can't force the person to take hold of the floatation device. We are not allowed to club him over the head and drag him to shore. We can argue that he is in a dangerous predicament and will soon be drowning if he does not accept assistance. We can try to convince the person that he is not making progress, but ultimately he has to surrender his pride. We can't even sit and wait for the victim to realize the predicament he is in, as that would let the hundreds of other beach patrons go without any lifeguard, all for the sake of one arrogant person.

The only option for lifeguards at this point is to tell the drowning person that if he or she wants help, we will come back out, but only if the victim calls for help in front of all the other beachgoers. Then we have to return to the shore.

Ultimately Jesus is a lifeguard who comes to us wanting to save our drowning souls, but often he is met with pride and a deluded sense of self-sufficiency. Jesus will not club us over the head and drag us to shore against our will. He waits patiently for us to realize that he is not only the best alternative but the only one.

When Jesus sends out others to rescue souls, however, he is very clear that if they do not find hearts that are receptive to salvation, they are to wipe the dust off their feet and move on to another place in search of those who need rescuing.

The first criterion to look for in someone whom you wish to rescue and disciple is that he or she have an internal sense of desperation that is greater than his or her pride. This means that the person is willing to take hold of the

Good News and receive the rescue can. We simply cannot rescue people who do not want to be rescued. Jesus himself will not even violate this truth.

1. People Who Are Desperate (Luke 5:30–32)

Most discipleship programs today begin with saved people who either are already committed or want to be more committed. Often we think that we should begin with the most committed people when we approach the disciple-making process, believing that this will assure us of greater success in the end. But this is actually the reverse of how the kingdom of God is advanced. Jesus begins with those who are most desperate for salvation. In Jesus's kingdom the losers become winners and those who appear to be winners end up last (Matt. 19:30; Mark 10:31; Luke 13:30).

Often we avoid needy people for pragmatic reasons—they can be very demanding. Christian leaders even have terms for these people. We don't want to be blatant about it, so we refer to them in acronyms: *very draining people* are VDPs, *extra-grace-required people* are EGRs. Have we actually developed a code for such people so that we can refer to them without exposing our true intent of avoiding them? Are we embarrassed by our lack of grace and compassion?

Many experts in Christian leadership recommend that leaders not invest their time in these people because they are a losing proposition. And it is true that needy people can drain you if they are not making progress and if the ministry is not equipped to provide adequate help. But if we don't help the needy, and we focus only on "healthy" people, we have missed the point of God's kingdom. The discipleship process must begin with people who have a real need for Christ.

There is a temptation to think that good people make good soil for the seed of the gospel. In our church, however, we have a saying: *Bad people make good soil. There's a lot of fertilizer in their lives.* Fruitful plants tend to grow best where the fertilizer is abundant. Some people are drowning in the fertilizer of poor decisions and acts of unrighteousness. We need to look for these people and begin to plant the seed of the kingdom there. Regarding this, Jesus said, "It is not those who are well who need a physician, but those who are sick. I have not come to call the righteous but sinners to repentance" (Luke 5:31–32).

It can be refreshing to offer immediate assistance to people who want help. When we see a life begin to change in radical ways because we've helped the person find Christ, we are reminded again of what Christianity is all about. This can be very encouraging to a busy Christian.

In my book *Cultivating a Life for God*, I list seven very important reasons that we must start the disciple-making process with people who *desperately* need Christ. I think they bear repeating here.[1]

1. Desperate sinners will hold on to Christ because their lives depend on it.
2. Desperate sinners will see their lives change more readily than those who are already doing "well."
3. Desperate sinners are more likely to confess their sin because it is more obvious.
4. Desperate sinners will become walking and talking billboards about the power of the gospel to other desperate sinners.
5. Desperate sinners usually have more strategic contact with other desperate sinners who need Jesus.
6. Desperate sinners are the very reason Jesus came and died. He delights to save them.
7. Desperate sinners who are transformed by the gospel bring greater glory to God because it makes the miraculous that much more manifest. Only God could do such a miracle!

2. People Who Will Stay Faithful (2 Tim. 2:2)

There is no doubt that desperate and drowning souls will feel a need for Christ. Unfortunately, someone who is very desperate is not always the easiest to help. This leads us to a second frustrating rescue, which illustrates the other criterion to consider in choosing people to disciple.

Once I swam out to rescue a victim in a strong rip current and had the opposite reaction to what I described above. I found a desperate man struggling to live and willing to do whatever it takes. This victim took the floatation device with enthusiasm; the problem was that when he found he couldn't climb up on top of it and be completely out of the water, he started pulling on the rope to get closer to me and then climbing up on my head! If I had succumbed to the panic, we would soon both have been drowning because of his desperation.

Actually it is quite common to hear of double drownings, when a rescuer becomes a victim because of uncontrolled panic. The greatest threat in the water is not big waves, strong currents, or man-eating sharks. By far, most drownings occur because of one thing: panic. If people would remain calm and relax, lives would be spared.

Fortunately, I was well trained and knew exactly what to do when this desperate victim started to climb on my head. I simply held my breath and went underwater. He let go quicker than you can imagine because I was going where he least wanted to be. I popped up again a few feet away and said, "Now, let's try this again. Take hold of this rescue can or you will die." Again, he didn't hear me, because panic had seized control of every part of his body and soon he was climbing up on my head again. What did I do? I submerged yet again, and he soon figured out that I was not going to be his floatation device and began to cooperate.

When lifeguards face panicking victims, they must remember not to let a sense of urgency dictate the plan of action. Keep calm or you will both be in trouble.

In making disciples, it is very possible to reach out to desperate sinners who will have such a sense of need that soon they are dragging you down with them. The Lord realized this long ago and he has given us another criterion to consider when choosing someone to rescue: choose people who will be faithful to the healing process. This second criterion, while not obvious until the disciple-making process begins, determines its success.

Paul wrote to Timothy about passing on the baton: "Entrust these [things you have heard from me] to *faithful* men who will be able to teach others also" (2 Tim. 2:2). If a man or woman who has entered the process is not faithful to what we are doing, he or she will usually drop out. Any disciple-making process should not continue if the members are unwilling to continue with the goals. This second criterion establishes the balance for the busy person who is concerned about being drained (or drowned) by a needy individual who doesn't really want progress.

A Recycling God

These two criteria work together to form balance in transformation without allowing an unhealthy codependency. This has been the way of God from the beginning. God loves to recycle. He transforms garbage into glory and turns trash into triumph.

God chooses whom he uses, and most often the choice comes from those the world does not choose. He loves to turn tax collectors into truth-givers and downcasts into disciples. He receives more glory when he uses weak things that amount to nothing, adds his presence and power, and turns them into men or women of substance and even legend. Every one of us who follows

Christ is a recycled disciple—made from raw garbage and transformed into something beautiful.

Here are just a few of the many examples of this in the Scriptures.

David and His Mighty Men

David, at a low point in his life, found himself alone in exile, seemingly out of place. He was a shepherd without a flock and a king without a kingdom. Taking refuge in a cave, his family came to him. Then others followed. They were the outcasts, those who didn't fit in. First Samuel 22:2 describes them: "Everyone who was in distress, and everyone who was in debt, and everyone who was discontented gathered to him; and he became captain over them. Now there were about four hundred men with him."

David was supposed to be a king of God's chosen people. He became captain of the crooked, marshal of the misfits, ruler of the rejects, emperor of the exiled. The people whom nobody wanted to have around became the people David befriended. They lived together and fought together. They became a family, a tribe, and eventually an army.

Soon they were referred to as David and his men (1 Sam. 27:3–4, 8). Just by being with him, they were nobler—more wanted, more valuable. Also they became fearless warriors. As David rose in stature and fame, they also rose to high esteem and became legends. Their deeds are recorded in Scripture and they are still spoken of today. They became "the mighty men" (2 Sam. 23:8–39). They had gone from hopeless to heroes.

Jesus and His Apostles

After a night of prayer, reflection, and great consideration, Jesus chose twelve men to be his special disciples. He would leave his kingdom in the hands of these chosen envoys. The only casting agency he looked to was the kind that had a worm on the end of the hook. The men he selected were not the most talented, best looking, wealthiest, or best educated. In fact he was known for turning those away (Luke 18:18–27). He went for tax collectors, fishermen, and zealots with an edge. They included outcasts and men of questionable reputation.

After selecting them, Jesus spent time with them, trained them, mentored them, and appointed them to lead (Mark 3:13–19). Others, even their enemies, would come to see a difference in their bold character because they had spent time with Jesus (Acts 4:13). These men would turn the Roman Empire on its head, and their names will adorn the foundation stones of the new temple of God in New Jerusalem.

Paul and the Corinthian Converts

When Paul was in Corinth, the sin capital of the empire, Jesus told him, "I have many people in this city" (Acts 18:10). Paul made many disciples out of the sinners in that corrupt and immoral place. Eventually a church was born out of the darkness. Later in a letter to them, he would say:

> For consider your calling, brethren, that there were not many wise according to the flesh, not many mighty, not many noble; but God has chosen the foolish things of the world to shame the wise, and God has chosen the weak things of the world to shame the things which are strong, and the base things of the world and the despised God has chosen, the things that are not, so that He may nullify the things that are, so that no man may boast before God.
>
> 1 Corinthians 1:26–29

He would remind them of their humble beginnings by telling them:

> Or do you not know that the unrighteous will not inherit the kingdom of God? Do not be deceived; neither fornicators, nor idolaters, nor adulterers, nor effeminate, nor homosexuals, nor thieves, nor the covetous, nor drunkards, nor revilers, nor swindlers, will inherit the kingdom of God. Such were some of you; but you were washed, but you were sanctified, but you were justified in the name of the Lord Jesus Christ and in the Spirit of our God.
>
> 1 Corinthians 6:9–11

God delights in turning misfits into mighty men and zeroes into heroes. In this way he is able to demonstrate so much more of his glorious attributes. His miraculous power is made obvious. His compassion is also shown when he takes a fisherman and makes him a foundation stone for a glorious kingdom. This is what the kingdom of God is all about, and we need to get back to it.

If we get to thinking that it is our best assets that make us most valued to the Lord, we are close to being useless. We must become acquainted with our weaknesses if we are to see him use us for great purposes. Even seemingly successful people need to come to understand their own brokenness and desperate need for Christ before they are of use in the kingdom.

Be Strong in Grace

I remember distinctly a strange conversation I had with an older pastor over the sink of a men's restroom. He smiled and said with a hint of frustration, "Take care of your prostate while you're young so things will be much easier when you're older." I thought, *That is sage advice; I think I will.* Then my next thought was *How do I do that?* Sometimes suggestions are not as easy as they first appear. There are some commands in the Bible that are not as easy to obey as you might think they are.

Paul wrote to Timothy: "You, therefore, my son, be strong in the grace that is in Christ Jesus" (2 Tim. 2:1). These are words that many of us have read dozens of times without ever stopping to ask, "How do I do that?" I understand how to be strong in body: the one who bench-presses the most wins the gold cup. I know what being strong in intelligence looks like: the one with the highest SAT scores receives the scholarship. I know how to be strong in talents and abilities: the one with the most points in the game has the gold medal placed around her neck on the center podium.

These standards are easy to understand. But how do you become strong in grace? Grace is God's strength compensating for our weakness. So to be strong in grace—to have the most grace—is to be strong in not being strong. In other words, being weaker in yourself is what it takes to be stronger in grace. This is not an easy thing to do for those of us with a hyperactive self-confidence.

I think that is why starting with desperate people willing to be faithful to an ongoing process of obedience is key to being strong in grace. Our natural inclinations are to search for strong and graceful people rather than people who can be strong in grace.

After reading some of my books and articles, people may be tempted to think that only those whose lives are in the toilet are qualified to serve God. I can understand why people would assume that, but let me explain further. Certainly those whose lives are circling the drain faster and faster are often more inclined to reach out for grace and hold on to it with white knuckles. But it is also very common for exceptional people to recognize their need for grace. I do not think that only those who are in the toilet in this life can be disciples of Christ.

The apostle Paul, who wrote the words we are studying, was the rising young star of the Sanhedrin. In a letter he wrote to the Philippians, he described his pedigree, saying he was a Hebrew of Hebrews, a Pharisee on the fast track to the heights of spiritual leadership (see Phil. 3:4–6). Paul was certainly a successful person who was admired by his peers and contemporaries as a passionate and intelligent man. No one saw him as a loser.

It is possible for people who are strong in intelligence to be strong in grace, but it is necessary for us to empty ourselves of one to make room for the other. Paul goes on to say, "But whatever things were gain for me, these things I have considered loss for the sake of Christ" (v. 7). He summed up all of his human assets as a loss. He gets even more crass than that. Using street language (some would say gutter language), he counts his past accomplishments as *skubala* (v. 8). You see, I can't really say in a Christian book what he said. (I suspect that our own cultural and literary standards would edit the Bible to be less of a book if it were written today.) I have seen the word translated as "rubbish," which is not at all close to the true meaning of the word, but it is certainly more culturally sanctified than what Paul wrote. King James translates *skubala* as "dung," which is closer to its meaning. The word was a strong and crass word for excrement. Suffice it to say "Skubala Happens."

So I guess I was wrong, you do need to start in the toilet to be qualified, but I want you to understand that you can get there voluntarily. It is not necessary that you be a loser to be useful to God; it just requires that you be willing to be one—like Paul was. Are you willing to count all your own personal strengths that others admire as a loss? The journey to true greatness begins in the port of a loser, even for those who are considered winners in life. You cannot transfer your greatness in the world into a position of greatness in God's kingdom. The two economies function on completely different currencies.

Jesus said, "Blessed are the spiritually bankrupt [my paraphrase], for theirs is the kingdom of heaven" (Matt. 5:3). To be great in the kingdom requires a willingness to be least on earth. The kingdom is reserved for the least and the last in this human "race." Christianity has been a little too clean in recent days. I believe we need to get dirtier to get holier. All of us, even the highly successful, must come to the place where we recognize that our lives are crap (that's a better word for *skubala*) when compared to the goodness of Christ and his righteousness. Jesus was adamant about this.

So you might be thinking, *I'm just an ordinary person.* Or you might be a guy who goes through life with your thumb and forefinger forming an L (symbolizing "loser") on your forehead. The good news is that you may be much closer to true greatness than you ever realized. Reach for his grace.

Then, again, you may be a superstar among your peers and considered the standard of success in whatever you do. You are also just a heartbeat away from significance way beyond your measly success. You too must reach out for God's powerful grace.

The challenge is that for any of us to reach out for God's grace, we must first let go of whatever it is we were using to keep afloat in this life, and that is scary. Letting go is hard—for both the loser and the leader of leaders. Yes, it is true, the successful "winner" has more to lose than the "loser." But sometimes our hopes and dreams hold more sway in our hearts than things that are actually real and tangible. The person down on her luck must put down her hope of better luck to come. It can be as hard to let go of the excuses we have and the evil done to us—the things that have made us the losers we are today—as it is for the winners to let go of the graduate degrees and accolades.

Our hearts become attached, cemented, and fused together with the things that have made us who we are. Those things can be drugs, sex, scars, power, possessions, enjoyment, beauty, admiration of others, or even hatred of others. When our core is fused to these things, they begin to make up our identity. To let go of these things is a death sentence for sure. But the only way to find life in God's kingdom is to let go of your own life and cling to his. You will find a much more potent and true identity in Christ than in whatever you leave behind. Like Paul, you will count whatever you leave behind as *skubala* when you look at it in hindsight.

More Dependent Not Less

Here is an example of what I think Paul is talking about. When Charles Colson was advisor to President Nixon, he associated with some of the most powerful people in the world. Later in life, however, in a moment of reflection while speaking at a prison event, he realized that it was at his point of greatest weakness that Jesus used him most. He writes:

As I sat on the platform, waiting my turn at the pulpit, my mind began to drift back in time . . . to scholarships and honors earned, cases argued and won, great decisions made from lofty government offices. My life had been the perfect success story, the great American dream fulfilled. But all at once I realized that it was *not* my success God had used to enable me to help those in this prison, or in hundreds of others just like it. My life of success was not what made this morning glorious—all my achievements meant nothing in God's economy. No, the real legacy of my life was my biggest failure—that I was an ex-convict. My greatest humiliation—being sent to prison—was the beginning of God's greatest use of my life; He chose the one experience in which I could not glory for His glory.

Confronted with this staggering truth, I discovered in those few moments in the prison chapel that my world was turned upside down. I understood with a jolt that I had been looking at life backward. But now I could see: only when I lost everything I thought made Chuck Colson a great guy had I found the true self God intended me to be and the true purpose of my life.[2]

Colson goes on to say:

It is not what we do that matters, but what a sovereign God chooses to do through us. God doesn't want our success; He wants us. He doesn't demand our achievements; He demands our obedience. The kingdom of God is a kingdom of paradox, where through the ugly defeat of a cross, a holy God is utterly glorified. Victory comes through defeat; healing through brokenness; finding self through losing self.[3]

When he wrote to the Corinthian believers, Paul remarked about his spiritual journey:

> And He [Jesus] has said to me, "My grace is sufficient for you, for power is perfected in weakness." Most gladly, therefore, I will rather boast about my weaknesses, so that the power of Christ may dwell in me. Therefore I am well content with weaknesses, with insults, with distresses, with persecutions, with difficulties, for Christ's sake; for when I am weak, then I am strong.
>
> 2 Corinthians 12:9–10

Even those of us who are walking with Christ through the years must recognize that we need his salvation as much today as when we first believed—if not more. The closer we get to our holy Savior, the more we should become aware of our own lostness. I once heard Billy Graham, who has walked with God much longer than I, say, "The closer I get to heaven, the more aware of hell I become."

There is a paradox in the salvation process. We may think that as we grow closer to Christ's likeness, sin decreases and our need for the gospel also decreases, but this assumption is wrong. While it may be true that our life of obedience will include a decrease in sin, at the same time we should become more aware of sin and the grip it has had on our lives. Thus we should develop a more dependent attitude toward our Savior, his sacrifice and his ongoing ministry in our lives.

It is interesting to see the apostle Paul's self-awareness change over time. In his earlier writings he refers to himself as equal to the most eminent of apostles (2 Cor. 12:11). Later he writes that he is least of the saints (Eph. 3:8). In one of his last writings he calls himself the foremost of all sinners (1 Tim. 1:15). Was his sin and disobedience actually increasing over that time? Of course not. He was getting closer to his Lord and thus becoming more aware of his own weaknesses in the light of Jesus's perfection. He knew his need for the gospel better at the end of his life than he did at the beginning.

Don't be too proud to accept Jesus's help. Reach out, take hold of the buoy of hope he offers, hold on tight—and go for the ride of your life. Realize that to be strong in his grace, you must be weak in your own strength. That is why some dimwit divers are a good example of the sort of raw material God delights in turning into heroes he can use. The good news is that if this is indeed the raw material of a real hero, we have lots of potential heroes all over the place. But it takes something bigger than ourselves to propel us to the stature of a real hero, and that is what the next chapter addresses.

4

○

This Is a Job for . . . Me?

A Heroic Call to a Larger-Than-Life Mission

Rookie school, or "lifeguard academy," is where lifeguards learn the most basic techniques of lifeguarding. When I was in rookie school, we worked our tails off with run-swim-run workouts. There was a sense in which the trainers wanted to screen out the rookies that were too weak or lazy to become good lifeguards, so they worked us much like a drill sergeant at boot camp. Some never made it through rookie school.

While rookie school was full of learning, it is not where we learned how to be lifeguards. We learned *about* lifeguards in rookie school, but we *became* lifeguards out on the beaches and in the surf, learning from real-life experience and often under the tutelage of seasoned veterans.

It was actually quite common for an old pro to tell you to forget everything you learned in rookie school and then tell you what really works out on the sand and in the waves. I can't recall a single lesson from rookie school, but I will always remember the men who showed me firsthand how to save lives.

In this chapter we will look at the way one seasoned veteran passed on the skill of saving lives to a younger rookie. Heroes learn best from other heroes. That is the whole point to Paul's letter to Timothy.

Last Words Are Lasting Words

Someone has said, "Last words are lasting words." The words we share with loved ones in the last moments of our life are usually very important. If you knew that you had just a few days left to live, how would you spend your time? Would you watch television? Read a novel? Lie out in the sun to get a tan? Go shopping at the neighborhood mall? I doubt it. Probably you would spend that time with those most important to you. And I doubt that you would talk about the weather or how the local baseball team was doing in the playoffs. Most of us would make sure that our words were memorable and significant, because they would be our last.

Second Timothy is Paul's last word and testament. Written in his final hours while in a dungeon on death row, Paul passed on his most pressing words to his apprentice and successor. As you would imagine, this is a very personal and passionate letter. At a time when one would look back over his life, Paul asks himself, *What will survive of my influence in this world?* In this very personal letter, he charges Timothy with the responsibility to carry on the great work after he is gone. Here we find the principles Paul wants passed on in the discipleship relationship. He shows us what ingredients are essential if we are to see lives changed and ministry multiplied and if we're to have an influence down through the generations that follow us.

Paul starts the second chapter by explaining the importance of multiplying disciples and leaders for the strength and future of the church. He says, "My son, be strong in the grace that is in Christ Jesus. The things which you have heard from me in the presence of many witnesses, entrust these to faithful men who will be able to teach others also" (vv. 1–2).

A hero can be made in a moment, but there are those for whom their entire life is a heroic tale. Those who die leaving behind a lifetime of heroism have a code that they live by, which helps them make the right choices in times of duress and conflict. These are men and women who are living for something bigger than themselves. They have a calling that is worthy of their life. This can become a legacy that is passed on to others.

The Most Noble Mission

There is no greater legacy to pass on than the mission Jesus gave to us originally—to go and make disciples of all the nations. These were Jesus's last words to his disciples. Last words are lasting words.

I will never forget the last words my mother said to me. She knew it was the end, and in moments like that you want your words to be significant.

She sat up in bed, miraculously sober despite much pain medication, and said good-bye to each of my immediate family. Then she asked me to read the last chapter of the Bible out loud for all to hear. Not only did she need to speak last words, she wanted to hear them. Only recently had she become a follower of Christ, and she had a hunger to know the message of a book she had no time to read herself, so she just wanted to hear the end. I read the last chapter to her, and then she sank back into the bed, and the blankets of the medication covered her lucidity once again. She passed into the presence of the Lord a few days later. I was grateful for that one brief and lucid moment when I got to see the hunger of her heart longing to hear God's Word and even share it with her loved ones.

Moments before Jesus left the planet, he called his eleven disciples to himself and said, "All authority has been given to Me in heaven and on earth. Go therefore and make disciples of all the nations, baptizing them in the name of the Father and the Son and the Holy Spirit, teaching them to observe all that I commanded you; and lo, I am with you always, even to the end of the age" (Matt. 28:18–20).

These are the last words of Jesus to his close companions. You cannot find words that are more lasting in their implication or intention. There is not a nobler mission than this. These words are for every follower of Christ. They carry within them a reproductive pattern of obedience-oriented training. Christ commands us to make disciples and to teach them to observe his commands, including the making of disciples. In so many ways, these few sentences are masterful. They contain within them all that is necessary to become the heroes of his kingdom that he desires.

The Scope of the Mission

Personally, I want to have influence that expands in both time and space. In other words, I want the influence of my life to go beyond the driving distance to my church and beyond my eulogy.

Jesus gave us a mission that is bigger than any of us, and bigger than all of us together. The scope of his mission goes to all the nations of the earth, throughout all of time. He said to "make disciples of all the nations . . . to the end of the age." This requires that we all carry a part of the legacy, and none of us carries the entirety of it.

This is an incredible commission. It is huge. It is all encompassing. It is worthy of both our life and our death.

So many have shed their blood and sacrificed their lives to pass this important work on to us. On the other hand, today we face little or no persecution in the West, and we fold and give in when we receive a glance from someone that may embarrass us. A slight word of sarcasm and we give up. I will say this: unless we realize the significance of this important work and are willing to face humiliation, rejection, and scorn, we will not be fit to carry on such an awesome legacy. We must go even farther than that; we must be willing to face death for it—because it is worth it.

The only way for this to be fulfilled is if we pass this great mission on to the next generation who will live longer than us and go farther than us. But of course, that leads us to the next observation about Jesus's words; they also contain a strategy for fulfillment.

The Strategy of the Mission

The task is to make disciples; in fact, that is the actual imperative of the passage in the original Greek language. The rest of the commands (going . . . baptizing . . . teaching) are participles carrying the weight of the imperative to make disciples. In other words, the main thing is to make disciples, and the rest of the passage is about how to go about doing it.

Inherent in Jesus's command is the reproduction of the very command itself. The command is not obeyed until the next generation is also carrying the mission forward. Simply making disciples is not enough; your disciples must also make disciples, or the commission has not been accomplished. In a very real sense, *your* final exam is not to be taken by you, but by another person. Others will be the test of your life and the fulfillment of this command. You do not graduate until others have passed the work on to the next generation.

In a day when knowledge is the barometer by which maturity is judged, we learn from Jesus's words that the real test is not what you know but what you obey. It is not enough to know facts about the Gospels and Epistles; we must put them into practice to fulfill the commission. Even obeying them is not enough. We do not fulfill this command until others are fulfilling it because of our influence.

The church in the West is educated beyond its obedience, and more education will not help. What is needed is more obedience. Knowledge is not enough. What you do with what you know is the important thing. Knowledge is not measured by the facts you know. Knowledge is measured by how you put into practice in real life what you know.

Most of the people reading this book already know enough to be useful in serving the Lord. But for some reason we have been trained to think that we do not know enough to do anything really important. I have heard that if you took all those who are starting churches in the world and made a composite of the average church planter, she would be eighteen years old, Chinese, having read very few books, and without seminary training. The average American Christian already knows more than this hero who is starting dozens of churches each year. While we emphasize knowledge at the expense of obedience, it isn't what you know; it's what you do with what you know that is important.

The Source of the Mission's Fulfillment

The enormous mission that Jesus gave was thrown out to very ordinary people. The idea of it would be laughable, if not for this final observation. Anyone looking at the eleven disciples and hearing Jesus's commission would have thought this work was dead in the water before it had ever begun. How on earth could an intelligent person such as Jesus think that a motley crew of misfits such as these fishermen and tax collectors could carry out such a huge plan?

Indeed, the idea would be foolish if not for the opening and closing words of the passage. Jesus begins with the words "All authority has been given to Me in heaven and on earth." It is not "*a lot* of authority"; it isn't even "*most* authority"; it is "*all* authority" found both in heaven and on earth. That is a lot of power. When you ask who has the most authority in heaven, the answer is simple: God. And Jesus has *that* authority.

The words for *authority* and *power* can be synonymous. With only this statement of authority, we can assume that Jesus's command needs to be taken very seriously, because it comes from the highest seat in the universe. And this assumption is true. But the statement is not to be taken alone. It is to be joined with what he says at the end: "I am with you always."

All authority of heaven and earth is with Jesus, and he is with us. That is an incredible source of power to fulfill the commission given to us. In speaking about this very idea, C. H. Spurgeon had this to say: "You have a factor here that is absolutely infinite, and what does it matter what other factors may be? 'I will do the best I can,' says one. Any fool can do that! He that believes in Christ attempts the impossible, and performs it."[1] Spurgeon is masterfully unlocking this powerful truth that we need to understand today. After looking at this truth, the question begs to be asked: With this powerful and present source, how could we not all be heroes?

When you consider all the obstacles to the Great Commission, there is not a single one that can withstand the authority of Jesus. What are the things keeping us from fulfilling the Great Commission? Is it a boss who will not permit you to share your religious viewpoint? Perhaps it is a law that keeps you from sharing the gospel on a public school campus. Perhaps it is a government that has outlawed Christianity in the entire country. The reality is that none of these obstacles compares with the authority of Jesus. Closed doors and human laws are nothing compared to all authority of heaven and earth. Jesus describes himself as the one "who opens [the door] and no one will shut [it], and who shuts and no one opens" (Rev. 3:7). When we obey Jesus in this Great Commission, all authority of heaven and earth goes with us in the work. If this is so, we should be seeing greater fruitfulness. The only reason we do not is that we do not go forth believing in this powerful truth.

Final Words

In college I had a close friend named Jim who struggled with cancer for as long as I knew him. Eventually the disease overcame his body and he went home to Jesus. I went to visit him one late afternoon after he had been brought home for his final days. As I walked into his room, I could smell death. Machines were beeping and lights flashed, indicating that he was getting the pain medication he needed and monitoring his vitals. I noticed a stark contrast: death was everywhere, but in his eyes there was so much life.

We had a short talk. At times like this you want to make every word count. He told me he loved me, and I said the same to him through the tears. As I was walking toward the door to leave and let him rest, he stopped me and said, "Neil, I have something very important I need to tell you, but I can't tell you until tomorrow. Can you come back tomorrow?" I said, "Of course. I will see you tomorrow."

That night Jim died. I never was able to hear from him what was so important and it has always bothered me.

I am so glad that we do not have to wonder what Jesus's or Paul's last words were. They are clear and compelling and they reveal what was on their hearts as they were about to leave this planet.

In his last words, Jesus has given us the code, the DNA, of a heroic mission—a mission larger than life. This is what captivated Paul, and it is what drove him to live the sort of life he did. It was his greatest desire to pass on the mission to his son in the faith.

We have seen Jesus's last words, and we are looking closely at Paul's last words—and there is a striking similarity. Both men, at the end of their lives on this earth, were telling their closest companions to make disciples who will make disciples—to the end of the age.

In the next chapter we will look a little closer at this idea.

More Powerful Than a Locomotive

The Unstoppable Power of Multiplication

I was not the first lifeguard in my family. My father watched the same beaches I did when he was in his twenties. Before that, even before Los Angeles County lifeguards were established, my grandfather watched the water nearby at a beach club. My kids have competed as junior lifeguards on the beaches of Southern California. We have four generations of lifesaving and surfing in my family.

The Coles first came to California in 1849 in search of gold, but what we found was in some ways better than gold; we found a home at the Pacific Ocean. The Coles swim, surf, scuba dive, kayak, and some have even been known to sail. We have salt water in our veins. We have passed our

Neil's kids, Erin, Zach, and Heather, at a Junior Lifeguard Competition at a beach just south of Venice.

love of the ocean down through the generations, and I am confident that my grandchildren will long for the smell of salt water in a cool breeze off the grand Pacific.

Legacies are usually something special, which is why they get passed on. In these modern days we do not often see families passing a heritage down to succeeding generations. I am honored to have received and passed on the noble call of saving lives.

A Refresher Course in Basic Math

Paul wrote 2 Timothy at the end of his life. His primary concern was that the special power and transformation of the Good News be passed on through the generations and not end with his death.

He wrote: "You therefore, my son, be strong in the grace that is in Christ Jesus. The things which you have heard from me in the presence of many witnesses, entrust these to faithful men who will be able to teach others also" (2 Tim. 2:1–2). How many generations are in this verse? Paul, Timothy, faithful men, others also—there are four generations in this verse.

Multiplication is a popular topic in missions and churches today. Unfortunately, much of what people call multiplying is really just addition. When a small group is added, it is often called multiplying. When another worship service is added on Sunday morning, it is often called church multiplication, but it is merely addition. Adding a venue for worship in your church is not multiplying a church, it is merely adding. I am not against addition, but let's not call addition multiplication.

Even if you add an additional church to your denomination, you are still not multiplying, at least not yet. In the early stage of multiplication, addition plays a part—for example, 2+2=4 and 2x2=4. The difference is found in the sum of succeeding generations. If you merely add two more, the sum is six, and you are adding by twos. But if you multiply, you get eight, then sixteen, and then you know you are multiplying.

It is true that addition has a role to play in multiplication. In fact, multiplication is when every part adds an equal part to the whole. I guess, in theory, you cannot have multiplication without addition. Addition is not a bad thing; in fact it is far better than subtraction or division (which many of our churches in the West are experiencing).

Addition is good, multiplication is better, way better. Addition produces incremental growth, but multiplication produces exponential growth. The difference is seen in the results of multiple generations. I have suggested to people: "Let's not call it multiplication until we get to the fourth generation." Until we get to the "others also," we have not succeeded in multiplication. It is possible for a strong leader to attract other leaders who, because they are leaders, will have followers. You can have three generations of influence without really multiplying. But to get to the fourth generation, everyone must be investing all they have into the next generation, and that is when you have multiplication. When we have great-granddaughter or great-grandson disciples, leaders, or churches, *then* we are multiplying.

The thing about math is it is a world of absolutes; there is one right answer and many wrong answers to every equation. But if processes are mixed up, the solutions are screwed up. In Christendom today we have poor math skills, and our results are wrong in the end because of it.

Multiplication Is an Imperative

I remember it like it was yesterday. I went to the Urbana Missions Conference in 1987 as a young pastor of a college ministry. Many speakers from all over the world urged me to be concerned for the world. A seed was planted in my heart that continues to bear fruit to this day.

The biggest news of the conference was a world record of monumental proportions: for the first time in history, the population had passed five billion people. I remember hearing people say that the current population of the world had exceeded the population of all of history combined. Wow, what an amazing time to be alive! What an incredible task was before us!

That was only two decades ago, which may seem like a lot for a young person, but in the scheme of history, it is not even a blip on the radar. Today the population has passed six billion and is almost halfway to seven billion. What took multiple millennia to reach is now happening in mere decades, because the population of the world is multiplying. The church in the West, however, is not. We must find a way to get back to multiplying again.

In his book *Disciples Are Made—Not Born*, Walter Henrichsen described a display at the Museum of Science and Industry in Chicago that featured a checkerboard with 1 grain of wheat on the first square, 2 on the second, 4 on the third, then 8, 16, 32, 64, 128, and so on. Somewhere down the board, there was so much grain of wheat that it was spilling over into neighboring squares—so the display ended there. Above the demonstration was a question: *At this rate of doubling each square, how much grain would you have on the checkerboard by the time you reached the sixty-fourth square?* To find the answer to this riddle, you punched a button on the console in front of you, and the answer flashed on a screen above the board: *Enough to cover the entire subcontinent of India, fifty feet deep!*[1] There would be 153 billion tons of rice—more than the world rice harvest for the next one thousand years.[2] Henrichsen concludes: "The reason that the church of Jesus Christ finds it so hard to stay on top of the Great Commission is that the population of the world is multiplying while the church is merely adding. Addition can never keep pace with multiplication."[3]

You may have heard the fable of a father who offered his two sons a choice of either one dollar a week for fifty-two weeks, or one cent the first week with the amount doubling the next week to just two cents and continuing to double for fifty-two weeks. One son took the buck; the other took a chance and accepted the penny. We all know who wins. The son who took the dollar would have fifty-two dollars at the end of the year. The one who began with a penny would have enough money to pay off the national debt by the end of the year and still have plenty left over.[4] That's a father with some deep pockets!

Multiplication begins slower than addition, but like a car rolling down a steep hill, it builds up momentum as it goes. A penny can become millions, and then billions, and within a short time, trillions.

To illustrate this concept, Christian Schwarz and Christoph Schalk, in their *Implementation Guide to Natural Church Development*, give the following example: "Imagine a water lily growing on a pond with a surface of 14,000 square feet. The leaf of this species of water lily has a surface of 15.5 square inches. At the beginning of the year the water lily has exactly one leaf. After one week there are two leaves. A week later, four. After sixteen weeks half of the water surface is covered with leaves."[5] The authors then ask, "How long will it take until the second half of the pond will also be covered? Another sixteen weeks? No. It will take just a single week and the pond will be completely covered."[6]

Multiplication may be costly, and in the initial stages slower than addition, but in the long run, it is the only way to fulfill the Great Commission in our generation.

Imagine what would happen in life if you got the two processes mixed up. What would happen if NASA engineers added when they should have multiplied? What would happen in your own household budget if you made the mistake of multiplying figures when you should have simply added? The results would be problematic at best, disastrous at worst. So why do we confuse the two when it comes to something as important as reaching the world for Christ?

Because addition is faster in the beginning and multiplication takes time, often we are content with addition growth. We choose the more immediate success and instant gratification of addition instead of waiting for the momentum that can build with multiplying. Don't be content with addition. Stop applauding the pathetic success we see in addition and start longing again for the incredible power of multiplication. This would mean, in practical terms, not to look for immediate or large results in the early days. Christian leaders would need to invest in the few rather than in the multitudes, much like Jesus did. Growth would need to come from each part rather than from a single source or strong personality. We would need to think of ways to equip people to serve rather than simply serving people.

The Power of Multiplicative Momentum

Of course, in our current context, the success promised by addition is hard to turn down. It is so rare to have a church ministry grow at all that when one grows fast through addition, it is very desirable. It is hard for leaders to turn away from the crowds and invest in the few, but that is exactly what Jesus did.

Jesus knew the power of multiplication and he was willing to wait for it. He rejected the pressure of the crowds and chose instead to spend his life with the few that would multiply. We need leaders who are willing to do the same.

Small things can make a big difference. A tiny microscopic virus is devastating the largest continent on the earth, one life at a time. HIV has no bias toward color, creed, or culture, yet it is altering entire societies. Ultimately governments and economies will succumb to its destructive agenda.

Governments are attempting to destroy terrorism by aggressively attacking the leadership of Al-Qaeda and other movements. But we use addition defense against a multiplicative strategy and we do not make any dent in stopping the terror. When we strike down one leader, two take his place. Every time one Islamic extremist is dead on the street, two more take up arms. A decentralized, subversive, cell-based strategy is hard to stop, and the harder you fight against it with conventional strategies, the more it fuels the problem.

The idea behind nuclear bombs is that the smallest of particles, set on fire, can multiply the devastation in a fast and exponential manner, causing a combustible chain reaction resulting in huge destruction.

The devil understands the simple power of multiplying small things and creating extensive damage. It is time for us to counter our enemy with a strategy that works.

I have found that there are small things that can have a big impact in a positive way. Jesus referred to the kingdom of God as a mustard seed, the smallest of all the seeds known to man at the time. He went on to say that it would grow into a large tree that cast a shadow across the entire planet and down through the ages of human history. He also spoke about the kingdom of God being like leaven; add just a little to a lump of dough and through reproduction, soon the entire loaf is transformed. It is time for God's kingdom to reawaken to the same principle: small things can make a big difference in this world. Whether it's a seed, a neutron, an AIDS virus, or a disciple, a small thing can have huge implications via multiplication.

Still Haunted by My Times Tables

I was not a good math student, which makes it somewhat ironic that now I am teaching some principles of multiplication. As a boy, I found it difficult to memorize my times tables. I felt like I was being haunted by the numbers while trying to commit them to memory. I am still haunted by the math but in a far different manner. Today it is not the memorized answers that haunt me, but the new questions. There are some questions that have haunted me for several years.

These questions have led me to a simpler way of living for Christ and of functioning in the family of God. Let me share some of these questions with you: What would your church do if one hundred people came to Christ tomorrow? You would probably rejoice and find some new seats for your church auditorium. What would your church do if one thousand people came to Christ this week? You would probably have to start adding many more services and hiring new staff. What would your church do if ten thousand came to Christ this month? Now you are stretched beyond imagination, but it would be possible to rent a venue to handle that size group. What would your church do if one million people came to Christ this year? Now you are beyond the limits of your idea of church. But the real question is not *What if?* but *How?* How can our churches be prepared for rapid expansion?

Now, let's get more personal with these ideas. Take your current goals for your ministry and multiply them by one million. If you hope to reach one hundred people this next year and you multiply that sum by one million, you come up with one hundred million people who will come to Christ in a year. Does that sound farfetched to you? Of course it does. It is so far from any reality we have ever experienced. But, humor me, what if it *could* happen, would your current ministry methods be able to handle that amount of growth? The answer is more than likely no. Your buildings could not hold such numbers. Your staff could not accommodate the needs of that many people, and you couldn't hire enough staff to do so. You couldn't add enough worship services to your weekend or even your week to satisfy that number of people. Everything about the way you see and do church would have to alter remarkably.

The truth is, if you do not have the ministry structure or systems to reach that new goal in your lifetime, you do not have the systems that will multiply. If this isn't possible, your ministry strategy is based on an addition model. You see, multiplication growth can reach exponential results and a momentum that is beyond anything we can imagine, based on all our addition-bound experience. We can talk about multiplication all we want, but if the only key on our calculator has a plus sign, we will never see multiplication happen.

You cannot use an addition strategy to produce a multiplicative result. This is just a reality. One thing that is always true in arithmetic is that it is always true. It makes sense and is absolute. Math is black and white, right and wrong. We cannot pretend that the methods of incremental growth we employ will result in exponential impact. That is fooling ourselves. And to think we can start with addition strategies and slowly adapt and evolve into a multiplicative method is also deluding ourselves. We are deceived in the same way that the United States was when we thought we could slowly adopt the metric system—inch by inch. You must die to the old to put on the new. Jesus said, "Unless a grain of wheat falls into the earth and dies, it remains alone; but if it dies, it bears much fruit" (John 12:24). If you are content with the results of addition and are unwilling to let go of the method to see exponential growth, you are foolish.

The Mishaps of Multigenerational Disciple Making

Getting to the fourth generation in reproduction is not easy. Much of our disciple-making materials today have the disciple following the one ahead of him or her. Of course this makes some sense, but without realizing it, this approach eventually sabotages itself.

Jesus said, "A disciple is not above his teacher. . . . It is enough for the disciple that he become like his teacher" (Matt. 10:24–25). In other words, the best you can hope to do is match the character, skills, and knowledge of your instructor. The following diagram demonstrates that, as you progress to the next generation and the one after that, a noticeable depreciation in quality occurs:

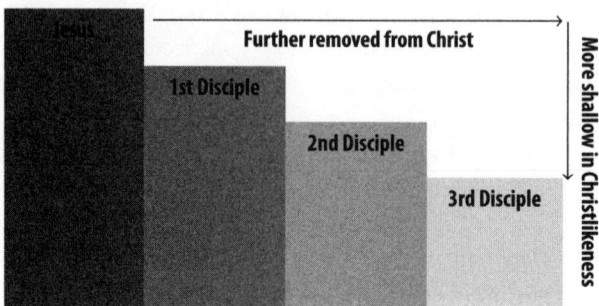

"A disciple is not above his teacher. . . . It is enough for the disciple that he become like his teacher" (Matt. 10:24–25).

Each generation is further removed from Christ and becomes more shallow in Christlikeness. It is much like making a photocopy of a photocopy of a photocopy. As the examples below demonstrate, the farther you go down the photocopy path, the more corruption becomes obvious and every flaw is passed down to all succeeding copies.

The Shortcomings of Multiple Generations of Copies Being Made

". . . but when they measure themselves by themselves and compare themselves with themselves, they are without understanding. . . . For I am jealous for you with a godly jealousy; for I betrothed you to one husband, so that to Christ I might present you as a pure virgin. But I am afraid that, as the serpent deceived Eve by his craftiness, your minds will be led astray from the simplicity and purity of devotion to Christ."
—2 Corinthians 10:12; 11:2–3

The solution is to make every copy from the Master, like the copy on the left. In other words, we need to make every disciple a first disciple. Our commission is not to make disciples of us, but disciples of Christ, and there is a big difference. This is actually the only way that disciples can excel beyond their human teachers and maintain the purity of God's kingdom through multiple generations of reproduction.

In the movie *Pay It Forward*,[7] starring Kevin Spacey, Helen Hunt, and Haley Joel Osment, a middle school boy is challenged by his social studies teacher to do more than just remember a few facts for a test. The teacher challenges each student in the class to try to come up with an idea that can change the world for the better.

One boy, played by Osment, takes the challenge to heart and comes up with a brilliant idea. During his oral report for the project, he says, "That's me," and draws a small circle. Then he draws three other circles below connected to the first by three lines and says, "And that's three other people, and I'm going to help them. But it has to be something real big, something they can't do on their own." He explains to his class that he doesn't expect them to pay him back but rather to pay it *forward* by doing three big things for three other people. He draws three other smaller circles under the first three with lines connecting them and goes on to sketch a growing pyramid of circles grouped in threes, all connected to the ones above by three lines.

Then he goes on to put into practice his idea by helping three people, who end up helping three other people, and a movement is born. Eventually the movement spreads to other states and keeps on going. One day a reporter whose car gets smashed receives the keys to a brand-new Jaguar with no strings attached from a wealthy attorney. The attorney simply calls it generosity between two strangers. When the reporter queries why he would do such an unusual thing, he simply says, "Just pay it forward. Do three big things for three other people."

The reporter starts hunting for a story only to find that a thief who was injured trying to escape from the law let the attorney's asthmatic daughter go ahead of him for care at the emergency room of a local hospital. Why did a criminal exhibit such kindness for a stranger? Because a homeless woman in Vegas had helped him out when he was desperate and challenged him to do three things for three other people. The idea behind this is simple, and yet it is profound. It is a multiplication movement that is passed along by all whom it touches. It all started with a middle school kid from a broken home in Las Vegas.

Small, simple ideas are the kind of things that will change the world. But what makes this work and what separates it from some multilevel marketing scheme is the simple idea that the favor has to be something big that the person cannot do for him- or herself and is passed forward without expectation of anything in return. First the favor is received and then it sticks in the heart of the recipient to such an extent that he or she can't help but pass it on to others. There isn't an initial selfish motivation behind it. That is what makes the whole thing "sticky" and motivates the ongoing movement. You see, if it were something simple and not big, like helping a lady with her groceries or opening a door for someone carrying a child, it wouldn't be remembered and it wouldn't tap into people's internal psyche. Because it is something big, they are motivated to return the favor by paying it forward.

The idea behind *Pay It Forward* has actually caught on, and some people have put the idea to work, starting a real movement of good deeds for others.[8] But the idea of paying it forward did not originate with this movie or even the novel on which it was based.

Jesus was the first to come up with the idea. He brings to each of us something so big, so special, that it captures our hearts forever—our own redemption from all our failures replaced with an abundant life of intimate connection with God. He did this when we couldn't do it ourselves. He gave us this big favor when we didn't deserve it. All he asks in return is that we pay it forward. "Freely you have received, freely give" (Matt. 10:8). "We love, because He first loved us" (1 John 4:19). Your own changed life should be motivation enough to pass it forward to others.

It doesn't matter if you are a high-powered attorney in LA or an awkward ninth grader from a broken home in Las Vegas. Anyone can be a part of the great bridge of life by passing forward the Good News of Jesus to others. You can play an important part in saving the lives of others and spreading the power of a movement that can change the world.

In the next chapter we will discern what sort of motivation can change the world.

The Heart of a Healthy Hero

Motivations That Make a World of Difference

In a city full of famous and powerful people who seek attention and media exposure, Lenny Skutnik was just an ordinary guy, unnoticed in a routine job at a government building in Washington, D.C. It was January 13, 1982, and one of the worst blizzards in that city's history had hit and was shutting down many of the businesses early, which had caused some unusual traffic on the bridges leaving the city center. Lenny was on his way home from work. The weather and commute were at the forefront of his mind as he approached the 14th Street bridge over the Potomac River, which was sealed with an inch-thick layer of ice.

Suddenly something violent ripped into his life, consuming all of his senses and thrusting him unexpectedly before dozens of cameras and microphones and into the heart of his nation. Within hours his picture and name were in almost everyone's living room on the evening news, and two weeks later he was standing with President Reagan and his wife, Nancy, at the State of the Union address.

At 3:59 p.m. that snowy day, Air Florida flight 90, a Boeing 737, took off from the National Airport. But there was ice on its wing, and this crippled the plane, rendering it unable to gain altitude. A few moments after takeoff, it crashed into the 14th Street bridge, killing seventy-eight people. All but four passengers and one crew member were lost in a moment. Miraculously these five people survived the crash, only to find themselves dying in the frozen water of the Potomac River.

Through the heroic efforts of the rescue workers on board a United States Park Police helicopter and one passenger named Arland Williams, who continued to pass the rescue lines to others, four passengers were dragged to shore where they were treated by paramedics and rushed to a nearby hospital. Williams, a self-sacrificing passenger, was stuck to part of the sinking plane, and became the only passenger to die by drowning.

Lenny Skutnik beside Nancy Reagan (on right) at the State of the Union address, where he was honored for his heroic service to the victims of the crash.

Another passenger, Priscilla Tirado, tried with everything she had to hold on to a rescue line to save her life, but her own body began to betray her. In second-stage hypothermia a person begins to lose feeling and control of her extremities because the body is using all of its blood to keep the internal organs alive. By the time third-stage hypothermia takes over, the victim loses the use of arms and legs, and even coherent thought begins to fade as the body starts to shut down. In conditions like those on the Potomac that day, stage-three hypothermia comes quickly.

Contrary to all her will, Priscilla's muscles simply would not grip the rope, and she fell back into the icy cold waters of imminent death. She called out desperately for someone to help her in one last gasp from her lungs. Lenny Skutnik could not hold himself back any longer. Without permission or a whole lot of forethought, he took off his shoes and jacket. In his short-sleeve shirt, he dove into the freezing water to rescue a complete stranger. He managed to get her to safety and saved her life, risking his own.

What would convince someone to do that? What would compel someone to dive into a freezing river? Why would this ordinary guy risk his life to try to save a stranger? Swimming against unseen currents and dodging chunks of broken ice, debris from the airplane, and floating bodies, all with hurricane force winds coming down on him from the blades of the helicopter above, Lenny was unyielding in pursuit of his goal. Clearly his motivation went beyond the norm. Unlike the firemen and emergency response team, who also displayed great bravery that day, he wasn't paid to do it. He wasn't working on a merit badge or thinking, *This will get me on the evening news.* He wasn't trying to save Priscilla because he knew she was such a good person. He didn't know her at all.

Something noble in this man's heart compelled him—motivated him—to rise above being ordinary to do something of such heroic proportions that a short time later the president would say, "Just two weeks ago, in the midst of a terrible tragedy on the Potomac, we saw again the spirit of American heroism at its finest . . . the heroism of one of our young government employees, Lenny Skutnik, who, when he saw a woman lose her grip on the helicopter line, dived into the water and dragged her to safety."

The Significance of Motivation

Motivation is such an important element of a productive life. It's what gets you up in the morning and brings you home at night. To lose your motivation is deadly. Motivation is the fuel of life.

Motivation is also a most powerful thing. In 1871 on a small hill in South Africa, a diamond was found, then another and another. Soon, without any concern for the environment, people were digging up so many diamonds in this place that eventually the hill disappeared entirely. But still the digging did not stop. So many diamonds were found that many people became very wealthy. They founded the town of Kimberley on the spot, and it had modern conveniences not found anywhere else on the continent of Africa. You have heard the expression "turning a mountain into a mole hill," but this goes farther, much farther. The people were so motivated that eventually the hill became a hole, the largest man-made hole on the earth. Focused motivation can literally move mountains aside and leave deep caverns in their place.

The hole in Kimberley where once there was a hill. Now filled with rainwater, the hole is in fact much deeper than it appears in this photo.

Motivation is a tricky thing. It can be clouded by all sorts of influences. It is not always an easy thing to discover or use. Much of what consumes the mind of the typical pastor today is figuring out how to motivate unmotivated people. How do we make people want to do the right thing?

If I could invent a simple pill or magic dust that would suddenly motivate people to do all that is good, I could make *billions* of dollars. But of course that would go directly against all the values of Christ and his kingdom. In the kingdom of God people choose love, rather than being compelled by someone or something to do so.

Types of Motivation

There are different kinds of motivation. Some motivations are *natural,* meaning all people on the planet share them universally. More ethereal or *spiritual* motivations are options to every person on the planet but only motivate us if we choose to let them. *External* motivations are forced on a person by an outside source. *Internal* motivations come from the heart of a person. If we lay these four different motivational factors on a chart, mapping out the possible configurations, it could look like the diagram below, where the internal is opposite the external and the natural is opposite the spiritual.

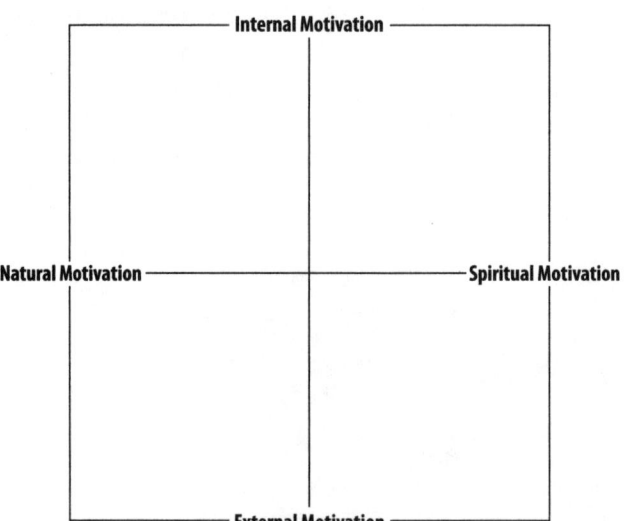

When motivation is charted in this way, we find four quadrants that demonstrate four different ways people are motivated.

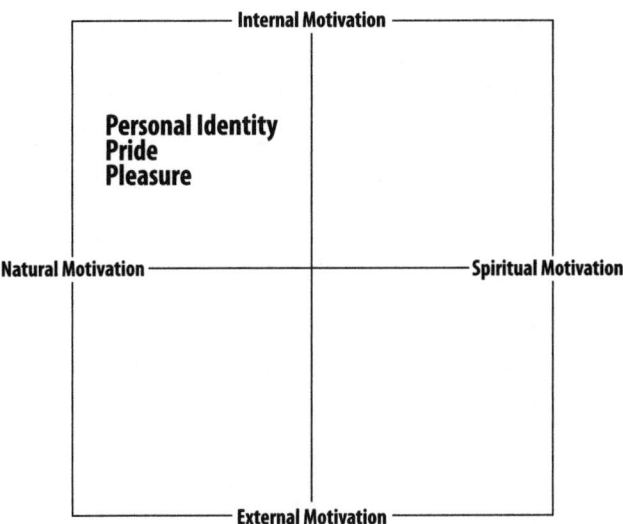

In the upper left quadrant is a person motivated internally in a natural way, the same as every person on the planet. Because it is natural, this is true for all people and reflects the way God designed us. Our own identity, our pride, and pleasures fall in this quadrant of motivation.

In the bottom left quadrant we find natural, external motivations, which are applied all around the world to get people to do what others want. In all cultures and nations people use the threat of pain, the pressure of peers' opinions, and the ever so useful paycheck to get people to do what they want.

In the lower right quadrant we find the external, spiritual motivations that are often employed by people to get others to behave the way they want. People use guilt, shame, and fear to compel others to behave in certain ways.

The upper right quadrant is the unique place of a person's heart that is influenced by internal, spiritual motivation. It is a longing from inside that some but not all feel. Internal, spiritual motivations are, in a real sense, the most valuable, but like most valuable things, they are also the motivations that are the most fragile. As such they are vulnerable to sin and neglect and can be replaced with callousness (Heb. 3:12–13). It is in this realm where we find a passion for truth, compassion for others, and a reverence for God.

Each kind of motivation creates particular results. External, spiritual motivations (the lower right quadrant) will always result in emotional bondage, whether it is inflicted by a dysfunctional parent wanting to corral a child or a cross pastor wanting to beat up on his congregation. External, natural motivation (lower left) will always result in a form of social slavery. Oh, don't get me wrong; it isn't evil to be paid by your employer, but when you accept money from your employer, he or she has some level of control over you. In one sense, he or she owns you for the job. The natural, internal motivation (upper left) fuels personal ambition. Only the internal, spiritual motivations can result in a sincere and selfless love.

Internal Motivation	
Results in personal ambition	Results in selfless love
Personal Identity Pride Pleasure	Passion for Truth Compassion for Others Reverence for God
Natural Motivation	**Spiritual Motivation**
Pain Peer Pressure Paycheck	Guilt Shame Fear
Results in social slavery	Results in emotional bondage
External Motivation	

Motivation is such an important part of the disciple's life that in 2 Timothy 2:3–13 Paul addresses the concern of motivation for the disciple. This passage has appeared to many to be a string of unrelated metaphors, each with its own lesson, but it is in fact a treatise on the motivations of a godly disciple. Paul lists three natural motivations that are internal and three spiritual motivations that are internal.

In this critical passage about the heart of a disciple who passes his or her influence on to the next generation, Paul devotes all his attention to motivations that are above the horizontal line of our chart. In the kingdom of God there is no room for external motivations. Try as we have over the years, making people behave in a godly way if it's not their will to do so is an exercise in futility.

The motivation for following Christ and reproducing disciples must be *internal* rather than *external*. As Paul wrote in a dungeon while awaiting execution, he appealed to Timothy passionately about internal motivation, something he could write about because he had lived it.

Soon Timothy would not have Paul to challenge him. That's the reason Paul wanted to be sure that Timothy had the internal motivation he needed. If the drive for making disciples does not come from within, the process will eventually break down and will not continue. Disciple making that truly re-produces is propelled by an intrinsic motivation. If we need someone looking over our shoulder to either commend us or correct us, we will fail to see any movement that changes the world. It is that simple. It is that important.

Proverbs 16:26 says, "A worker's appetite works for him, for his hunger urges him on." I don't usually have to motivate myself to eat. Hunger does that for me. Most of us do not need external motivation to eat, though we may need it *not* to eat. The food industry thrives because we all have an internal drive to eat. Another industry that does well, but exists to motivate us not to eat, is the diet industry. You would think that the two are in competition, but in reality, the diet business does best when the food industry does well. Ultimately, the food industry taps our internal motivation and is far more successful than the diet industry, which utilizes external motivations.

Paul appeals to the internal motivations that will keep Timothy going even in the face of hardship and setbacks. He uses several analogies and admonitions to demonstrate the drive we need to have that will see us through even when we suffer hardship. He begins with natural, internal motivations. The thing about natural motivations that we must understand as Christians is that we cannot be rid of them; they are a part of being human. Rather than pretend we don't have them, Paul shows us that we need to surrender them to Christ so that they become sanctified.

Natural Motivations

1. *A desire to make those to whom you are responsible proud* (2:3–4). Paul writes: "No soldier in active service entangles himself in the affairs of everyday life, so that he may please the one who enlisted him as a soldier" (v. 4).
2. *A desire to be the best we can be* (2:5; 4:6–8). Paul describes this motivation when he says, "If anyone competes as an athlete, he does not win the prize unless he competes according to the rules" (2:5).
3. *A desire to benefit from the results of our efforts* (2:6). Paul says, "The hard-working farmer ought to be the first to receive his share of the crops."

But this is just the beginning of motivation for a follower of Christ. Even when transformed by the gospel, these natural motivations are not enough. If these are all we have as motives, we are no different from billions of others on the planet. And we are to be different. There should be something about us that the world cannot understand; we should reveal a part of God to the world. So Paul goes on to address internal, spiritual motivations.

Spiritual Motivations

1. *Moved by the love of Christ, demonstrated in his sacrifice for our sins* (2:8–9). Paul charges: "Remember Jesus Christ, risen from the dead, descendant of David, according to my gospel, for which I suffer hardship even to imprisonment as a criminal; but the word of God is not imprisoned."

2. *A compassion for the lost and dying souls in this world* (2:10). Paul describes his own motivation with these words: "For this reason I endure all things for the sake of those who are chosen, that they also may obtain the salvation which is in Christ Jesus and with it eternal glory."

3. *Inspiration rooted in the character of God* (2:11–13). Paul reminds us, in poetic fashion, of God's faithful character. He says, "It is a trustworthy statement: For if we died with Him, we will also live with Him; if we endure, we will also reign with Him; if we deny Him, He also will deny us; if we are faithless, He remains faithful, for He cannot deny Himself."

These motivations are not natural; indeed, they are *super*natural. When the world encounters someone with these motivations, the world cannot understand or stop that person.

This is where the Christian life is meant to be lived, in the fourth quadrant. This is where love comes from. Most of what the world thinks is love is really a selfish desire for personal fulfillment. Occasionally true love is seen, a reflected image of God found in his created people. It was from this place that Jesus saved the world.

Paul: An Example of Internal, Spiritual Motivation

Paul was writing to Timothy about the keys to a heart that would die for another. Paul had intimate knowledge of this. In a letter to the Corinthians he shares what I consider his résumé. Those in Corinth had been led astray and told not to believe in Paul's apostolic gift or calling. So he wrote to them to remind them of his true credentials as an apostle (2 Cor. 11:22–29).

One of his "qualifications" is that he was "beaten times without number." Anyone who has ever been beaten remembers it and probably remembers every blow. Being beaten is not something one easily forgets. I wonder how many times Paul would have to be beaten up before he would lose count?

He goes on to say, "Five times I received from the Jews thirty-nine lashes." One of the reasons it was thirty-nine lashes and not thirty-eight or forty is because forty strikes of the whip were considered lethal. Thirty-eight would be too little and forty too much. The whip used in such an instance became known as a "cat of nine tails," because it was made up of several whips with lead weights attached at the end. The whips would be woven together at the handle. Often pieces of sharp broken bone were laced in some of the tails to tear away at the flesh when the whip was withdrawn from its victim's body. This scourging with a "cat of nine tails," similar to what is shown so graphically in Mel Gibson's film *The Passion of the Christ*, was horrific and evil. Paul went through it not just once, twice, three times, or four, but five times. His back must have been one giant scar.

"Three times," he says, "I was beaten with rods." The same back that had already received 195 lashes with a cat of nine tails, also received a caning—not once, not twice, but three times!

He says, "Three times I was shipwrecked, a night and a day I have spent in the deep." I have not met many people who have been shipwrecked at all, let alone three times. If Paul gets on the cruise ship, get off at the next port, because the boat is probably going down. I am just grateful Paul was not around during the time of air travel.

Paul also says, "Once I was stoned." This statement is incredible. It is not a comment on his days in the drug culture of the sixties. There are not many people in history who can write on their résumé that they have been executed; Paul could. When we get to heaven, we will not find very many people, perhaps only one, who can say they were executed twice. Paul was stoned in Lystra (Acts 14:19–20) and left dead under a pile of rocks. Then, his life came back, his lungs filled with air, and he rose from the pile, brushed off the dust, and walked right back into town to preach to the people. What sort of motivation is this? Where does it come from? How can someone like this be stopped?

Paul had a motivation that goes well beyond anything else the world has ever seen. It is not often that we see someone who is willing to suffer and die for his beliefs, but it does happen. This sort of love is not natural; it is otherworldly and only possible by the abiding presence of the Holy Spirit and a heart willing to surrender to the love of Jesus.

Internal versus External Motivations

The motivations below the horizontal are not uncommon at all. Many churches devote much of their time, energy, and resources to working below the horizontal axis. Some throw guilt, shame, and fear at people to hold them ransom to behavior that is fitting for the church. But I think the external motivation we are most guilty of employing in the church today is in the external, natural quadrant. We pay people to do the needed work. In the Western church we tend to invest our money in our deficiencies, with the result that we develop more deficiencies. When we need youth supervision, we hire a youth pastor. If we need better music on our stage, we hire musicians. If we want our kids cared for, we hire children's workers. We use money to make sure that the work is done and done well. Why? Because external motivation works.

Imagine you started a business, a McDonald's franchise because there were only a few of the restaurants in your town. Would you hire workers or make a call for volunteers? Of course you would hire workers, because who would want to contribute their time and energy flipping burgers for the cause of over nine billion served? External motivation works, and it is not always wrong. In some contexts it is the right alternative.

Both internal and external motivations work. But the church is not a business. It is meant to be a movement. If we resort to paying people to serve, we have started down a path that cannot result in transformation.

Many pastors have felt the pressure of visiting sick parishioners in the hospital. If the pastor doesn't call on the sick, often he or she will be in serious trouble. While laypeople may not understand many things about the spiritual kingdom, they do understand being an employee. The pastor will soon be reminded that he is paid to be the pastor and one of his tasks is to visit the sick.

But what if he does visit? Does it make you feel loved knowing that he is paid to come call on you in your moment of need? We don't know; maybe he would come anyway. I am sure many would. But we can't really know for sure because he *is* paid to do it. You see, real love does not come from this quadrant. It comes only from the internal, spiritual quadrant. It comes when we "remember Jesus Christ, risen from the dead" (2 Tim. 2:8). We love *only* because he first loved us. This is why Jesus was so careful to instruct us to take the bread and cup regularly—to remember him and the body broken and the blood shed for us. This is where the internal, spiritual motivation comes from. When we forget Jesus Christ and him crucified, things of less value motivate us.

All the motivations below the midline in the diagram result only in manipulation. Human efforts to control the outcome of other people's actions will not spread a grassroots movement. Even if they could, the effort would be lost, because only what is done in love will last (1 Cor. 13:1–3; 2 Cor. 5:9–15).

While it is right to sanctify our natural hearts, if the only motivation we have is found in the upper left quadrant, we will be no different from anybody else on the planet. Ultimately the natural motives can be useful for God's kingdom, but only if they are in tandem with internal, spiritual motives. Without the all-encompassing love found in the upper right quadrant, the internal, natural motivations will result in selfish ambition.

Unleashed, the motivations found in the upper right quadrant can turn the world upside down. They are so powerful that nothing on the planet can stop them. These motivations can initiate a movement, which, once the momentum is released, cannot be stopped. These motivations can actually rise

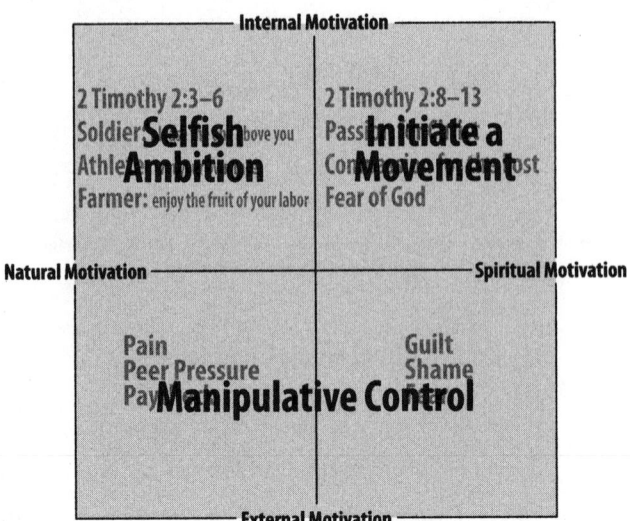

within people to such an extent that death itself cannot stop them, because the motivations pass on to others in a chain reaction. Death serves only to spread them further. Wherever the church has faced its greatest persecution, these motivations have won the day.

Someone once said, "The blood of the saints is the seed of the church." This is true. Satan has little he can do to stop people motivated like this, except to tempt them to settle for the lesser motivations of the other three quadrants. I suspect this is one key reason the church in the West is so stagnant and lifeless; we are not living in the upper right quadrant.

All of these motivational incentives are internal drives that will cause someone to delay immediate gratification to aspire to a greater cause. Paul urges Timothy to remind the church of these things (2 Tim. 2:14). These are the motivations that create a hunger for Christ and a drive to stay the course in the face of opposition (vv. 3, 9).

The key to effective disciple making and multiplying is tapping internal motivation. Many discipleship methods, however, resort to external motivation, which is much weaker. We have people sign a "contract" (or we spiritualize it and call it a "covenant"), stating we will fulfill the obligations of the method. Or, as some encourage us to do today, we keep an empty chair in the meeting to remind us to reach out to others. If empty chairs ever did win people to Christ, most of our churches would be experiencing revival. How many of us really share the gospel so that a chair will be filled? It would be far better if our motive were to see heaven filled. Pardon my expression, but I really mean it when I say, *to hell with the empty chairs!*

Once I had a boss who would fine us a dollar for every minute we were late to a staff meeting. If we have to resort to this kind of tactic, we have already lost the battle. When meetings leave staff feeling better for having been there, the leader does not have to resort to such manipulation to get the meetings started on time. By adding the fine, he actually made the meetings *less* attractive. If one were a few minutes late, it was better to find an excuse not to go at all.

If disciples do not *want* to move forward, but do so only out of guilt and obligation, the discipling process will end as soon as the pressure is removed. Even while the external compulsion is present, the process will lack quality because the disciples lack enthusiasm.

The Best Motivation

The basis of Christianity is the new covenant, in which God writes his law, not on tablets of stone but on human hearts (2 Cor. 3:1–11). The reason that Christianity continues is not because we have better rules than other religions or stiffer punishments for breaking the rules. The reason that the church continues generation after generation is because God changes hearts by regeneration. Christianity begins in a heart that is set on fire from heaven and cannot be quenched on earth. Any incentive less than that will ultimately hurt the cause rather than help it. The good news of salvation by grace through the death and resurrection of Jesus is the spark that will change a heart and provide incentive for obedience the rest of our lives. The powerful presence and influence of King Jesus in our daily life is what empowers us to transform ourselves and the world around us.

If the Spirit of God does not grip our hearts and move us to invest our lives in the most important cause of all, no manipulative tactics, gimmicks, and persuasions will get the job done. In fact this very idea is what separates true Christianity from all other forms of religion. It is the gospel that transforms a soul from within that is the essence of our faith. Everything we are and do should stem from this. The rest of the religious world appeals to external motivation and good works to merit a better life. If we appeal to the same, we offer nothing better than what the false religions and cults offer today. Christianity begins with the assumption that none of us merits life; we are absolutely dependent on help from above.

A while ago I had a very enlightening conversation about this with a self-avowed Satanist. Yes, we sometimes find light in the darkest of places. He was a very intelligent young man with a photographic memory. He would read and memorize entire books, sometimes as much as a new book every day. He had read every sacred writing he could find including the Bible in his quest for spiritual enlightenment.

His name was Josh and we had built a relationship over the months. In my book *Organic Church*, I actually tell more of this story, but a portion of it bears repeating here.[1] I saw him walking down the street and offered him a ride. He climbed into my old red T-Bird and suddenly made a shocking announcement: "I'm thinking about changing my religion."

My first thought was, any change is a step in the right direction, but I refrained from saying it out loud. I asked, "Josh, what are you thinking of changing your religion to?"

He said, "I'm either going to become a Buddhist or a Christian."

At that point I could have made an attempt to discredit Buddhism so that he would have to choose Christianity, but I didn't. I've learned from experience not to go that route, because then he would only end up defending Buddhism, and I would unintentionally push him closer to it. Instead, I asked him why on earth he would choose to become a Christian, so that he could defend the truth of Christ.

The Satanist made a very profound observation that I think we Christians should listen to. He said, "I have studied all the major religions and read most of the sacred writings and I have found one important difference between Christianity and all the other religions—grace." He went on to elaborate, "The fact that God would give us all his goodness when we do not deserve it and cannot earn it is remarkable. But I don't think grace is anymore evident than in the sacrifice of Christ for our sin. The fact that he would willingly pay the penalty for our sins even though we are awful people and he is so good is hard to ignore." With some tears in his eyes, this Satanist then said, "And that is why I think I may become a Christian."

I have heard the gospel preached by a lot of different people but never more compellingly than by this Satan worshiper. If a Satanist can see the internal, spiritual motivations that flow from the very heart of God as the best part of who we are, why can't we? Why can't we see that it is the freedom and grace found in Christ's life and death that can empower and embolden us to do great works beyond anything that can be accomplished with other means of motivation?

If you were given the choice of going into business with an all-volunteer staff or a paid staff, which would you choose? Most would opt for paid workers over volunteers because it is easier to motivate them to do the job the way it should be done. With financial remuneration, one can add bonuses, extra commission, a raise, or other incentives. On the other hand, one can also threaten a loss of job or a drop in income if the work is less than desirable. External motivation *does* produce results.

If you were given a choice of going to battle against a volunteer army or an army of paid mercenaries, which would you choose? I would choose the paid workers. Why? Nobody in their right mind will take a bullet for a buck! Few men will risk their lives for the sake of a paycheck. That just wouldn't make sense. What kind of bonus is worth dying for? This is one reason why the Iraqi army rolled over so easily when the US military first invaded Iraq. They were on assignment motivated strictly by external influence rather than a cause. But an army of men who are willing to give their lives for a cause is hard to beat, which the United States discovered while Iraq was under their occupation. The Soviet Union discovered this in Afghanistan. Superior weapons are often no match for hearts sold out to a cause worth dying for.

The church is an army of volunteers in a battle for the souls of people. We must be willing to "suffer hardship . . . as a good soldier of Christ Jesus" (2 Tim. 2:3). This is the kind of motivation that can turn a world upside down. We need to stop functioning as a business, concerned with the bottom line, and start acting like soldiers who are at war fighting for a cause worth dying for. We have weapons in this war that are so much more powerful than external means (2 Cor. 10:3–5). Love, peace, humility, prayer, truth, grace, hope—spiritual means to transform lives—are available to us. Why would we opt for less?

The kind of discipleship that will make an impact on the next generation will be the sort that grabs the heart of the disciple. Our methods must tap the disciple's intrinsic motivation rooted in a vital relationship with God (Rom. 2:28–29). Our discipleship must have no less a goal than a transformed life. Conformity to external standards is not enough. We must set hearts aflame with passion for Christ.

If we can't see our *own lives* changed by the power of the gospel, we have no right to expect to see the *world* changed by our message. If the gospel is not more important to us than life itself, the world will not be attracted to it. If they can't see that we value the gospel, why would we expect them to?

Freedom of Choice

Few have been as effective as Hudson Taylor at stirring up a desire to take the gospel to those who need it most. Taylor recruited hundreds to serve in the China Inland Mission. Once he commented on the subject of motivation to fulfill the mission and create a movement. "In the study of the divine word," he said, "I have learned that to obtain successful laborers we do not need elaborate appeals for help. [What we need is] first earnest prayer to God to thrust forth laborers, and second, the deepening of the spiritual life of the church, so that people should be unable to stay at home."[2]

There is nothing more futile than trying to get unmotivated people to be moved. My life is too short to spend it trying to manipulate unmotivated people to do important things. I would much rather give my life to a few motivated people who will make a difference.

In the comedy *Bruce Almighty*, God grants his powers, with one hitch, to a man played by Jim Carrey. Carrey's character, Bruce, is told he cannot violate free will. With his newfound omnipotence, Bruce becomes arrogant and changes so much that the love of his life begins to slip away from his grasp. He tries desperately to *make* her love him but fails completely. Finally, he asks God (played by Morgan Freeman), "How do you make someone love you without affecting free will?" At which God laughs and replies, "Welcome to my world, son. You come up with an answer to that one, you let me know."

Certain actions can be compelled, but love is always a choice of free will. God left the tree in the garden for a reason: without a choice we could never love, and love is the baseline of all that is truly spiritual and holy. It is the fulfillment of all that is right. Without a choice we are incapable of love and are only involuntary slaves operating under compulsion or robotic creatures that merely act on impulse.

Perhaps one reason we often opt for lesser means of motivating people (i.e., appealing to the other three quadrants of motivation) is because we fear people may choose the wrong things. After all, they often do. That's the thing about free will: people will often make the wrong choice. But if we do not allow people the freedom to make wrong choices then, by default, we do not allow them to make the right choice either. So love must be chosen over other options, or it isn't love.

Try telling your spouse someday, "I love you, because I said I would and now I have to." How well do you think that would go over? That isn't love; it is obligation. I don't love my wife because Dr. Phil tells me I have to. Love may lead to obligations, but it always starts with a choice and each of those obligations remains a choice.

When we resort to external means of motivating people, we may get them to behave according to our prescribed patterns but we lose something in the process. We lose the most important thing—love. I, for one, refuse to live in a home or church that is moral in its behavior but does not love.

So to win the best prize, we must risk losing it. That is the great gamble behind the spiritual nature of God's kingdom. It is definitely worth the risk.

Actually Jesus took the greatest risk in this universal enterprise, and I for one am glad he did. He never violates our choice, but woos us to follow him with his love for us.

What Will You Leave Behind?

Paul could leave this planet victoriously (2 Tim. 4:7–8) because he left behind someone who could carry the work to the next generation. We would all do well to ask ourselves, *If I were to die today, what of significance would I leave behind?* We should share Paul's concern for lasting influence and begin to invest in transformed disciples who can take the message of the gospel to the next generation. Who is the Timothy in your life? Who will carry on after you're gone? Christianity's very survival depends on the lives that we leave behind, lives that have been changed and prepared to carry on after us.

Goals should be more than targets to shoot for. Goals should provide a level of accountability to keep us on track. I have set three goals for my life in ministry:

1. That more churches would be started the year after my death than all the churches started during my life (this would indicate in the best possible measure that we are indeed multiplying).
2. That a handful of leaders into whom I have poured my life would far surpass my own influence in this world.
3. That the books I write will still be relevant and read seventy years after my death (this is a goal to keep me focused on transferable concepts that rise above a trend or cultural phenomenon).

What do you want to leave behind? Will this world be better off for your brief presence? If you had only a year left, what would you do with your limited time? If today were your last, how would you spend it? To whom will you pass the baton in this cosmic, historic relay race?

When we were trained as lifeguards, we were told emphatically that if our own lives were endangered, we were to back away from the rescue. This makes sense; the lifeguard service does not want two victims. But I remember distinctly when the trainer also said, "If you choose to place your own life in harm's way, that is your choice and there will not be any penalty. But we cannot ask you to do this." As I have already related, there were a couple of times when my life was in jeopardy in the line of duty. In those times it was not my paycheck that motivated me; it was not my desire to be valued by my peers. In those moments it was motivation from within, a desire to save a life that was all consuming. This kind of love is always a choice.

Having the right motivation is crucial. In the next chapter we will discover from 2 Timothy what it takes to become prepared and equipped to do every good work God has for us.

7

Who Needs a Utility Belt?

Being Prepared and Equipped for a Great Work

Prepared but Not Equipped

It was a warm July afternoon with temperatures in the low nineties in the St. Louis area. A church took some of its volunteers for an outing at a park along the Meramec River in Ballwin, Missouri, to honor their service to the church. The sacrificial nature of these people would soon be demonstrated in a dramatic yet tragic fashion for the nation to see and mourn.

The slow moving river on a sunny afternoon was deceptively calm. No one would ever suspect the unrelenting power that courses through it. There were close to fifty kids there and the children sought fun and relief from the heat in the cool waters of the river.

One young boy playing a little too far out slipped into water where he could no longer touch the bottom. Suddenly what appeared to be a slow and calm flow of cool water proved to be a constant and unforgiving current. As the boy was drifting quickly down the river, a couple of the older kids went to rescue him, and in fact did save his life, but in the process found themselves swept into a far more dangerous part of the river. Five young people ages ten to seventeen died trying to save one another in a sad story of sacrifice. Four of the five were siblings. The young boy who would have drowned was saved in part because of the sacrificial compassion of the other children who sadly gave their lives in the rescue.

When I first read this story in the newspaper, I was moved to tears. I was at once struck by the courage and compassion of the young children who gave their lives, one after another. I was also saddened by the tragedy of this great loss that could have been prevented. With the right equipment and training, this tragedy might not have happened.

It is not uncommon to read stories such as this, though in this case the number of victims is extreme and adds to the heartbreak. Many people are prepared to help others in a rescue situation, but unfortunately they are often ill equipped to do so. It is very common to hear of would-be rescuers who become victims. If you are not equipped to do the job, it is not enough to be willing to jump in the water.

Equipped but Not Prepared

On another July weekend at a Santa Monica beach, I saw a situation where the rescuer was equipped but not prepared. The surf had been rising for several hours and had topped out at sets of twelve-to-fifteen-foot waves. All the lifeguards were on duty because a sunny weekend will always bring large crowds, and the big surf meant we would face a lot of rip currents and weak swimmers. Sure enough, it was a busy day. I was only a second-year guard at the time, practically a rookie.

Early in the morning I remember watching the beginning of a rescue in this huge surf. It involved an old friend who was also a lifeguard and a couple years older than I. He was someone I always looked up to. He and I competed with and against each other in high school, both in swimming and water polo. He was one of the best swimmers I had ever known—in a pool. The ocean, however, is different. Currents, waves, hidden obstacles, all make the ocean more hostile than the pool. The ocean hits back.

While we were standing together in a backup posture, about to join other lifeguards in a large rescue operation, he shared with me that he was afraid and didn't want to go in the water. He asked me if I would go in instead and let him stay behind on the beach. I was shocked and a little disappointed in my friend, whom I had admired. But I was glad to enter the chaos of the big surf.

This friend was equipped for the job but not prepared to venture in. He was an excellent swimmer, much better than I was. He was carrying a rescue can and was fully trained as a lifeguard, but skills and knowledge are often not enough. He was not prepared for the moment.

To be useful to our Lord, it is not enough to be prepared if we are not equipped. It is also not enough to be equipped if we are not prepared to do the work. Paul gives us clear instruction in how to be both prepared and equipped to do any good work God calls us to. In this chapter we will uncover what is necessary for every disciple to be prepared and equipped.

Spiritual Resuscitation

As lifeguards, we were taught how to resuscitate drowned victims. Cardio-pulmonary resuscitation (CPR) was a vital part of our training. We all hoped we would never have to use the skill but we were prepared if it was needed. Those of us who never had to use the skill liked to think it was because we were good lifeguards who rescued victims before they drowned, but it may just be God's grace, what the world likes to call dumb luck.

It is amazing, but even after someone's heart has stopped beating and he or she is no longer breathing, in some cases CPR can bring the person back to life. CPR technique has remained relatively the same through the years, but there have been some improvements. That is the reason lifeguards must be recertified every year. A good lifeguard is always prepared and always up to date in his skills.

In a similar way, a follower of Christ must also be prepared and equipped for every possible good work that he or she may be called to do.

The word *disciple* carries the idea of discipline. Paul tells Timothy and us in this last letter that there are two essential disciplines necessary to make disciples. These are the disciplines needed to prepare and equip ordinary people to do extraordinary work for the Lord. Both elements are necessary for effective disciple making. They go together and are as essential to the process as exhaling and inhaling are to breathing. In fact they are much like breathing. They are the CPR of people who need life. It is what gets their heart started for Jesus and is as simple as "out with the bad air and in with the good." Exhaling, inhaling, and communication are necessary for spiritual resuscitation.

Exhaling

In the Christian life, *exhaling* is confessing your sins to one another (2 Tim. 2:19–21). Paul wrote to Timothy:

"Everyone who names the name of the Lord is to abstain from wickedness."

Now in a large house there are not only gold and silver vessels, but also vessels of wood and of earthenware, and some to honor and some to dishonor. Therefore, if anyone cleanses himself from these things, he will be a vessel for honor, sanctified, useful to the Master, prepared for every good work.

The first discipline necessary for a disciple to grow into usefulness is the confession of sin. Unless we are cleansed from sin, we will not be useful or honoring to the Lord. Christians are people of confession. John wrote, "If we confess our sins, He is faithful and righteous to forgive us our sins and to cleanse us from all unrighteousness" (1 John 1:9). Without confession there is no cleansing. When we do confess our sins, we become cleansed and honorable, and our message becomes acceptable.

Paul likens us to vessels. By vessels, Paul means containers. Some are vessels of honor and some of dishonor. We all have daily contact with both kinds of vessels. A friend of mine is a plumber. He works with vessels of dishonor—toilets. My dog may want to drink water from a toilet, but I would never do so; it is a vessel of dishonor. My wife, Dana, and I used to have a weekly ritual every Monday evening, which involved vessels of dishonor. After I had settled down in bed and almost fallen asleep, she would graciously remind me that I needed to take our two vessels of dishonor out to the curb so that the truck of dishonor could take the contents to the dump of dishonor. Now that we have a teenage son, the ritual has changed and we both remind him to do the job.

While speaking to a congregation, I once held up two different vessels to illustrate the difference between a vessel of honor and one of dishonor. Both were guaranteed to be sanitized and full of clean and cool water. One was a crystal goblet, the other a bedpan. No matter how clean it is, none of us would want to drink from a bedpan; it is a vessel of dishonor. But if you came to my home and I served you dinner with our fine china and crystal, you would gladly receive it because it would be an honor. Paul is showing us, by this example, that when we are cleansed by confessing our sins, we become vessels of honor; as such, our message is more readily received.

The real difference between a vessel of honor and one of dishonor can be summarized simply: with a vessel of dishonor, you want to make deposits but not withdrawals. One experience we can all relate to is when we push the lever on the toilet and the water starts to rise instead of descend. This scenario is so intense (especially as a guest in someone else's home) that we lose our mind and start talking to porcelain as if it could understand us. We might even resort to making deals with it. This is because we want nothing to do with the contents of a vessel of dishonor. But with a vessel of honor, we are happy to receive its contents.

King David, a man after God's heart, was not a perfect man. He sinned in some of the most grievous ways imaginable—adultery, murder, lies, and cover-up. But he turned back to God. In his confession to God for his involvement in the Bathsheba scandal, he said: "Create in me a clean heart, O God, and renew a steadfast spirit within me. . . . Then I will teach transgressors Your ways, and sinners will be converted to You" (Ps. 51:10, 13). The way to have our message received by lost souls is to have our souls cleansed by confessing our sin.

Confession is verbal agreement. When police officers want a confession, they are looking for the perpetrator to agree with the charges. When we confess our sins to God, we are saying we agree with God that our sinful behavior is wrong and unholy.

In addition to confessing our sins to God, there is a place in the Christian life for confessing our sins to others of a common belief and purpose. James says that healing comes to us when we confess our sins to one another in a supportive environment of prayer (James 5:16).

Since the Reformation, Protestant churches seem to have discarded the idea of confession of sins to others. In a rush to be separate from Roman Catholics, they lost a valuable and needed part of spiritual formation. Not only does James tell us that if we confess our sins to one another, we will be healed, John also explains that it is a necessary part of being a true Christian. It is our only path to righteousness, as I will explain below.

As Protestants we believe wholeheartedly with confession of sins to God, just not with one another. We cite 1 John 1:9: "If we confess our sins, He is faithful and righteous to forgive us our sins and to cleanse us from all unrighteousness." This verse by itself seems to indicate that we need to confess privately, in our hearts to God and not involve others in the dynamic. But the context of this pivotal verse is confession to other people not just to God. Hear the context:

This is the message we have heard from Him and announce to you, that God is Light, and in Him there is no darkness at all. If we say that we have fellowship with Him and yet walk in the darkness, we lie and do not practice the truth; but if we walk in the Light, as He Himself is in the Light, *we have fellowship with one another*, and the blood of Jesus His Son cleanses us from all sin. If we say that we have no sin, we are deceiving ourselves and the truth is not in us. If we confess our sins, He is faithful and righteous to forgive us our sins and to cleanse us from all unrighteousness. If we say that we have not sinned, we make Him a liar and His word is not in us.

1 John 1:5–10

We can agree that verses 6–8 and 10 have to do with fellowship with one another. Why would we assume something different in verse 9 about confessing our sins? There is simply no escaping the fact that this whole idea of confessing our sins is somehow tied into our relationship with one another. It is not simply a spiritual matter between you and God; it is a matter between you and the others in God's spiritual family. Our fellowship with one another is contingent on our being open and walking in the light. If we do not open up and confess our sins to others, we are not even in the truth. It is that important.

I am not advocating going into a dark booth, sliding a window open and saying, "Bless me, father, for I have sinned." Unless of course, he says, "Yeah me too; you go first." It is mutual confession, one to another, that brings cleansing, healing, and Christ's righteousness. I am not advocating another priesthood; I am advocating the same priesthood that Jesus set up—the priesthood of all believers.

A Believable Message

Confessing sin regularly will make others more receptive to the message we bring. Often we think that if we confess our inner secrets to others, we will lose credibility in their eyes. Many have found, however, that the opposite is true. When we have the courage to confess our inadequacies, we often *gain* credibility in the eyes of others because we demonstrate humility, honesty, courage, and a willingness to take sin and righteousness seriously. We are seen as authentic, brave, and, most of all, *human.* This will tend to raise us in stature, not tear us down. It is important to make our confessions in a safe place where confidentiality is a value, but often our fears of exposure are unwarranted. On the other hand, when there is no confession, often there is suspicion and hypocrisy. People know that humans are fallible. When we pretend not to have faults, it raises suspicion not credibility.

The most common reason that unbelievers give for rejecting the gospel is that Christians are hypocrites. Whether pointing out the Crusades a thousand years ago or the latest televangelist's fall from grace ten minutes ago, without a doubt the number one excuse people give for rejecting our message is that Christians are hypocritical. Perhaps there is a little too much truth in these complaints. The world sees the label on the outside of our vessels, but they want no part of the contents. They are telling us that they do not want to receive what we offer, because they see an inconsistency between our message and our lives. A better label on the outside is not going to make us any more attractive to the lost. What is needed is a heart transplant. A new life from within that is clean and full of light is what will turn things around so that we are no longer shunned as undesirable, but sought out as life bearers.

Do we really think that others believe we don't sin? Do we really think that we can keep our masks on and fool people into thinking we don't give in to temptations and have flaws? Of course not. So when we do confess our sins, it substantiates our authenticity rather than chipping away at our credibility.

In our relationship with God this is especially true. We can never fool him with our masks. He knows how many hairs we have on our heads (Matt. 10:30) and he also knows what thoughts we have in them. We can hide nothing from almighty God. So when we confess our sins, he isn't shocked. There are no hidden scandals in heaven. When we confess our sins, we don't embarrass God; in fact, we please him. In the psalm mentioned above, David writes: "You do not delight in sacrifice, otherwise I would give it; You are not pleased with burnt offering. The sacrifices of God are a broken spirit; a broken and a contrite heart, O God, You will not despise" (Ps. 51:16–17).

A Dangerous Cover-up

Working at the beach in Southern California (especially Venice Beach) allows the opportunity to meet all sorts of people from all walks of life. The last few years of my lifeguarding, I worked in a supervisory tower. I had the shift that opened the beach each morning at 7 a.m. It was my responsibility to wash and fuel the emergency response vehicle and patrol the whole section of beach until other guards started arriving and checking in.

Every morning I also provided the wake-up call for several homeless people who slept under the lifeguard towers. I got to know them personally, buying them coffee or an occasional breakfast, and I found out what interesting lives some of them had lived and how circumstances had brought them to such a state of hopelessness. I befriended one younger man who had recently been released from prison but had nowhere to go. I bought him breakfast every now and then and we would talk. For a week I didn't see him at the beach and I assumed it was a good sign.

Then on one particularly hot and busy weekend day, he flagged me over away from my tower and the other lifeguards. I saw a panic in his eyes and knew something was wrong. He was very secretive and hesitant to talk with me. I asked him what was wrong, and he said he was hurt. I asked where and why, and he said, "I hurt my foot." I told him to show me where he hurt himself. When he rolled up his pant leg, I saw the nastiest wound I have ever seen. I can't describe in detail all that I saw without turning your stomach. Even the color of his foot was turning green. I asked him what happened. At first he wouldn't tell me. I insisted that he tell me or I wouldn't know how to help him. Eventually he told me that his ex-wife had shot him.

Apparently she had a restraining order to keep him away, but in the desperation of homelessness, he went to see her anyway, and she shot him. The problem is that this had happened a week earlier. Out of fear of being caught, he ran or limped off to hide out. Being on parole he had broken the law by going to see his wife, and now he was afraid to go to the hospital for fear they would report the gunshot, which is legally mandated, and he would have to go back to prison. So he wrapped up the wound in a stolen towel and hoped for the best.

A week on the streets with a bullet in his foot was lethal. The infection of a wound that has not been cleaned or treated was poisoning his whole body. I told him he had to go to the hospital immediately. He adamantly refused. I told him, "Listen, this is serious. You will be fortunate if you get to keep your foot, but if you let the wound continue in its infection, the poison of this infection will soon kill you." The thought of death was scarier than prison, and he finally relented.

I radioed for the paramedics. Of course the headquarters needed to know what sort of injury to report when they called the paramedics, so I told them it was a gunshot. This information immediately released a whole chain reaction of events.

The first response I heard was a request to repeat what I had just said. Unlike the lifeguards on TV, most of us do not usually have to respond to gunshots. Because I had to make the call on the radio, every lifeguard vehicle on the beach heard it, and the buzz on the radio was immediate. Every emergency vehicle within miles of my tower was sent scrambling. Some were afraid that they would be shot at. Immediately the police were summoned. I could hear the adrenalin pumping through the questions they started firing at me. "Is your life in danger? Is there a suspect to apprehend? Are patrons under immediate threat?" It was not easy for me to find a pause long enough to say that it was a week-old wound but urgent nonetheless. Once I was able to explain it, the tensions eased.

The paramedic arrived, looked at the wound, wrapped it up, and immediately transported the man to the hospital. Unfortunately, he never returned to let me know what happened. I often wonder what became of him.

This episode provided me with a visual lesson that I have kept with me to this day. When we sin or are hurt by others, we carry a wound in our soul. Most of us think like ex-cons on parole in fear of being found out. We try to cover over the wound and go on with our life, content to walk with a limp, hoping that with time all things will heal, but they won't. Wounds that are covered up but not cleansed will infect and poison our soul. Our fears of being caught can cause us to cover up wounds that do not have to be lethal, but because we fail to open them up and cleanse them, they infect and spread the wound to other areas of our spiritual life. These wounds, left covered up for fear of being found out, slowly kill us. The solution is always to open up the wound and clean it out. We must remove the invading substance that causes the infection, or the wound will never heal.

Each of us knows how hard it is to confess the darkness, sin, and inadequacies of our soul. This is universal, though more challenging in some cultures than in others.[1] Since the very first sin ever committed, we have struggled to come to terms with our fallen nature. Adam hid in the garden. First, he covered up his shame with a fig leaf. Our cover-ups are often more revealing than we would like them to be. Once Adam had wrapped himself in a leaf, he hid in the woods. Soon God called for him and drew a confession out of him, and Adam quickly resorted to shifting the blame to others. We have not progressed much through the ages.

God describes his kingdom as a kingdom of light. Light exposes and dissipates all darkness. We hide in darkness, but in the light everything is open and disclosed. God himself is clothed in light.

There is freedom in the light. All the bondage that we held on to in the darkness dissipates, and we are left in the grace and freedom of Christ. The Christian life is not a life of secrets. There is something powerful about living a life fully disclosed. Secrets eat away at our soul. They take constant effort to maintain. And what good do they do? But a person who has no secrets, no guile, is free and strong. Confession and disclosure are the path to freedom, wholeness, and healing of one's soul.

We are deceived into thinking that confession will destroy relationships; in fact the opposite is the case. When we hold on to secrets, we have to lie about ourselves to the people around us, and this destroys our relationships, just as Adam and Eve found themselves blaming each other in the grand cover-up. A man and wife who have no secrets, however, will find their relationship to be real, honest, and intimate. They will know each other.

The only way to heal the wounds of our soul is to open them up and cleanse them. Covering up infected wounds can be a deadly game and will not only bring bondage but will also prevent healing and health. We simply must learn to open up the book of our lives and share what is within in a safe and honest relationship.

When we confess our sins and are cleansed, we become "useful to the Master, prepared for every good work."

Inhaling

In the Christian life, inhaling is planting God's Word in your heart (2 Tim. 3:16–17). The regular intake of Scripture is the second discipline needed to be useful to the Master. Again Paul writes to Timothy: "All Scripture is inspired by God and profitable for teaching, for reproof, for correction, for training in righteousness; so that the man of God may be adequate, equipped for every good work."

The truth is clear: it is the Word of God that changes lives. It can keep us from sin (Ps. 119:9–11). It performs open-heart surgery on our souls so that we can be cured of our sin (Heb. 4:12). It provides us with direction (Ps. 119:105). It is what sets us apart for God's purpose (John 17:17). We are foolish to think that we can equip people with anything other than the Word of God. No amount of books, tools, or sermons can replace a steady diet of God's Word for equipping God's people.

For a few summers I worked at a tower directly in front of the division headquarters for all of the LA County lifeguards. It is a tall round building overlooking most of Venice Beach. Up four flights of stairs are the offices of the highest-ranking lifeguards. It is the tallest building for miles around and for a young lifeguard, it could be intimidating working in its shadow.

Ave 23 tower with the division headquarters behind it.

I was not envied for working in this tower. It was constantly under the watchful eyes of the most influential men in the agency. A mistake could set your whole career back.

Every day I would see the chief come down and go for a workout. I would say, "Hi, Chief," and he would graciously nod his head, but that was the extent of any conversation I ever had with him. He remained high up in the offices over my head, while I remained alert and cautious down below, trying not to make any big mistakes in front of the boss and his staff.

All of us have been in a situation similar to this. In the world there is a hierarchy that leaves some at the top and others below. Rarely is there communication between the top dogs and the peons at the bottom.

I have never received a call from the president of the United States. He doesn't even know I exist, and he isn't really interested in my opinion of world affairs, so he isn't pursuing communication with me. But what if he did? Wouldn't it be weird if all of a sudden the president wanted to meet with you and search out your thoughts and feelings about important matters? How would you feel if he wanted to give you important assignments in his administration? Well, you may not ever get to meet the president and advise him about anything, but the God who rules over the universe does want to sit down and talk with you about important things every day. That is incredible. All we have to do is make some time for him. If the president called and asked if he could have a half hour of your time today to talk about important things, you wouldn't tell him you were too busy for such a meeting. It doesn't matter what political party you voted for; if the president wanted your audience personally, you would make time. But so often we get too busy to give God time. We take his Word for granted, forgetting that it contains words of life.

Often I ask audiences if they like to read instruction manuals. Usually there are a small handful of people who do; the rest of us do not. We are the ones who use only about 10 percent of our computer software capabilities, and our VCR is still blinking "12:00" (and yes, we still have VCRs). The few who read the instructions use their equipment much more effectively than the rest of us.

Then I ask the audiences if they have ever received a love letter from someone they really have a thing for. When they raise their hands, I ask them how they read their love letters. "Did you read the first line, 'Dear Joseph,' and then set the letter down to meditate on the deeper meaning of those words rather than going ahead to read the rest? Of course not!"

How do people read love letters? They read the whole letter, every word, all the way through, and then they read it again and again. They even smell the letter, wanting to consume every part of it. They may even take it with them in their coat pocket or purse, so that if they end up waiting for a bus or in line at the bank, they can take it out and read it again.

We must begin to see God's Word as a personal love letter that God has written to us. It's not just an instruction manual. Yet often we approach it like an instruction manual. When something goes wrong, we turn to the troubleshooting section (the concordance) to find the text that addresses our problem, and then we read just that paragraph divorced of context, flow, and unity of thought.

The intake of Scripture to transform a life from within is a strong theme throughout Paul's last letter. He challenges Timothy to "present (himself) approved to God as a workman who does not need to be ashamed, accurately handling the word of truth" (2 Tim. 2:15). Timothy was reminded that he was taught the Scriptures by spiritual parents even from a young age (3:14–15). Paul commands Timothy to "preach the word" in all times no matter how receptive people are (4:2).

The word translated "inspired" in 2 Timothy 3:16 means literally "God-breathed." All Scripture is born on the very breath of God. We breathe in what he breathes out. This is a form of spiritual resuscitation that resurrects our souls and rejuvenates our lives. We must see ourselves as dead victims of a drowning in whom Jesus has breathed new life. His Word is as necessary to our survival as breath itself.

Preparing and Equipping

When we confess our sins, we exhale the bad air. When we read and meditate on the Scripture, we inhale the good air. Breathing requires both.

Paul indicates that our cleansing from sin *prepares* us for every good work, while our reading of Scripture *equips* us for those works. One makes us ready to be used; the other gives us the equipment to do it. It is useless and even dangerous to have equipment that you are not prepared to use. But likewise, we cannot be effective by simply being prepared to do a job if we don't have the equipment to get it done.

The word translated as "equipped" means to be fully outfitted and supplied. In some ancient literature, the word was used in relation to a fully stocked rescue boat.[2] Without a steady intake of God's Word, we are not equipped for the work of search and rescue.

If we built a new house on a lot without clearing away the old one that stood there, we would not have a safe and suitable home to live in. Before building the new, there must first be a deconstruction phase where the old is cleared away. Once this has been adequately addressed, we are ready to build a new house in its place. If we tore down the old house but never built a new one, we would find ourselves dangerously exposed and vulnerable to all sorts of health problems.

Confessing our sins is the deconstruction phase—clearing out all the wrong assumptions and admitting to the faulty behaviors that have damaged our lives. Once this has been done, the truth of God's Word enters in and builds a strong place on a good foundation.

Effective disciple making requires both of these disciplines working together to transform a life from the inside out. You would think that all of us are experts on breathing. I have been doing it all my life. I'm so skilled I can even breathe in my sleep, and I'm not that good at multitasking! The sad reality is that spiritually we have lost the art of confession and Scripture intake, and the results are lethal. We might as well give up on breathing.

The Universal Pattern

Paul uses another analogy to teach this same idea. Often he refers to taking off the old man and putting on the new. Like clothes, we must first take off the old before we can put on the new. When I use this analogy, I ask, "What would happen if I decided to wear these same clothes for a year and never take them off? What if I worked in them, played in them, slept in them, and relaxed in them, but never took them off? A year later I would smell so bad, people couldn't stand to be within forty miles of me.

"Now suppose someone told me to put on some new clothes, so I went and got a new set of clothes and put them on—over the old ones. I would still stink, and now I have contaminated another set of clothes. The only way to be really clean and healthy is to first take off the old—get naked—and then put on the new."

This is the pattern Paul continues to set up and reinforce in every place he ever works. It is essential for the Christian life. It is as essential spiritually as breathing is physically.

Paul established this universal pattern of taking off the old and putting on the new everywhere he went to produce quality disciples who could, in turn, pass on the pattern to others. My friend and mentor Thom Wolf is a biblical genius. He was the first to unlock from the New Testament the missional concepts of *oikos*[3] and *person of peace*.[4] It was Thom who first revealed this discipleship pattern to me in the New Testament, and since then, I can see it everywhere.[5] For multiplication to occur from one life to another, certain characteristics must be evident in the people so that a simple pattern emerges that is reproductive. Paul had such a pattern and constantly referred his spiritual disciples to it.[6]

The pattern needs to have the following four characteristics if it is to initiate a multiplication movement:

1. It must be *incarnational*: The pattern must be internal and work its way out into behavior. Paul challenged the Philippians to follow his example and observe others who live by the same pattern (see Phil. 3:17).
2. It must be *viral*: The pattern must be contagious and simple enough to pass on to other succeeding generations. In 2 Timothy 2:2 Paul refers to this pattern when he reminds Timothy of the things he heard from him among many witnesses and is now passed on into three additional generations. (I dealt with this in more depth in chapter 5.)
3. It must be *transformational*: Because the pattern is so life changing, others, strongly affected by its positive transformative nature, will pass it on. Paul writes to the Roman believers, before he had even visited them: "Though you were slaves of sin, you became obedient from the heart to that form of teaching to which you were committed" (Rom. 6:17).
4. It must be *universal*: The pattern must work across all racial, economic, political, social, language, and cultural barriers if it is to change the world. Paul wrote to the Corinthians about the pattern and said, "Be imitators of me. For this reason I have sent to you Timothy, who is my beloved and faithful child in the Lord, and he will remind you of my ways which are in Christ, just as I teach everywhere in every church" (1 Cor. 4:16–17).

Spiritual breathing, or putting off and putting on, is definitely part of the universal pattern,[7] as is seen in the following exhortations from the New Testament:

- To the Colossians Paul writes to put aside anger, wrath, malice, slander, abusive speech, and lying. In their place they are to put on the new self, specifically: compassion, kindness, gentleness, patience, forgiveness, love, and peace (see Col. 3:8–14).
- To the Ephesians Paul writes: "Lay aside the old self . . . and put on the new self" (Eph. 4:22–24).
- To the Romans he writes: "Lay aside the deeds of darkness and put on the armor of light. . . . put on the Lord Jesus Christ" (Rom. 13:12–14).

- James says, "Putting aside all filthiness and all that remains of wickedness, in humility receive the word implanted, which is able to save your souls" (1:21).
- Peter writes: "Therefore, putting aside all malice and all deceit and hypocrisy and envy and all slander, like newborn babies, long for the pure milk of the word, so that by it you may grow in respect to salvation" (1 Peter 2:1–2).

It seems clear that the Christian life is to involve an intentional removal of the old life and a replacing of it with the new life found in God's Word, so that we can be prepared and equipped for the great works God has in store for us. I firmly believe that this pattern is as necessary for the Christian life as breathing is for the physical life. Confessing sins and receiving the Scriptures are vitally important catalysts for life change. I do not believe life change can really be possible without them.

I was meeting weekly for a time with a young man who was once the leader of a very dangerous Hispanic gang. He had left the gang and was hiding out in the desert in fear for his life. I met for many weeks with him, and we set the agenda to confess our sins to one another and read a whole book of the Bible every week.

After meeting with him several times, I found he was very willing to confess his sins, which were very interesting indeed. But whenever I asked him if he had finished the reading we were doing together, he consistently said no. In fact he never did any of the reading at all. One morning over coffee, I told him I wanted him to do something for me. I said, as I looked down at my watch, "When I tell you to, I want you to exhale the air in your lungs and keep exhaling until I say to stop. Ready, go."

He exhaled—and exhaled—and finally he had no more air in his lungs to push out, but still I kept looking down at my watch and telling him to exhale more. Finally, desperate for air, he disobeyed and sucked in two lungs full of oxygen.

I asked him, "Did the air feel good when you sucked it in?"

"Yeah."

Then I asked, "What would happen to you if you didn't inhale?"

"I would be dead."

"That's what you are doing spiritually. You are willing to confess and exhale the sin in your life, but if you don't start inhaling soon, you will start to die spiritually."

Peter tells us:

For you have been born again not of seed which is perishable but imperishable, that is, through the living and enduring word of God. . . . Therefore, putting aside all malice and all deceit and hypocrisy and envy and all slander, like newborn babies, long for the pure milk of the word, so that by it you may grow in respect to salvation, if you have tasted the kindness of the Lord.

1 Peter 1:23; 2:1–3

Peter agrees with Paul on the two elements needed for growth in a disciple's life: continual cleansing from sin and a steady diet of God's Word. There are, of course, several other spiritual disciplines that are needed for growth of the disciple, such as prayer and worship. My purpose is not to exclude any others, but rather to reduce the disciple's spiritual transformation down to the most essential elements needed to induce growth and multiplication. These two disciplines are the foundation for the others.

Of course, if your lungs are full, more inhaling will not do any good. In the same way, if we have not made room in our soul for the Word of God by first confessing, the Word may not penetrate and transform as it should. When we are exhaling the darkness and inhaling the light, the Word will transform us from within.

The New Testament presents this pattern repeatedly but most of our Christian education methods have abandoned this powerful, simple, and transformative process. Often we encourage Bible reading, but without confession there isn't room within for the fresh and powerful Word of God to work. Lungs full of seawater have no room for fresh oxygen; the water must first be pushed out. Putting new clothes on over the old ones does not effect change. I want to be careful not to say it is fruitless work, but I will say strongly that receiving the Word in a soul that has cleansed itself by confession is powerful and will bring about a transformation of the soul.

Communicating

There is a third idea with which Paul concludes this letter, and it is related to spiritual breathing. It is the act of communicating. In a real sense, this is the great work that we are all being prepared and equipped to do (2 Tim. 4:1–5).

Paul has made it clear that confessing one's sin and receiving the truth of God's Word can actually breathe life back into a dying soul and get his or her heart beating once again. Then he ends his letter to Timothy with this challenge: "Preach the Word. Be ready in season and out of season. Reprove, rebuke, exhort with great patience. . . . Do *the work* of sharing the *good* news" (my translation).

Paul has repeatedly used a couple of words together to make a point, and we need to pay attention to this. He has said that confession and cleansing prepare us for every *good work* (2 Tim. 2:21). Consuming the Scriptures equips us for every *good work* (2 Tim. 3:16–17). And now in chapter 4 he challenges us to *the work* of sharing the *good* news (v. 2). In each of these sentences he combines the words *work* with *good*. Yes, work is good, but there is a specific work that is truly good. Sharing the truth with others who have need of it is the *good work* we are being prepared and equipped to do. This is ultimately about being prepared and equipped to do the good work of search and rescue.

We are not fit to share the Good News of God's kingdom unless first we are transformed by it. Personal transformation precedes community transformation. In the same way, trying to communicate when you cannot breathe is a lesson in futility.

A few years ago I was at a meeting with some fellow servants of the Lord, and we were all hoping to get a grant to keep our ministries going another year. There were about twenty ministries at this gathering, each represented by the leader and one other administrative person. We all were in a seminar listening to the speaker, and at various points throughout the day someone would come up behind one of us, tap us on the shoulder, and we would go two at a time to a small room to speak to the billionaire who was funding the grant.

I remember being nervous, wondering what would happen to our emerging family of church planters if we didn't get the funding. I realize that I am not to be a respecter of persons, but on this occasion I blew it. When I was tapped on the shoulder, a lump came to my throat that would not leave for a long while.

I went in to meet with the billionaire along with the representative of a highly successful, well-known ministry. At first I was relieved when the other guy was asked to go first. After he described every church plant as growing to over three hundred people without a single failure, I suddenly felt very inferior. I know I should not have felt that way, but I am human. We intentionally plan small, simple churches that meet in homes and the marketplace. We expect a large percentage of churches not to survive; in fact we encourage it. Because we do not pay each church planter, or rent facilities, there is little to risk. The people involved with the churches that don't make it are assimilated back into the mother church, retooled and sent out again later. (You can read more about the churches we start in the book *Organic Church*).

When it came time for me to share, my nervousness took hold, and I was short of breath. As I started describing our work with very shallow breaths, I realized that I had been so tense that for a long while I had not been fully breathing. I could no longer get any words out. I actually had to excuse myself for a few seconds, and turn and breathe. Then I could carry on.

After the meetings I felt like I had made a fool of myself. The only thing that would have been worse was if I had puked on the guy. I felt like a failure.

God was gracious, though. The billionaire actually liked what I had to say, saw the potential behind our strategy, and mentioned that he would like to keep track of what would come of it. We got the funding for another year.

But I learned in a very real way that *to communicate, you have got to breathe.* There is no other way. When disciples are regularly exhaling the sin of their lives and inhaling the Word of God, they will be prepared and equipped for the good work of sharing God's Good News with others.

Perhaps the reason Christians in the West are so ineffective at communicating the gospel is because they are not breathing. They may attempt to shout the message, but without any air in their lungs, nothing comes out that makes sense to the unbelieving world.

Those who do not know Christ personally find it hard to hear what we have to say. They examine our lives and see the label on the outside and the contents on the inside and say, "No thanks." What we need is new life, a renewed heart, and fresh air in our lungs. Then we will be prepared and equipped for the greatest work of all.

Summary: Spiritual CPR

CPR stands for cardiopulmonary resuscitation. It involves breathing life back into a dead person's lungs and restarting their heart. That is what is necessary in a believer's soul as well. In a real sense we need spiritual CPR:

- Confessing our sins one to another
- Planting God's Word in our heart
- Reaching out to others with the message of the gospel

Once we were all dead in our sins and we needed Christ to resuscitate us spiritually so that we could have new life, breathe, and be ready to do his work. This simple pattern, laid out by Paul and repeated numerous times in the New Testament, is what is needed if we are to be prepared and equipped to do his good works in an effective way.

If indeed confessing sins to one another is important, then establishing the right context in which to do so is very significant. In the next chapter we will deal with the best context for practicing spiritual breathing.

Every Hero Needs a Sidekick and Every Sidekick Is a Hero

All of Us Need Backup

It was a gray morning with the usual coastal low clouds hovering over the beach. It would burn away by noon to reveal another active day on the public beaches. The mornings were always a special time for me. The quiet solitude with the constant sound of the waves gave me a chance to reflect and pray. During those mornings, I would often rehearse memorized passages of Scripture, sing worship songs to my God, and have some very important talks with my Creator while I waited for the busier part of the day. This particular morning all of that was interrupted by a very serious threat that developed rapidly on my beach. Two rival gangs came together on the beach near my tower. The testosterone, voices, and heat elevated quickly.

My first thought was to let them do their business and then they would leave, but it soon became apparent that they were not going to slow down the showdown. I picked up the phone and called the tower just south of me, then the one to the north. I told each of them what was transpiring and that I was going in to break this up armed only with my bright red rescue can. We carry the rescue can at all times so that we are always prepared for *any* emergency. You would be surprised at how important this can be.

The stretch of beach where the gang fight was about to happen. The tower in the foreground, where I was stationed at the time, is called Westminster.

Neil holding his rescue can at the same beach where this incident took place.

Another reason lifeguards always carry the rescue can with them is to be easily spotted by other lifeguards. On a busy day with thousands of beach patrons, you can often see lifeguards holding their rescue can above their head or waving it back and forth. This is not because they are bored or hyped-up on caffeine; it is so that other lifeguards can easily spot them. Second only in importance to watching the water is watching fellow lifeguards. That way a lifeguard is never alone and backup is always only a few minutes away.

I have never appreciated backup more than I did that morning when I walked between two angry gang members, put my big red plastic rescue can in a guy's face and said, "Get off my beach!" I pointed at both towers on either side of us and said lifeguards were watching us right now, ready to call the police. "Take this somewhere else. Get off my beach!"

Both of the testosterone-driven gang members in the middle of the mix muttered something under their breath that I can't write here, but they also left in a hurry. All the tattoos and hanging baggy pants walked off my beach.

I'd be a fool to think that my bright red plastic rescue can scared them off. It was because they knew I had backup. I wonder if I would have had the courage to walk into danger and face it with such authority if I had been alone.

In this adventure of the Christian life, we are not to be alone. As we walk into the darkness to set captives free, we must rely on our backup.

I live in Los Angeles, which is full of larger-than-life personalities. Lakers games in LA are the centerpiece for showboating celebrities and egos. People who don't even like sports go to games just to be seen. For a while we ruled the National Basketball Association with Shaq and Kobe leading our team to three titles in a row.

Both these guys have tremendous egos. Shaq used to call himself Superman, and had the "S" logo tattooed on his arm and displayed on his cars and clothes. Eventually the two egos of Shaq and Kobe could no longer fit in the Staples Center at the same time, so Shaq left. Kobe remarked at that time, "I'm tired of being a sidekick."

Being a sidekick can be hard; you have to support the other guy, often at your own expense. It requires humility. But the truth is, we all need a sidekick, and we should all strive to be one as well. We must lay aside our own ego and desire for the limelight and lift our brother or sister up ahead of ourselves. To win in this great contest of light against darkness, we must buckle down and work together.

Lives change in the context of community. "Lone Ranger Christian" is an oxymoron. We need each other to stand against sin in our lives.

Groups of Two or Three

In 2 Timothy, the passage we've been looking at, Paul says, "Now flee from youthful lusts and pursue righteousness, faith, love and peace, *with those who call on the Lord from a pure heart*" (2:22). Note the use of the plural nouns in the verse we looked at earlier regarding multiplying disciples. Paul wrote: "The things you have heard from me in the presence of many *witnesses*, entrust these to faithful *men* who will be able to teach *others* also" (2:2).

I believe that the best context for life change is a community of two or three. Consistently throughout God's Word there is reference to two or three. The phrase "two or three" is mentioned at least ten times in the Bible. It seems to consistently say "two or three" not "two or more," for that could be endless numbers. It also doesn't say "three or less," for that could also include a solo disciple not in relation to others. No, the perfect size group for life change in the Bible seems to allow for options, but only two: two or three.

The grouping of two or three is found everywhere in the Bible, but nowhere in our churches. We have made attendance in large celebratory meetings practically mandatory. We have enthusiastically encouraged small groups of twelve to fifteen people. But the one sized group that is specifically prescribed almost a dozen times in the Bible is not very often encouraged in the church. And we wonder why our people are not changing.

Following are six biblical reasons why I think a group of two to three is the best context for disciple making and multiplying:

1. Community

Ecclesiastes 4:9–12 says:

> Two are better than one because they have a good return for their labor. For if either of them falls, the one will lift up his companion. But woe to the one who falls when there is not another to lift him up. Furthermore, if two lie down together they keep warm, but how can one be warm alone? And if one can overpower him who is alone, two can resist him. A cord of three strands is not quickly torn apart.

Life change does not occur in a vacuum; it happens in relationship with others. From the beginning, God has said, "It is not good for the man to be alone" (Gen. 2:18). God designed us with a need for community.

While a community can be a larger group than three, a group of three can be the strongest form of community. For most, it is difficult to have the kind of close-knit relational bond that can change our life with more than three people at any one time. The best context for a life-changing community is in a group of two or three.

2. Accountability

First Timothy 5:19 says, "Do not receive an accusation against an elder except on the basis of two or three witnesses." When it comes to leveling a rebuke against a spiritual leader, we need to make sure we are accountable to one or two others who can substantiate what is said. All leaders must be accountable to others. Few things would ever get done in life without some degree of accountability. In the pursuit of godliness we need accountability to one another. There are at least twenty-eight "one another" admonitions in the New Testament. Many more if you count those that are repeated. We need each other.

It is difficult to be held accountable to a multitude of people who do not know you well. A group of two or three has a greater degree of strength in accountability. A person can find support with a group of two or three people who can know and understand his or her life.

3. Confidentiality

Jesus said, "If your brother sins, go and show him his fault in private; if he listens to you, you have won your brother. But if he does not listen to you, take one or two more with you, so that by the mouth of two or three witnesses every fact may be confirmed. If he refuses to listen to them, tell it to the church" (Matt. 18:15–17).

Since confession of sin is needed for cleansing and preparing oneself for a life of service, a safe place for it is essential. Rarely do people feel comfortable confessing their sins to a large group of people they don't know. A small coed cell group is also not a safe place to share your darkest secrets. A group of two or three others of your same gender, who know and care about you and who also are sharing their own struggles, is as safe a place as you can find.

Confidentiality is much easier to control in a context of two or three. This is especially true when each participant is vulnerable and equally at risk of exposure. If confidentiality is indeed broken, there is a short list of suspects to consider.

In these verses the Lord specifically indicated that it is best to have a group of two or three when confronting sin to maintain confidentiality.

4. Communication

Paul wrote to the Corinthians: "When you assemble, each one has a psalm, has a teaching, has a revelation, has a tongue, has an interpretation. Let all things be done for edification. If anyone speaks in a tongue, it should be by two or at the most three, and each in turn, and one must interpret." He goes on to say, "Let two or three prophets speak, and let the others pass judgment" (1 Cor. 14:26–29).

It is certainly easier to communicate with fewer people. The more voices you add to the equation, the more confusion results and breakdowns occur. Paul counsels the Corinthian church that they should limit the number of people speaking to two or three at a time, with clear interpretation.

Today our attention span is not that great, and we have technological gadgets that do much of our thinking. I have to look down at my wrist now to know what day of the week or month it is. With short attention spans, it is hard for us to receive more than two or three messages at one time. In a context that was challenged by a lack of order, Paul recommended that we limit our intake to two or three messages at once.

Two or three is a perfect size group for clear communication. When the group is limited to this size, it is virtually impossible for a person to hide in the crowd and not be involved. It is also hard for one person to dominate the conversation.

5. Flexibility

In Matthew 18:20 Jesus says, "For where two or three have gathered together in My name, I am there in their midst." Certainly there is more behind the words Jesus spoke than flexibility, but it is one advantage of a group this size.

Most of us have had the experience of trying to coordinate the calendars of a handful of busy people. An advantage to a group of two or three is that there is a better opportunity to coordinate schedules for a meeting time that suits all.

A second logistical advantage to a group of two or three is that they can meet almost anywhere. Groups can meet in a restaurant for coffee, in a gym while working out, at a park where their children can play and they can walk together. There is no need for a host or hostess with this size group.

6. Reproducibility

As I have already mentioned, simple things multiply easier than complex things. A group of two or three can multiply much easier than a group of ten to fifteen. All that is needed to multiply such a group is to find one more person and multiply into two groups of two. If we cannot see multiplication at this level, we will not see it at higher, more complex levels of church life. If we can't multiply groups of two or three, we will not multiply a cell group or a worship service or a congregation.

This is the most basic unit of the church—*two or three believers held together by the presence of Jesus Christ and the truth of his Word in pursuit of his kingdom life.* By initiating multiplication here, at the base unit, we can infuse the very genetic code of the church with the value of reproduction. If we truly wish to see the power of multiplication released in our church, it is best to initiate the momentum here at the grassroots level. If we can't reproduce disciples, we will never reproduce leaders. If we can't reproduce leaders, we will never reproduce churches. If we can't reproduce churches, we will never see a true movement.

Church planting is my calling and passion. It dawned on me one day, however, that I could not find a single verse in all of the Bible that commands us to plant or multiply churches. It's just not there! The command that God gave was to make and multiply disciples—not cell groups or churches. Jesus wants to build his kingdom through church planting and multiplication, but his plan is to do so by multiplying disciples. It begins here—with the basic unit of the church—then it spreads through every pore in the body of Christ. But if we do not start here, if we skip this God-ordained step, we can work and work and work until we turn blue and drop dead and we will not see multiplication happen.

All reproduction begins on the smallest level possible. When speaking about the beginning and growth of life in his kingdom, Jesus uses the analogies of seeds and leaven. We must first learn to reproduce disciples before we can reproduce leaders, churches, and movements.

One Final Reason

If none of the evidence listed above is enough to convince you of the biblical precedent for groups of two or three, this last reason is sure to clench the debate. *Even the Godhead exists in a community of three!* Jesus used the community of the Godhead to teach us how we are to function in relationship to one another (John 17:11, 21). Perhaps there really is something special, even spiritual, about a group of two or three.

J. R. R. Tolkien seemed to understand the potent force of two or three. In the epic quest to destroy a rising evil in *The Lord of the Rings*, a band of brothers was formed called the fellowship of the ring. Over the course of the journey, the band was split up into three groups of two or three, each smaller group tackling a different conquest. It is in these smaller groups that they actually destroy the ring and defeat the dark lord Sauron. A group of two or three is indeed a formidable force.

One scene in *The Lord of the Rings* movies that always brings a tear to my eye is when Frodo Baggins and his loyal companion Samwise Gamgee are exhausted, thirsty, and collapsed on the side of Mt. Doom in their attempt to destroy the dark and evil ring of power.

Frodo and Sam were alone in a dark place, surrounded by evil and constantly hiding from the ever watchful eye of the dark lord. As the ring bearer, it was Frodo's task and his task alone to carry the heavy weight to its conclusion. But he was not alone. Sam would never leave his side.

In this particular scene, Sam tries to encourage Frodo with a description of the simple beauties of their home—the Shire. There is nothing like a reminder of what we are fighting for to motivate us to carry on, but in this case, all Frodo could see in his mind's eye was the evil eye of the dark lord bearing down on him with all the weight carried around his neck.

In righteous indignation, Sam spits out the words, "Then let's be done with it! I may not be able to carry it [the ring] for you, but I can carry you!" And with that, Sam lifts Frodo up over his shoulders and proceeds one step after another up the steep bank of loose rocks with his friend on his shoulders.

What a picture of the value of being in a small group of two or three to bear one another's burdens and thus fulfill the love of Christ! All of us bear a ring of sorts, some special and unique calling that weighs on us. We cannot carry these loads alone; we all need a friend like Sam who will carry us in times when we do not have the strength to go on. We all need backup in this life. Every hero needs a sidekick and every sidekick is a hero.

In the next chapter I will describe the rescue that stands out in my own mind as the most significant. It illustrates the need for us to be ready and available in our search and rescue efforts.

9

The Boy Scouts Have It Right

Be Prepared

Of all the rescues that I made in my days at the beach, one stands out as the most meaningful. I hope it can teach us something about the importance of being alert, available, and ready to take initiative in the midst of our busy lives.

One day each week I worked what is usually a slow tower called Ave 23 on Venice Beach (see photo on p. 112). When I worked there, the tower was tall and sat up high on the berm above a rock jetty. The real purpose for the tower's placement was for it to be a bridge of vision and coverage. The tower was manned mostly to provide backup for the guards at either of the two towers beside it because their vision was blocked by the high berm and jetty. Consequently those who work this tower usually get to watch the action more than participate in it. To be paid to go to the beach every day and watch other people work is a nice gig if you can get it.

On the north side of the jetty was a popular surfing spot. On the south side was a popular stretch of beach good for sunbathing and swimming. The southern strip of beach had a steep berm and the waves tended to be mostly shore break (where the waves crash right on the beach).

Another reason that this tower exists is to keep people from climbing on the rock jetty, which can be dangerous. On this particular day the surf was big, and the people were enjoying it. I was sitting down, comfortable, in my high tower, listening to music, watching life happen. I noticed some local surfers, climbing out on the jetty to get a good view of the waves. I remember thinking, *They're all right. They know the conditions and probably won't get hurt. They climb those same rocks every day after the lifeguard goes off duty. They won't get hurt.* I was about to let them go, but my conscience kicked in and wouldn't let *me* go.

Wrestling with myself I finally decided: *This is what I'm supposed to do. It's what I'm paid to do.* Finally, I got up out of my comfortable chair, turned off the music, put on my jacket and sunglasses, grabbed my rescue can, slid down the ladder, walked down the berm to the water's edge, and called out to the young people (who were pretending not to hear me).

As I was waiting for a response, I did something that is natural and instinctive for all lifeguards—something we have been trained and ingrained to do. I glanced around at the water in my area. No matter what else we may be called on to do, watching the water was never an option for lifeguards but always the prime directive of utmost importance. This is what lifeguards must do. It is why we are there. It is so important that we were programmed to do so by constant reinforcement, training, and education until it finally became habitual. Even to this day, whenever I go to the beach, I still scan the water looking for potential problems, identifying weak swimmers, and spotting potentially dangerous riptides. The lifeguard has a prime directive: watch the water and save lives. It's that simple. Everything else must come second.

I looked south over my shoulder and turned back to finish yelling at the kids on the rocks. Suddenly something I just saw to the south registered and jolted me with adrenaline. I saw, about 150 feet away, a large wave crash on the beach, knocking a toddler off his feet, and dragging him back into the ocean. Quickly a mother got off her blanket and ran after him.

This is the kind of moment that defines a lifeguard. It is the culmination of all his or her training and working. The lifeguard can never truly anticipate a moment like this but must be ready for it at any time, because it can come without warning. Often it lasts only a few seconds and is never more than a few minutes. As quickly as it comes, it is done. Not to be ready is lethal. A moment like this is the reason lifeguards exist.

Immediately I took off sprinting down the beach. I tossed my very expensive sunglasses into the wind (never to be seen again). I tore my jacket off and threw it down in the sand. I unwound my rescue can and put it on over my shoulder. By the time I reached the place where I had originally seen the child and mother, I could no longer see either. All I saw was the Pacific Ocean spread out before me.

When an adult is fighting hard not to drown, they do something we call "climbing the ladder." There is no ladder, it's just wishful thinking, but it appears as though they are trying to will into existence an imaginary ladder. With all their strength they usually rise once, then twice and three times before they surrender to the silence of the water. Small children know nothing about the ladder; they just drop and never rise again.

The odds of rescuing someone after he has submerged in the ocean are very small. When you factor in the vastness of the ocean, the smallness of a child, the poor visibility of the water, and the ocean currents and waves, you begin to see how hopeless a rescue is once a child has submerged. Finding a needle in a haystack is a daunting challenge, but imagine looking for a needle with all the straw constantly moving, and you will get an idea of how impossible this situation is. Unfortunately, a beach that has shore break usually means the water gets deep immediately.

Time is of the essence for obvious reasons. In most cases, after three minutes, brain damage occurs because of lack of oxygen. But in the ocean another fatal danger exists. If someone aspirates salt water, the eventual damage to the lungs can be fatal. Some live through the ordeal, only to drown days later in lungs full of infection. Instinctively I dove into the water in roughly the place where I last saw the child. As I dove under the water with my arms and fingers stretched out wide, trying to rescue this child by Braille, intuitively I uttered a prayer that I would somehow find him in time. "Oh, God, help me find this kid!"

Jackpot! I felt flesh. It was the torso of a small boy. Instantly, without seeing anything, I planted my feet and shot my hands up through the surface of the water lifting the boy up into the air to breathe. After he had gasped and sucked in a lung full of oxygen, I rose to the surface myself to get air. I immediately began walking up toward the beach, holding the boy in my arms. He still hadn't begun to cry because he was trying to hold on to every molecule of air he could consume. As I fought the strong force of water being sucked back out to another incoming wave, I felt the strap around my neck tug hard against me. I looked back and found Mom holding on tightly to the rescue can on the other end of the rope. I managed to drag the three of us up to the warm sand.

I put my ear to the boy's back to listen for any gurgling from aspirated seawater and heard nothing but clean lungs. Of course, by now, everyone on the beach could hear those lungs screaming—*a most welcome sound!*

This boy is a man today because I was busy doing the things that lifeguards are supposed to be doing. I was down on the wet sand, close enough to reach the boy before it was too late. If I had been up in the comfortable tower, removed from the sand and water, I am confident that I wouldn't have made it

A view from the place where this rescue was made back toward the Ave 23 tower. Some things have changed since the day I made the rescue. The beach has become more flat and the sandy bottom has become shallower, thus eliminating the shore break. The tower was once a tall, cylindrical, enclosed lookout post with a ladder and now has a more traditional tower and ramp.

in time to save this child. But being busy down on the beach wasn't enough. I never would have seen the boy if I hadn't remembered my prime directive and scanned to see if there was anyone in the water who needed to be rescued.

Life can keep us busy, but it is there in the midst of our busyness that we need to open our eyes and see if there is anyone in desperate need of saving. The moment we have been called on to save a drowning soul can come in the midst of our busyness, and we need to be prepared. Jesus was a busy man, but he never lost sight of his prime directive—to seek and to save those who are lost (see Matt. 9:35–38; Luke 19:10).

Every one of us can bring the Savior to drowning men, women, and children who are distressed and sinking fast. But first we have to see them and be close enough to reach them in their time of need. Our purpose here on earth goes beyond basking in the goodness of the Son. We are called to help others who cannot help themselves.

Be Ready

As Paul comes to the conclusion of this letter to Timothy, there is an increased sense of urgency. These are the last of his last words, and they are said with strength and passion. As you read them, and consider the disappointment that Demas, Titus, and others were at the end of Paul's life, you can see that he wants to instill in his spiritual son something that Timothy will not soon forget. He says, "I solemnly charge you in the presence of God and of Christ Jesus, who is to judge the living and the dead, and by His appearing and His kingdom: preach the word; be ready in season and out of season; reprove, rebuke, exhort, with great patience and instruction" (2 Tim. 4:1–2).

That's intense language. Solemnly charged, in the presence of God, but not just God, also of Christ Jesus, who is to judge the living and the dead. Yikes, pay attention, Timothy. Paul wants to make sure he is always alert, always ready. He goes on to add: "Be sober in all things, endure hardship, do the work of [telling others the Good News],[1] fulfill your ministry" (2 Tim. 4:5). Whether we find ourselves in a season of fruitfulness or not, we are to continue in the work of being a hero for God's kingdom.

The phrase "preach the word" can be misleading. We tend to read our own experience into the Scriptures. Preaching has become something done on Sunday, from behind a pulpit, to a congregation of Christians. In the New Testament, however, this is not the way the word would have been understood.

Another inaccurate way of interpreting the word *preach* is to think of it as referring to a self-righteous, stern, and overbearing lecture pointed at the shamefulness of our lives. When we say someone is "preachy," we think of this sort of thing, but that is not what Timothy would have understood when he read these words from Paul.

When Paul uses the word *preach* in his epistles, most often he is not referring to a pastor teaching his or her flock, but rather a Christian sharing the Good News of Jesus with those who have not yet chosen to follow him. In this letter Paul describes the process as being done "with great patience and instruction" (v. 2). That doesn't sound preachy. In another place he describes the way we are to interact with others, saying we "must not be quarrelsome, but be kind to all, able to teach, patient when wronged, with gentleness correcting those who are in opposition, if perhaps God may grant them repentance leading to the knowledge of the truth, and they may come to their senses and escape from the snare of the devil, having been held captive by him to do his will" (2:24–26).

Paul does not want us to be obnoxious Bible thumpers, but he doesn't want us to be passive saints who are ashamed to tell people the great news that Jesus is real and present either. Unfortunately, we often get deceived into thinking that the best thing we can do for Jesus is to be kind and not say a word for fear we will turn people off. I am very much in favor of living a life that is compelling because of Christ, but we should not ever be ashamed to tell people why we live such a life. If telling others the Good News is out of fashion, let's be unfashionable. We must come to terms with the fact that the message of God's kingdom here on earth is worth telling others. We must value it enough that it becomes hard not to tell people. But as Paul points out so well, we must do so with patience and kindness.

Love should be what compels us (2 Cor. 5:14), not trying to prove that we are right or others are wrong. That is a foolish waste of time. Love is not rude and obnoxious at another's expense, but it is not silent either. We should care enough to tell people the great news about Jesus.

As Paul describes at the end of chapter 2, our desire should be that "they may come to their senses and escape from the snare of the devil, having been held captive by him to do his will." Not caring about these things is cold indifference that is anything but heroic. Perhaps we are more concerned with our own reputation than the freedom of others. I am really not sure which is worse: rude, obnoxious preaching or cold, self-serving indifference. It is not enough that we tell people the Good News; we must live it and love it so much that we cannot help but share it with others.

Perhaps we do not really believe that the news is that good. How else can we explain our passive indifference? Chuck Swindoll alludes to a relevant court case in the state of Massachusetts back in the late 1920s:

> It concerned a man who had been walking along a pier when suddenly he tripped over a rope and fell into the cold, deep waters of that ocean bay. He came up sputtering, screaming for help, then sank beneath the surface. For some reason he was unable to swim or stay afloat. His friends heard his faint cries in the distance, but they were too far away to rescue him. But within only a few yards was a young man lounging on a deck chair, sunbathing. Not only could the sunbather hear the drowning man plead, "Help, I can't swim," he was also an excellent swimmer.
>
> But the tragedy is that he did nothing. He only turned his head to watch indifferently as the man finally sank and drowned.
>
> The family of the victim was so upset by that display of extreme indifference, that they sued the sunbather. The result? They lost the case. With a measure of reluctance the court ruled that the man on the dock had no legal responsibility whatsoever to try to save the drowning man's life.[2]

Swindoll goes on to say, "You and I have a legal right to mind our own business—to turn a deaf ear to anyone in need, to continue sunbathing while someone is drowning. We are not obligated to respond. Indifference may not be illegal, but it is certainly immoral!"[3]

I cannot accept that if we love Jesus, we will be able to sit back and sunbathe while millions around us drown. We cannot afford to turn a deaf ear to those who are drowning. Indifference is not an option for any follower of Christ. Indifference is an insult to the initiative and sacrifice of Christ.

Be Capable

As I've said, I was not the first lifeguard in my family. I am a third-generation ocean lifeguard in Southern California. My grandfather, father, and uncles all watched the same beaches that I did with one dramatic difference: I made *many* more rescues. There were some times when I would make more rescues in a single day than they had in a whole summer. My father used to be amazed at that fact, even a little skeptical. I used to say that it was due to the increase in the population in our area, all the while knowing the real reason: my dad and his brother can't see! They are both extremely nearsighted. They were outstanding watermen; in fact, my uncle, Peter Cole, is a legendary big wave surfer in Hawaii, where he still surfs even in his seventies. But it doesn't matter how good your lifeguarding skills are if you can't see those who are drowning.

You may wonder how in the world these men could be hired by the city of Los Angeles to watch the beaches when their vision was so bad. There is an explanation, but it only makes matters worse. They had a surfing buddy named Buzzy who was in excellent physical condition. At the time, Buzzy couldn't swim very well, but he also wanted to lifeguard. They worked together to pass the qualifying exams. Buzzy would show up to take their eye test in the physical exam while my father would show up and take the swim test under Buzzy's name. What's worse than a lifeguard who can't see? One who can't swim.

In case you're wondering, the testing process is far more scrutinizing now. Yes, it's safe to go back in the water. Eventually Buzzy also grew to become an outstanding waterman and a pioneer big wave rider in Hawaii with my uncle.

This comical tragedy is a good illustration of a crying need in the church today. We need believers who can *see* those who are lost and drowning and who are also *able* to rescue them. It isn't enough to be capable of reaching people and making disciples, while remaining blind to those who need to be reached. It also doesn't help to be able to see the harvest if we don't have the ability to make disciples. I contend that we are not doing well at either.

Be Where the Action Is

This world needs heroes. One does not become a hero without risk, and the greater the risk, the greater the heroism. Jesus calls us to abandon our own life for his sake and the sake of the Good News (Luke 9:23–27). When the people of God move out of their safe towers and into the raging surf of this world to save those who are drowning, heroes will be born. But we must abandon our own lives to do so.

I have met Christians, many of them, who do not know any people who are not Christians. These are people who went to Christian schools from preschool through college and then went on to be employed by a Christian organization. It is impossible to fulfill Christ's Great Commission if you never encounter a person who is not already one of his followers.

Many Christians have a "circle-the-wagons" posture in this world. We have created a Christian ghetto where we have no input from or to the world around us. In practically every town of America you can find "Christian Yellow Pages," so you can hire only Christian plumbers to install Christian pipes in your Christian house—and never have to encounter a real non-Christian!

Perhaps you find yourself in such a predicament. You may not ever have intended to be so secluded and separated, but there you are. It is time to take a chance. Somewhere deep in your heart is a longing to see God do miraculous things in your life, but if you stay safe way behind the frontlines, you will never be in a place to see God work. How do you spell faith? R-I-S-K. You simply cannot live a vibrant life of faith in a safe and protected place. If you do not have any current story of how God has stepped in and rescued you, you are probably not living with enough risk. I seriously doubt that God would have parted the sea for Moses and his family while they were on a nice vacation at the Red Sea Beach Resort. It was only when Moses found himself cornered, with Pharaoh's army pressing down on him—all because he followed God obediently—that the sea parted. If you want to see God work miracles, you too will have to venture out in faith into the waters of risk.

We must be willing to go into harm's way for the sake of others to see the hand of God intervene on our behalf. I go to greater lengths on this subject in my book *Organic Church*. Suffice it to say, to be a hero who saves those who are drowning, you must get out of your safe tower and get your feet wet.

Take a moment. Scan the waters that God has assigned you to watch. Where is the extreme danger? Do you see people drowning? Pray. Pray for God to save people and to quench the fires that are raging in the spiritual world around us. But also look for proactive ways to bring the kingdom of God to your community in grace and truth. We do not need to continue just reacting to the world crises; we can take the initiative and make a difference at the grassroots level by simply doing the things Jesus told us to do.

In the next chapter I tell a story that explains why I am no longer working the beaches as a lifeguard. The point of the chapter, however, is how we must never give up but press on "till death do us part."

10

More Than a Catchphrase

Never Give Up! Never Surrender!

After some years of lifeguarding I had the opportunity to take a test to become a year-round, full-time lifeguard. At that same time I was asked to come on staff as the pastor of the college group at the large church I was attending. This was an obvious fork in the road of my life. One path was to continue further in the career I enjoyed and could do well. The other was to launch into a new world of church ministry, leadership development, and sharing the gospel. The lifeguard career move would provide a sizeable increase in financial income and security; the other choice would mean only a few hundred dollars a month to support a brand-new family. One choice would save lives; the other would save souls.

The process to become a year-round, career lifeguard involved two parts: a written exam and an oral interview. From the information gleaned from these two processes, all the candidates are on a list that is divided into groups. Hiring would begin at the top of the list.

While I was weighing my career options, I went ahead and took the written test without studying and scored about average. I was in the middle of a pack of about fifty other lifeguards.

As I pondered what the Lord wanted me to do, I felt clearly that he was leading me down a new path. I realized that every life I ever saved on the beach would one day die. I chose the path that was to save souls rather than lives. My heart to bring the gospel to lost souls was so strong that I chose to take the oral exam for the lifeguarding position just for the opportunity to share the lifesaving message of Christ with the interviewers.

The first thing I noticed as I walked into the headquarters for the oral interview was how nervous all the other candidates were. It was also strange to see people I usually only see in bathing suits and T-shirts dressed in suits and ties or dresses and heels. I was at ease because I knew that I wouldn't take the job even if I got it. Unlike the others who were busy studying flash cards, I did not study or memorize anything for this interview. My only thought was to search and pray for any opportunity to share the Good News of Christ.

I was invited into a small room with three lifeguard captains from other agencies. I just responded honestly to all of their questions from experience. I was at ease and must have appeared very confident. At the very end, one of the captains asked me, "So what makes you a good lifeguard?" This was my opportunity.

I said, "If I am a good lifeguard, it is because my relationship to the ocean is much like my relationship to God." All three looked back at me with a curious and odd expression. I went on, "I love the ocean and feel most at home when I am in the water. I play in the ocean and enjoy it. But I also know what the ocean can do, and I fear it with a healthy respect. That is how I feel about God. I love him and enjoy him, but I also know what he can do, and I have a healthy fear of God that shapes my life and character. That is what makes me a good lifeguard."

The men stood and said, "Thanks for your time." They shook my hand and opened the door for me to leave. I walked out feeling really good, even though I was sure I had blown that interview and wouldn't get the job.

I was mistaken. I got one of the highest scores on the oral exam and ended up in one of the top spots for the position. My lieutenant couldn't understand why I wouldn't take the job.

Flying without Parachutes

After the test scores had been added up, I sent in a letter of resignation. I felt that I needed to burn the bridge behind me so that I wouldn't look back in the course of ministry hardships thinking I made a mistake and try to go back. In a sense, I felt I needed to toss the parachute so that I would be more committed to flying the path before me, and not bail out when rough turbulence struck.

In my twenties I had a sense of call to save souls that shaped decisions in my life. I still do. Today I understand that all of us make the same decision. Sure, for most of us it may not require a change of career, but we still have a choice to make. Will I choose a life that will take as many souls with me to heaven as I possibly can or will I just go to work?

I have since realized that someone can be just as effective serving Christ and saving souls as a lifeguard as any pastor, but this was a step down a path that I had to make myself, led by the Spirit of God. It was a decision I had to make with certitude and without room for compromise.

My decision, in the context of my own history, in no way means that someone pursuing a call in a regular job is less committed to seeing souls saved than someone in vocational ministry, and in fact doing so can often lead to greater influence. The whole message of this book (and my life) is that God has ordained ordinary people to be a part of extraordinary works.

I believe that some of the greatest heroes today are people who have left "full-time ministry roles" to start businesses or enter new "secular" careers for the purpose of having greater influence in the world.[1] Some of my friends have left salaried ministry jobs and are now starting businesses, like window washing or opening a coffeehouse or getting a real estate license. I have another friend who went back to school to become an attorney and recently passed the bar exam. These are heroes. They, too, are willing to die to an old path to strike out into uncharted waters for the sake of God's kingdom.

When Cortez landed in America, his first order to his men was to burn their ships. Retreat was not an option. They were now committed to this life, come hell or high water. Because of this, the men were motivated to move forward in their mission.

The Cost of Multiplied Significance

Decisions, such as those my friends have made, require dying to the old life. We all need to choose a life that will make the most impact for the Savior. Many wait until they near the end to evaluate whether their life will have lasting significance. Several years ago I learned that we can determine early in life to have a lasting impact. Every morning we can choose to live a life of significance. The apostle Paul tells us that he died daily. Death sobers our perspective and challenges us to choose our words and actions in light of eternity. Solomon, one of the wisest men to have lived, once said, "It is better to go to a house of mourning than to go to a house of feasting, because that is the end of every man, and the living takes it to heart" (Eccles. 7:2).

While it may sound morbid, I often ask myself the question, *If I died today would the fruit of my life continue after me?* A good look at death will certainly sharpen your priorities and focus your life. Jesus calls us to die every day to our old way of life so that we can birth the new way.

There is a cost involved with multiplication. For the salmon, the cost is death. It swims upstream, lays its eggs in the sand, and then dies. Grain also dies to reproduce. Jesus said, "Truly, truly, I say to you, unless a grain of wheat falls into the earth and dies, it remains alone; but if it dies, it bears much fruit. He who loves his life loses it, and he who hates his life in this world will keep it to life eternal" (John 12:24–25).

As disciples, we must deny ourselves and pick up our cross and follow Christ. This is all about surrender. This is about confession and repentance. This is about obedience. Where these attitudes and actions exist, there is a dying of self, and reproduction will come.

A hero is one who embraces death, for Jesus, for him- or herself, for the sake of others. A favorite story of mine that exhibits the courage and sacrifice of a hero is from a volunteer at a local hospital. The hero was a five-year-old brother to Liza, who was suffering from a serious disease. Liza needed a transfusion, and her little brother was the best match. Liza's doctor explained the situation to him and asked the little boy if he would be willing to give his blood to his sister. He hesitated for just a moment, took a deep breath, and said, "Yes, I'll do it if it will save Liza."

As the transfusion progressed, he lay on a bed next to his sister. Everyone smiled as they saw the color return to Liza's cheeks. But the boy's face grew pale and his smile faded. He looked up at the doctor and asked with a trembling voice, "Will I start to die right away?"[2]

He had thought that he was going to give his sister all of his blood. Real heroes come in all sizes, and that is a real hero.

Jesus was also willing to give all of his blood, his life, so that we could live. How could we do anything less?

The Last Lonely Lap

Usually we think of Paul as being successful. He is seen today as the apostle who laid the foundation for the church as we know it. He effectively brought the gospel to at least four people groups and started a church-planting movement that forever altered history. He is still the apostle to the Gentiles, and his influence is stronger today than it was even in his own time. We see his success and yearn for such an experience in our own day and time.

But at the end of his life, Paul does not feel celebrated or honored by his peers for his accomplishments. The people in Asia with whom he had such success (Acts 19–20) had turned on him (2 Tim. 1:15). Some of his favorite disciples have fallen away (4:10). Some have hurt him in deep ways that do not easily heal (v. 14). He is facing his execution, cold, feeling idle, and alone, but for a single faithful companion named Luke (v. 11). And perhaps worst of all, this isn't the first time he has been in this place. He mentions that in his first stand before the justice system of Rome, everyone but Jesus abandoned him (vv. 16–17).

Despite a life of faithfulness and constant suffering, at the end he finds himself alone, yet again, without regrets. From this place he looks ahead and sees his impending execution. He writes: "I am already being poured out as a drink offering, and the time of my departure has come" (v. 6).

More Than a Catchphrase

The movie *Galaxy Quest*, a comical spoof of the original *Star Trek* franchise, stars Tim Allen as the Captain Kirk character. He is a middle-aged, forever-typecast, out-of-work actor who will do anything for a buck, but who still loves the attention of his fans. He is not a hero but plays one on TV. In the movie he and his loveable fellow cast members are surprisingly placed in a real situation where they are no longer pretending to be heroic but must actually find a way to be heroes.

Now this part can get confusing. Never mind the fact that you are watching actors, pretending to be actors who pretend to be heroes and actually become heroes—at least that's what they pretend to be! In this movie they do find that they actually can be heroic, even though they are not the special people they portray on TV; at least that is what the imaginary characters who pretend to be actors do. We have yet to see whether Tim Allen, Sigourney Weaver, Alan Rickman, and Tony Shaloub are real heroes.

Allen's character has a catchphrase: *Never give up! Never surrender!* In the end, this philosophy gets the group through the adventure. For true heroes, this catchphrase would be appropriate in the face of the battles faced in our real world. Paul used similar words that were more than a mere catchphrase. "I have fought the good fight," Paul says, "I have finished the course, I have kept the faith" (2 Tim. 4:7). Paul was not an actor, pretending to be a hero; he was the real deal.

As I serve the Lord, I am finding that there are fewer people than you would imagine who are able to say at the end of their life words like this. As

I mentioned at the start of this book, the only applause that really counts is at the finish line. A true hero faces the finish line with strength, nobility, courage, and faith. Though he may not have been celebrated at the end of his life, he was a success, and he dies the champion that he truly is.

Passing the Test

In my junior year of high school I had the privilege of being a small part of a very competitive swim team. We were good enough to win, and everyone expected that we would. It was one of those rare times when the best all came together on one team.

In our league there was just one other rival team that could compete with us—Westchester High. Before the city finals we faced this rival at the league finals. We were waiting to peak at the city championships, so we did not prepare as we could have for the league finals, which were a preliminary event leading up to the citywide finals.

Westchester, however, knew that if they were ever going to beat us, it was here at the league finals when we would not be as ready, so they worked hard to peak at this meet. As a result, they swam better than expected, and we did not. At the league finals we went head-to-head through all the events. At each race the two teams would seem to trade the lead in points. The championship came down to the last race—the 200-yard freestyle relay. The team that won this event would win the meet and be the league champions.

Our team had a secret weapon. His name was Zach. He was the fastest sprinter in the league. Unfortunately, he hadn't been able to show his talent until this moment due to a serious injury to his shoulder. He swam in just enough meets to qualify for the final meets. All season long he was restricted from doing any normal swim workouts. He worked out hard, as hard as anyone else, but he couldn't use his arms, so he ran on the treadmill, used the weights, and kicked underwater laps, holding his breath to keep his cardiovascular endurance strong.

All his training was for this one moment. Zach was our anchor, or last swimmer, our greatest hope to win the championship. As if it were in some grand script, the first three legs of the relay were neck and neck. All the weight of our team fell on the untested and surgically repaired shoulders of Zach. He rose to the test. He swam with no hesitation, no reservation, no thoughts except touching the wall first. He moved into a clear first place as he gave everything he had. In the last few strokes his shoulder popped out of socket and through the pain Zach managed to touch the wall first. It was moving. All the people in the stands were on their feet cheering. It was an indoor stadium (natatorium), and the noise was so loud that you could feel your skin vibrating.

We won. We won the relay—the meet—the league championship. The year was ours. All the sacrifice and early morning workouts paid off. In one glorious moment of struggle and endurance, our team pulled together and tasted victory.

In the thrill of the moment, without thinking, one of our team members, whose name I will not mention nor forget, jumped into the water to embrace Zach and help lift him out of the water. Unfortunately, one of the other teams had not yet finished the race. This simple and spontaneous act, lacking in forethought, but full of the best intentions, automatically disqualified our relay team.

I will never forget the sinking feeling that came over all of us as we began to realize what had just happened. It spread across the whole audience like a cold wave.

We lost. We lost the relay—the meet—and the league championship. In one tragic moment of thoughtless emotional reaction, our team was made to taste the bitterness of defeat and disgrace. All the sacrifice, all the hard work, and all the year's effort came to a crashing defeat.

I have never been on a more quiet bus ride returning from the meet. The air seemed to have been sucked out of our lungs. We could barely breathe, let alone speak. Besides, we had nothing to say.

When I participated in triathlons, there was no one disappointed when I didn't win. No one expected me to win. I was merely a participant. Finishing was *my* victory. But when it is a race you can and should win, when you do all that is necessary to win, and you lose in the end because of a thoughtless mistake, that is the worst sort of tragedy. Don't do that!

Paul wrote to the Corinthian church:

> Do you not know that those who run in a race all run, but only one receives the prize? Run in such a way that you may win. Everyone who competes in the games exercises self-control in all things. They then do it to receive a perishable wreath, but we an imperishable. Therefore I run in such a way, as not without aim; I box in such a way, as not beating the air; but I discipline my body and make it my slave, so that, after I have preached to others, I myself will not be disqualified.
>
> 1 Corinthians 9:24–27

The greatest test of a hero is at the end of his life, his final exam. Paul took that test and passed it with flying colors. He became an example to Timothy and to us.

When I resigned as a lifeguard, it was not the end. It was a new beginning. I have been a part of seeing many souls saved since that day, and I do not regret ending one career to start a new calling. Of course there comes an occasional warm summer day when I am under a lot of stress, and I wish I could just climb up a ramp to a tower and go back to watching for riptides again. But I have never regretted the decision I made all those years ago.

The reason Paul could stare death in the face with complete resolve is he understood it not as an ending but a new beginning. Death has no sting to one who is part of Christ's kingdom. When we hold on to Christ with everything we've got and hold on to nothing else, we have nothing to lose. Someone who has nothing to lose is a dangerous man or woman. Paul was such a man. Peering from a dark cave to his own execution days away, he saw only good things.

While under arrest in the same city years earlier, he wrote to the Philippians: "For to me, to live is Christ and to die is gain" (Phil. 1:21). Now, under arrest in Rome yet again, this time without much hope of release, he writes to Timothy about his first imprisonment, saying, "The Lord stood with me and strengthened me, so that through me the proclamation might be fully accomplished, and that all the Gentiles might hear; and I was rescued out of the lion's mouth" (2 Tim. 4:17). Then without hesitation, he speaks about his new vantage point as he faces certain death in the days ahead: "The Lord will rescue me from every evil deed, and will bring me safely to His heavenly kingdom; to Him be the glory forever and ever. Amen" (v. 18).

To Paul, death is a rescue operation. It is a graduation from the kingdom of God on earth to the fullest experience of the kingdom in the very physical presence of the King. Even the most heroic of us needs to be rescued. Even lifeguards need to be rescued. Death, for Paul, is not the end but the beginning.

Practical Exercises at the End of This Section of the Book

Perhaps you need to write a metaphorical resignation letter yourself. Resign from anything that is keeping you from becoming the self-sacrificial hero that God is calling you to be.

Or perhaps you should write an epitaph for yourself. Think about how your life might end and the things for which you most want to be remembered. To quote a pizza commercial: "What do you want on your tombstone?"

Such exercises bring focus to our lives, so that we, too, like Paul, may press toward the goal and determine not to be disqualified. You will not be disappointed. Death brings life in this spiritual kingdom.

In the next section of the book, I will build on all of this section, presenting a simple way to go about making and multiplying disciples.

A SYSTEM FOR MAKING AND MULTIPLYING DISCIPLES

In the previous section I elaborated on the principles from 2 Timothy that develop healthy, growing, and reproductive disciples who can make heroic differences in this life. Based on these principles, I will now demonstrate a simple and powerful way to make and multiply disciples, a method anyone can do.

This section updates and expands work I've done in books and training materials on Life Transformation Groups (LTGs) over the past fifteen years. Even if you have attended training events or read previous books, you will find this section worthwhile.[1]

11

Falling into a Powerful Current

Discovering and Releasing Life Transformation Groups

I really never thought much about becoming a lifeguard while I was growing up. The days of my father's lifeguarding had long passed by the time I was old enough to remember things. Then one day toward the end of my senior year in high school, my best friend told me he was going to try out, so I figured I'd try out as well. Both of us were on the swim and water polo teams in our school, and we used to surf a lot in the summers.

I went with Ted to the lifeguard headquarters and filled out an application. Then early one Saturday morning, in the coldest time of the year, we joined about two hundred others at the beach in Santa Monica to try out. They wrote numbers on our shoulders with indelible markers, lined us up behind a line, and when the gun went off, we all ran into the frigid March water like crazy people scrambling to be in the top seventy-five to get the job. All my years of swimming helped, but actually, it was my water polo experience and my familiarity with the ocean from surfing all those years that made the difference. Most of the people were collegiate-level swimmers. My friend and I were still high school punks, but I knew how to use a rip current to get out faster. I knew how to pull, push, wrestle, and kick competitors in the water. I also knew how to catch a wave on my way in. As a result of years of training that I didn't even realize I was getting, I did well on the test. Much of what I did for fun as I was growing up actually prepared me for that moment. I was in the top half of those who passed the test to make it to the next level—rookie school.

Rookie school was a week of intense training. It was competitive and harsh, probably the closest thing to boot camp I will experience. The instructors were like drill sergeants who were doing everything they could to screen out those who couldn't cut it. It was their personal mission to discourage people from continuing.

Some of the training we receive in life is formal and intentional, like rookie school. There is much training in life, however, that we receive in unexpected ways. Without our always being aware of it, God prepares us to be ready for what he has in store for us. There is nothing in our life experience that God cannot redeem and use for his purpose. Even my experiences as a lifeguard twenty years ago, just simple stories from my past, I now realize were important lessons, the full meaning and usefulness of which I am still discovering. Often we underestimate the experiences we have and the lessons they teach us.

In many ways I stumbled into figuring out how to make disciples in a simple and reproducible way. It was not forethought and genius on my part that designed the Life Transformation Groups, which I will describe in detail in the chapters that follow. I have always longed to see spontaneous multiplication of disciples, so I was drawn to study it in history and could recognize

it when it was in front of me, so in a sense God prepared me without my even knowing it, using my own passions and desires.

The Strong Pull of a Rip Current

One of the most important lessons a lifeguard must master is the ability to spot a rip current, commonly known as a riptide, though it really isn't tidal. Some people refer to it as an "undertow" but this is also a misnomer, because the current doesn't

Neil in his first stationed tower shortly after rookie school.

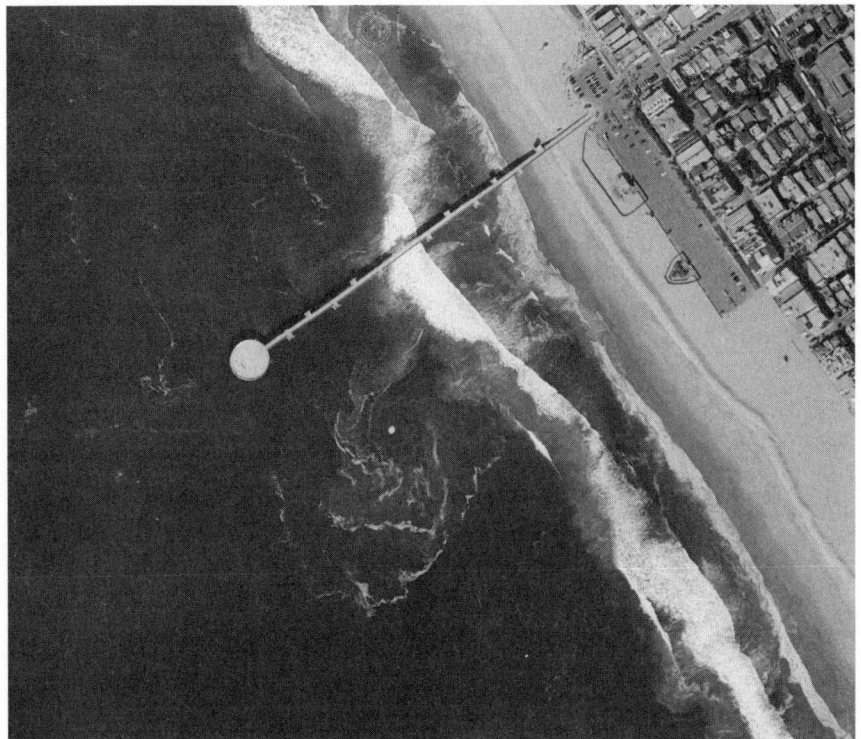

A satellite picture of a strong rip current sucking through high surf just south of the Venice pier where I used to work.

take you *under*; it takes you *out* past the waves. When the waves are large, the rip current can be strong, almost like a river, sucking all who enter it out to deeper water.

The formation of a rip current depends on many factors: the size and angle of the swells coming in, the shape of the beach and bottom, as well as any other obstacles deflecting the normal wave patterns, such as a rock jetty or a pier. By far, most rescues are made in "rips"—the reason it is so important for lifeguards to master identifying them.

When you are in a rip current, you must not fight against it. This will only cause fatigue and increased anxiety. In fact fatigue and anxiety are far more dangerous than the rip itself. It is recommended that you try swimming laterally, parallel to shore for a time until you are out of the current and then you can swim back to shore. The reality is that a rip current doesn't usually have to be so scary. It will pull you out past the waves, and then it will stop. As lifeguards and surfers know, rip currents can actually assist us in getting out to our destination faster. And they can even knock the waves down a foot or two in the process, making it an even easier gateway to the lineup (where waves build and are formed before they break).

There is a real sense in which my life has been in a strong rip current, and I have enjoyed the ride while other forces have done all the work. In this chapter I will tell the story of how, floating along in a strong current, I happened to discover Life Transformation Groups.

In my freshman year of college at Cal State University Long Beach, I started following Christ. From the start, I had a strong desire to be a part of something akin to the book of Acts and invested my life in disciple making, missions, and leadership development, especially with college students. I joined up with a local church that had a strong collegiate ministry and eventually became the pastor of their campus-oriented ministry while I was in seminary.

I have followed Christ for twenty-six years and in some respects little has changed. I am still working on college campuses, developing leaders, starting churches, and sending missionaries out, and I still long to see the book of Acts coming alive today in our time. For eight years I was pastor of a conventional church and in the last ten years I have been leading a ministry that trains and mobilizes church planters called Church Multiplication Associates.[1]

Early on I was hungry for any type of curriculum I could use that would help me fulfill my calling.

The Pitfalls of Discipleship Curricula

As I said, I have always had a drive to make disciples and have always had multiplication as a value in disciple making. I have used many of the materials and curricula available, some with more success than others. Every system that I used failed in some way. Often I would get bored with it after one or two times through the material. Once the leader is bored, the group is doomed. I also found that none of the materials encouraged reproduction. Rarely did I see multiple generations of Christians being produced.

Eventually I took to developing my own materials, naively believing that if I could just develop the right curriculum, it would set disciples loose and revival would come. I gathered the best of everything I could, tailored it for our ministry context (the university campus), and added some new stuff. I thought, *Surely this material will work.* Unfortunately, after spending months developing it, I was bored with it before I even started, and it never got past the first semester of use. Through painful trial and error, I discovered that the curriculum was not the key to multiplying disciples, leaders, churches, or movements. There are four common problems of a curriculum approach to disciple making.

1. *Leadership malnutrition.* One common problem of discipleship systems available today is that the leader often feels that he or she is not being adequately nourished and resourced. Meeting is piled on meeting to make sure that people at every level of the organization are being helped, and soon leadership becomes too time consuming.

Leaders of groups must be fed. A leader is one who, by definition, leads and influences the group. If the leader stops growing, he or she will lead the group toward stagnation and mediocrity.

2. *Leadership bottleneck.* Usually discipleship curricula require a leader of the group, which means that to reproduce disciples, you must first reproduce leaders. This is more difficult than reproducing disciples, and frankly, backwards. I have found that if you are good at making disciples who multiply, leadership recruitment and development are easy. But if you are not good at making disciples, you will always have a leadership void. No matter how many people you recruit to fill holes, when you use this backwards approach, you will never have enough leaders.

3. *A false linear approach to leadership development.* Another problem with discipleship curricula is that they are usually linear in their application, which means that you start in book one and progress in chronological order until you finish or graduate from the course. Life, however, is not linear, but mosaic, and it doesn't wait until we get to workbook number three before introducing the problems covered in that section.

4. *Borrowed authority.* A final problem with most curricula is that they use the Bible to substantiate their authority but don't usually empower the disciple to use the Bible as the authority in his or her life. A dependency can easily be created in the disciple on experts to decipher the true meaning of Scriptures. Usually the materials have the disciple look up a verse (often out of context) and fill in what is assumed it means in a fill-in-the-blank type workbook, never having actually read the whole passage in context.

Rediscovering the Best Discipleship Manual

Eventually I resorted to reading with my groups the newest and best books that were published and then discussing the reading together once a week. I was in the midst of a very good book when I started to get bored again. I

wasn't bored with the book; I just didn't see the lives of my disciples changing as a result of reading it.

In frustration, I asked, "What book could we read that would actually
change people's lives?" Then I heard the Holy Spirit whisper in my ear, "Duh!"
(which of course is the Greek word for *duh*). "The Bible." It is amazing how
invested we can be in bankrupt systems so that we simply do not see the
obvious staring right at us.

I started using the Bible for discipleship, and I have never gone back to
anything else. I told the group, "Put away the book we've been reading, or
read it on your own. This week I want you to read Proverbs." They thought
they were getting off the hook, so they were excited. Then they asked which
Proverbs I wanted them to read. Their countenance changed quickly when
I said, "All of them." "In a week?" one asked. "Yes, thirty-one chapters in a
week."

I was blown away at what the Holy Spirit was showing me throughout the
week as I read all of Proverbs. Wisdom began to just ooze out of my heart as I
walked through the week with a head and heart full of God's truth. I couldn't
wait to share this excitement with the others.

When we got back together, I asked them how their week was, expecting
a similar excitement, but they shrugged and said, "It was okay." Then I asked
them how much of Proverbs they had read. None had read more than seven
chapters. I told them, "You guys don't know what you're missing. This is awesome. You've got to try it. Let's do it again this week. Start over at chapter
one and read all thirty-one chapters this week."

When we got together the following week, I discovered that the guys
were not taking me seriously. While I had finished the reading and had
an even better week than the one before, the person the closest to completing the reading was at about chapter twelve. At this point I started to
take it a little personally, and in frustration I said, "Okay, we're going to
read Proverbs again. And if any one of you doesn't finish the reading, we
will read it again and again until we all show up at the same time with the
reading done."

In the cartoon world, a little lightbulb would have gone on over my head.
Hmm, I thought, *that's not a bad idea.* I kept it in my mind. We proceeded
to read Proverbs again. I couldn't wait to jump back into the reading.

Four weeks later we had all finished reading Proverbs. I had read the book
four times in four weeks, and it felt like a breath of fresh air had come across
my face. This was exciting and powerful. This was a means of feeding myself
as much as my disciples. I was hearing directly from God about all sorts of
things in my life.

Lessons Learned through Trial and Error

Then we went on to another book of the Bible, reading it in the same way. It took only a few weeks before I saw a complete turnover of the group. Those whom I thought I was discipling all left when I raised the bar. But God brought others who were hungry. The first was a young man named Kenny.

Kenny had been living a self-destructive life as an alcoholic and was experimenting with drugs. When I first met Kenny, his parents were in our church, but he was caught in the world. He'd already been in jail, had a couple DUIs, had his driver's license suspended, and had been in an accident. He came to church one morning when I was preaching a message on the consequences of sin, and I could tell that the Spirit was convicting him. Immediately after the message, I walked up to him and asked if he wanted to join our discipleship group.

I could sense that God was working in his heart so I refused any answer but yes. He told me he couldn't join us because he couldn't drive due to a suspended license. I told him I would pick him up at 5:45 Wednesday morning. He agreed. I arrived at 5:45 and honked my horn. After getting dressed he joined me, and we went to the group together. After a few weeks of reading the Bible, Kenny began to have a change of heart. He became a new creation; old things began to pass away as new things began to emerge. He asked if he could be baptized.

Four other young people, David, Dan, Pam, and Andrea, began meeting with us, and we soon outgrew the booth we were using in a restaurant. We needed to move to a larger booth. The entire group had changed and was now made up of motivated people. I remember mistakenly thinking this could be the solution to church growth. God was interested in so much more than church growth. He was interested in church health and multiplication.

The Bible reading was beginning to have an effect on our lives. We settled into a pattern of reading about thirty chapters of the Bible each week. When we got together, we discussed the reading, without any study questions, workbook, or facilitator guide. We were accountable to each other to finish together so that we could move on to another book.

Until that time, for my devotions, I would usually read the passage that I was to preach that week. Or, another way to put it, I would study for my sermons instead of having devotions. Don't get me wrong, the Scriptures would impact my life and in so doing bring a freshness to my sermons and make them very personal. But when we began reading so much Scripture, I knew that I would have to read a designated portion of Scripture each day apart from the text that I was preaching from if I had any hope at all of keeping up with the group. For the first time in a long time, I actually had a devotional time when I was intent on listening to what God had to say to me, rather than what he wanted to say to others. I began to change dramatically.

I was hearing from God in my Bible reading and I developed a great appetite for Scripture. Kenny and the others did as well. After a couple of months this way, someone approached me after church on Sunday and asked me a question that sent me into a discovery process. He asked, "Hey, Neil, what are you doing differently? Whatever it is, it's working. Keep doing it. Your preaching is so much more powerful."

This intrigued me and I began to ask myself why my preaching was more powerful. The answer was that I was infused so much more with Scripture that it was bound to affect my preaching. I began to wonder what other ways this group would affect our church. From that point on, I began to look at the group with the eye of an explorer. I was in a discovery process, so I began journaling and writing down observations. I was on a quest, which has since led me to several books and resources and new ways of seeing the kingdom of God grow and expand.

The Size of the Group

One of the first things I noticed was that when the group started to grow, just when I expected us to break loose and need to rent a meeting room, it would dwindle back down to three. A short time later, it would begin to grow, and again it would come back down to three. It would never die; it just wouldn't grow beyond three. The enthusiasm would never diminish, lives didn't stop changing, but the group did not grow as I had expected.

Finally, I listened to the Lord and figured out what he was trying to tell me. The group had a natural size that worked best. Rather than force the group to be something unnatural, I decided to keep the group limited to three—and multiply the groups. After this, I started noticing all the times the grouping of "two or three" is mentioned in the Bible (see chapter 8). This decision made an immediate impact on the group. Within one year that one group became approximately ten groups. It is possible that there were as many as twenty groups in our church the following year.

Kenny's growth continued as he was reading the Bible and making applications to his life. He developed relationships at church. He went back to school. I began encouraging Kenny to share his newfound faith with those he used to party with. Though he never would say so, he was less than enthusiastic about bringing up Christ with his old drinking buddies. I wanted him to do so before the relational ties became cold and the opportunity was lost.

Kenny's best friend was not a Christian. They continued to have fun together as buddies. One day they decided to go into business together. To celebrate they went out to dinner. Kenny's friend ordered two margaritas and had them set down before them. Kenny resisted at first, reminding his friend that he didn't drink anymore. But his friend persisted, insisting that they celebrate together like the good old days. Kenny gave in and had one drink. Then another, and another, and sure enough, they were back to the "good" old days. Late that night they were driving home in Kenny's truck. Kenny was not driving because his license was still suspended.

They were driving up a hill and approaching an intersection when the light turned red. Kenny said to his friend, "Go for it; you'll make it." They didn't. The truck was hit directly on the driver's side by a car heading east. When Kenny awoke, the truck was on his arm, glass was all over the place, and the paramedics were preparing to fly him via helicopter to an emergency trauma center. Later he found out that his friend had been killed instantly.

I received the call that Kenny was hurt early that morning and immediately drove out to see him. He still had glass and dried blood in his hair, but he was going to recover fully. He lost some feeling in his arm, but the doctors suspected that he would regain full use of it, and he did.

We talked a little. He was still shaken. I knew this was a significant moment in Kenny's life, so I chose my words carefully. I looked him in the eye and asked him, "Kenny, what do you think God is trying to tell you?"

With his lip quivering and his eyes full of tears, he looked up at me and said, "I just can't believe that my best friend is in hell right now, and there is nothing that I can do about it."

Kenny would never be the same again. From that day on he has been sober and has had a heart to share the gospel with those around him. One day, while skiing with friends from college, he met a pretty girl who wasn't a Christian. He thought she was cute, but he knew he couldn't date a non-Christian, so he led her to Christ and then they began dating. After Carol received the Lord, she quickly began to grow in her new faith. Eventually they were married and together they make a dynamic team. Carol began meeting with another growing believer in our church—Pam. Another young woman accepted Christ, was baptized, and joined their group. Soon after the group multiplied.

Both Kenny and Carol have a heart for sharing the gospel with the lost that flows from their own salvation experiences. For a time Kenny became one of the youth pastors at my church. Today he and Carol still have a passion for reaching troubled teens who are in the same bondage from which he was released.

Character Accountability Questions

I learned many valuable things from Kenny. I saw a need to introduce an element of accountability to our meetings. I began to ask him each week, "So how many days of sobriety has it been so far?" This was my way of (not so) subtly holding him accountable. Eventually I started asking, "Have you given in to a personal addiction this week? Explain." I did this because I have found that people with addictive behaviors can often find other means of falling into bondage. To God's glory Kenny did not.

I had been studying John Wesley and the beginning of the Methodist movement. They used to ask one another accountability questions in small groups to keep in touch with each other and to keep one another accountable for their spiritual growth. I came up with "Character Conversation Questions." The questions have been adapted and altered several times since (and now we have eleven questions we ask), but they have always been a simple way to hold one another accountable. They allow us to confess our sins to one another without feeling like we are intruding into personal areas that are none of our business. Using a simple card with these questions on it allows us to bring up deep issues of the soul without any of us feeling like the "sin police."

I also found the need to integrate accountability for evangelism into our meetings, so one of the questions deals with witnessing to our faith.

Gender Specific Groups

With the introduction of the questions, I knew the groups could not be coed. I encouraged the women to begin groups of their own. I also challenged them to come up with questions that relate best to their own needs, which they did. Eventually the questions became a list that can be appropriate for both sexes. In appendix 1 there are lists of sample questions that have been used all over the world and in history. Once I started using the Character Conversation Questions, I saw real multiplication begin.

Spontaneous Multiplication

At first, I wasn't even expecting the groups to multiply. I was having a nice time alone at the restaurant where my group met. One day our usual waitress, Michelle, came up to me and said, "You should be really proud of Kenny."

Thinking this was a good opportunity to let Kenny's testimony work, I said, "I am, but why do you think that I should be?"

She said, "His group is doing real well."

I was puzzled and asked, "Kenny has a group?"

She said, "Yeah, every Monday morning they have more and more young people who are excited about learning the Bible."

This is how I found out that my group had multiplied.

Eventually Michelle came to our church, probably just out of curiosity for what was changing these lives. One thing she discovered is that it wasn't the church or the preaching that was changing lives. I would add it wasn't the LTG system either. It was simply implanting the seed of God's kingdom in good soil that was changing these lives—starting with my own.

Soon after, Kenny left that group and began another. The first group he had started went on without him to give birth to three or four others and eventually became the foundation of a new ministry to young singles.

Strategic Prayer Focus

The last piece of the puzzle came to me when I was hoping that Kenny and others would reach out to their friends and relatives and talk about the new life they had experienced. We had already included an accountability question regarding their personal testimony. I didn't want to make it something pushy or manipulative. I looked at the New Testament's words regarding salvation and made a list of the passages that were pertinent. One of them was Luke 10:2 where Jesus remarks that the harvest is plentiful and all that is lacking is workers. Then he presents a solution—pray to the Lord of the harvest to send out workers. How simple yet profound! I took the list of verses on salvation and wrote strategic prayers for people's souls and included the prayers on the back of the card with the accountability questions (see chapter 13 for the prayers and references).

Life Transformation Groups Go Global

Eventually we published the idea of Life Transformation Groups in a resource that few have seen called *Raising Leaders for the Harvest*.[2] On the third tape of the resource I explained all about LTGs. What we found was amazing. The third tape would be spread all over the place and was constantly being pirated.

At this time I left the church I was at and moved to Long Beach, California, to start new churches. Very quickly a small team of us, some from my previous church, led many young people to Christ, and each one was immediately immersed in an LTG. Lives changed rapidly, and the churches we started carried an enthusiasm and life I had never seen before. My book *Organic Church* chronicles many of the remarkable stories from this time.

Many people have been in small groups or house churches before. But how many have been in a house church or cell group where all the participants are newly transformed and reading thirty chapters of Scripture each week, confessing their sins to one another, and begging God for the souls of their lost friends and family members?

John was one of our early disciples who came to Christ from a background of drugs. When we first met him, he had just been released from prison for possession with intent to sell. John quickly led his friend he used to party with, Mike, to the Lord. He baptized him and began meeting with him in an LTG. Mike grew very fast in the Lord and started his own groups. Eventually, both men led some pretty girls to Christ, baptized them, and married them. I am not saying this is the solution to all the problems of single people, but I will say there is nothing more attractive than a changed life that is infused with confidence in God's love and presence.

Mike reunited with an aunt and uncle in central California who are pastors of a church there. Seeing his enthusiasm and rapid growth, they gave him an old cassette tape with the printing all rubbed off from excessive use. It was a message they felt he needed to hear.

On the way home he played the tape. As the speaker started, he thought the voice sounded familiar. As the teacher kept talking, he started to describe LTGs. Mike announced loudly in his car, "Hey, that's Neil! That's my pastor!" It was an orphaned third tape from the resource we produced. It was so far removed from the rest of the tapes that no one even knew where it had come from.

Eventually I wrote the book *Cultivating a Life for God*, which explains the LTG concept and has made the spread of this idea even easier. We also published a simple fourfold brochure, which explains LTGs, and there is a tear-off card containing the questions and prayers to begin using right away.[3]

Over the years I have collected letters explaining how LTGs penetrated yet another language and culture in another part of the world. While in Australia I encountered a man who told me he had been doing an LTG for months. That was encouraging in and of itself, but then he told me how he spoke with a missionary friend in Sri Lanka who was frustrated with all the lifeless ways of disciple making he had tried. The Aussie explained the concept over the phone, and LTGs went from Australia to Sri Lanka in no time. Who knows where it has gone from there? We have found this simple idea in dozens of nations around the world. I even had a pastor tell me I need to try this new idea called LTGs. I listened politely and told him, "That's a good idea. I think I will."

Steve, a pastor of a large church in the Pacific Northwest, read an advertisement for the new release of *Cultivating a Life for God*, promising a new method that will transform lives and quickly multiply disciples spontaneously with barely any effort. He was furious at the brazen promises used to sell a product that could never live up to its claims. Convinced that it was a blatant lie to sell more books, he decided to write a stern letter to rebuke the Christian publisher. Believing that he had to read the book first and gather ammunition for his letter, he bought the book and read it.

After he read the book, he did write a letter but not the one he first assumed he would write. He wrote an explanation of his initial judgment and ordered many more books. He found that the book did indeed have a potential solution for transforming lives and multiplying disciples. Since then, his church has ordered hundreds of copies of the book and has seen many lives changed and multiplied. This former skeptic has also spread the concept to many other churches in his own area and even as far away as the southern tip of the continent of Africa.

All these stories are testimony to the power of God's Word in lives ready to receive it. These are not stories of the glories of the LTG concept. The system is simple, which makes it easy to use and pass on, but the power is in God's Word, confession of sin, and prayer, all in the context of safe and vulnerable relationships.

I am not confused about this, and it would help if you weren't either. There isn't a method or system that will change a life. It is the Good News of God's kingdom that changes a life. It is the power of God's truth that transforms a willing soul. It is regularly confessing sin to one another that brings healing. It is begging God for the souls of the hurting people around you that changes your heart. The system is just a simple, easily accessible package for those things; that's all.

It has been fifteen years since that first group began. Not a week has gone by in those fifteen years that I have not been in a Life Transformation Group. I stick to it, not because I am the author, not to prove it works, not to authenticate my writings, but for one simple reason—I need it.

I have seen many disciples grow weary and stop meeting in an LTG. In about two to three months' time, they realize what they are missing and often will get another group started. Once the current has hold of you, it is hard to bail out.

In the next chapter I will share why a simple method is so necessary and effective for such a profound task as making disciples.

12

The Value of Simplicity

Less Is More

In the past year my wife and I have had four surgeries between us. None was serious, but then again, when they put you under and cut open your body, it's not a walk in the park. I was amazed by all the complex and powerful equipment that modern hospitals use today to save lives.

As a lifeguard, however, a single tool is the most important one in saving lives—the rescue can. Sometimes called a rescue tube, it is very simple, yet also very profound in its significance. The typical rescue can is a hard plastic tube shaped like a big red bullet with three handles. It is about two and a half feet long and twelve inches wide in the middle. At the pointed end, a three-foot nylon rope is attached with a black strap at its end. The strap forms a circle that a lifeguard would fling quickly over his or her head and shoulder so that the rescue can floats along behind as the guard swims.

It doesn't take a rocket scientist to figure out how to use the rescue can. It is so simple that anyone can see how it operates. There are no electronic components, switches, moving parts, or digital readouts. It doesn't require batteries or special training. It just floats. But of course that is what you want

A rescue can hanging from a tower.

A lifeguard on a rescue with a rescue tube trailing behind him.

most when you are sinking—something that floats and is able to get you to shore. The only skill one needs to use it is the ability to hold on.

In the following chapters I will explain a simple system that is easy to do and yet does exactly what is needed to develop strong men and women of God who will pass their courageous faith on to others.

When Paul wrote to Timothy, he reminded him several times of the very simple yet profound words that he had passed on to him. "Retain the standard of sound words which you have heard from me" (2 Tim. 1:13). "The things which you have heard from me . . . entrust these to faithful men" (2:2). But it was more than just words that Paul passed on to Timothy. He writes in the opening chapter, "I remind you to kindle afresh the gift of God which is in you through the laying on of my hands" (1:6). Later he reminds Timothy that he followed much more than his words alone. He says, "Now you followed my teaching, conduct, purpose, faith, patience, love, perseverance, persecutions, and sufferings" (3:10–11). He continues, "You, however, continue in the things you have learned and become convinced of, knowing from whom you have learned them" (v. 14).

The things that Paul passed on to Timothy were substantive and simple. They had to be simple if he was to expect Timothy to pass them on to others who in turn would do the same.

After a few decades of serving the Lord in developing disciples, leaders, churches, and movements, I have discovered something that is very potent. If you can package something extremely powerful in something extremely simple, it can have a profound impact on the world.

We seem to do things backwards. Often we package the powerful things in complex systems that are not easily passed on to others. What ends up happening is that the complex system itself draws too much attention and the powerful truths of Scripture and redemptive relationships get lost in the system. We make the package complex and end up minimizing the potency of what can actually change a life in the process.

For example, as I pointed out earlier, many discipleship courses use the method of asking a disciple to turn to a verse in the Bible and find there the curriculum author's preconceived truth. Then the disciple is to write down the truth in a fill-in-the-blank workbook. The purpose, of course, is to help the new disciple grow. All that really happens is that the idea put forward by the author of the workbook is reinforced. Which do we actually think will be more life transforming, doing that, or actually reading an entire book of the Bible from start to finish repetitively? And of course we could save a lot of money and effort by not producing such workbooks if we simply had disciples read the Bible.

In our quest to be part of a powerful movement of God's kingdom, we often are tempted to think the solution will come from a complex composite of things that produce the longed-for results. We cry out to the heavens for a solution that will finally change the church forever. Many people travel every year to new seminars and conferences, buying the latest books and binders full of new methods in their search for the answer. The primal scream of our hearts is a search for spiritual success that will ultimately change the world. Albert Einstein once commented, "When the solution is simple, God is answering."

Power

There is something special about the power of simplicity. Many of the most profound things in life are indeed simple. Simple, however, does not mean simplistic. We tend to overlook simple things, thinking that anything of value and substance will be complex, require professional oversight, and be very expensive. A valuable maxim I have integrated into all I do is this: Less is more. Simplicity is a step *beyond* complexity. It takes great skill and effort to make something simple. It is easy to create something that is complex, but to design something that is simple and yet profound is a creative challenge. It takes great skill to know what is absolutely essential and what can be discarded.

Jesus said, "Come to Me, all who are weary and heavy-laden, and I will give you rest. Take My yoke upon you and learn from Me, for I am gentle and humble in heart, and you will find rest for your souls. For My yoke is easy and My burden is light"(Matt. 11:28–30). For most, discipleship has become so complicated that it is no longer an easy burden and a light load. But Jesus intends for the Christian life to be easy and light and to bring rest to our souls. Fulfillment of the Great Commission is meant to be restful not stressful.

Endurance

Another truth about simplicity is that simple things last, while complex things breaks down. When we approach disciple making—wanting to pass the baton on to succeeding generations—we must refine the process so that it is simple and transferable. Simplicity is the key to the fulfillment of the Great Commission in this generation. If the process is complex, it will break down early in the transference to the next generation of disciples. The more complex the process is, the greater the giftedness needed to keep it going. The simpler the process, the more available it is to the broader Christian populace.

Perhaps the reason that we do not see multiplication of disciples more often is that we are trying to do too much too soon in the process. We fail to grasp the fact that discipleship—following Christ in simple obedience—is a lifelong pursuit. Unfortunately, we attempt to teach our disciples so much in the first year that we unintentionally sabotage the following years by intimidating them into thinking it is way too hard for common people to do. We tend to overestimate what we can do in a year and underestimate what we can do in three years.

Being Unforgettable and Transferable

In the bestselling book *The Tipping Point*, Malcolm Gladwell says any epidemic type of expansion requires a "stickiness factor."[1] In other words, the pattern must stick with people in such a way that it is unforgettable and easily passed on to others. It is not enough that it is easy, it must also capture the imagination and affection of those who will pass it on.

Paul passed on to Timothy truths that were so profound that he would not forget them. They gripped his life and never left him. At the same time, however, the things Paul passed on were simple enough that Timothy could in turn pass them on to others who could then pass them on to still others.

The gospel itself is the most profound truth humankind has ever received, yet it is simple enough for a child to understand and pass on to others. It is not enough that people *can* pass it on; it is necessary that they will *want* to pass it on. The gospel is good news, and like a profound secret, it should be something that we all want to tell others.

We need systems that are practical and profound. They must be both simple and significant—significant enough to tap into the Christian's internal motivation, yet simple enough that they can be easily passed on from disciple to disciple. Such a system can strengthen the church and allow growth that is qualitative and quantitative.

In *Organic Church* I give simple criteria we at Church Multiplication Associates[2] use to determine if our tools or strategies are worth producing. These criteria are adapted from Thom Wolf.[3] When we go about thinking up a new strategy we ask ourselves, can it be . . .

- *Received personally.* Does it have a profound implication? It must be internalized and must transform the soul of the follower.
- *Repeated easily.* Does it have a simple application? It must be able to be passed on after only a brief encounter.
- *Reproduced strategically.* Can it be universally communicated? It must pass on globally by being translated into a variety of cultural contexts and languages.

The Focus on What Is Important

Another reason simple methods are better than complex methods is that they do not take the glory away from Christ. There are many times, unfortunately, that methods can be so impressive that people cease to notice Christ. If people are so impressed with our wineskins—systems and strategies—that they stop noticing the wine—the message and person of Christ—there is a big problem. Simple strategies keep the focus on Christ, not on the plans or the people dreaming up the plans. Our Lord chooses to put his glory in weak vessels so that he retains all the glory.

Jesus spoke of wine and wineskins (Luke 5:36–39). Wineskins are important because they carry the wine, but without the wine, the skins are useless. It is good to give some thought to ministry systems, but the systems should not be the main thing. In fact, if done right, they should hardly be noticed at all because the life of Christ has captivated our attention and affection. Simple systems are more likely to allow for this.

Easily Reproducible

One final reason that simple methods are important is that multiplication becomes much more feasible. Reproduction comes from a natural desire and ability inherent in all healthy living things. Similarly, reproduction of churches should not be hard. It should be natural and even pleasurable. The fact that reproduction is thought to be so hard and painful for churches is evidence of how far removed we are from being healthy and natural. Reproduction is the result of intimacy, and we are created to enjoy intimacy. Even among churches, reproduction is the product of intimacy with Christ, his mission, his spiritual family, and the lost world.

All reproduction begins at the molecular level and develops from the micro to the macro, from the simple to the complex. It is the same in the kingdom of God. We each began life as a zygote. A zygote is a cell formed by the union of a male seed and a female egg. Life multiplies from there. The moment that conception occurs, all the DNA necessary for the formation, growth, and development of a mature person is intact. The DNA never changes—it just leads the multiplication process within every tiny cell to form the complete body. The same can be said for the body of Christ.[4]

In the next chapter I will describe the Life Transformation Group System.

13

○

A Tool Easily Passed to Others

The Life Transformation Group System

One interesting piece of trivia from my lifeguarding days is that I may actually be the only lifeguard to have ever made a water rescue behind his tower!

During the winter of 1983, there was such strong storm surf combined with high tides that the entrance to the pier where my tower sat was washed away. The pier remained closed to the public for more than a year until they could replace the entrance with new pilings and road. During that summer, we had to park the truck next to the pier and climb onto the roof of the truck to be able to get up to the pier and then the tower.

During a couple days of strong surf and high tides that summer, we could see how the pier was washed away. The waves were so strong that a constant river of water started gushing from the south side of the pier up and behind the pier and tower and then washing into the ocean on the north side. Most towers would be pulled back to higher sand when the tides and surf were this high, but the tower I was at sat up on the pier so it remained where it was, surrounded by rushing water on all sides (see photo on p. 51).

On one of those afternoons, I was returning from a patrol in the truck and was about to try to navigate back to the tower when I heard my name yelled by my fellow lifeguard still up in the tower. I looked up and he was pointing to a person who had stumbled into the strong current passing around behind the pier and tower. Frankly, I am very impressed with my colleague's lifeguarding skills. It is our job to watch the water, but to see a rescue behind you is remarkable.

I watched the victim helplessly heading around the back of the pier where he would then head out toward the ocean in the current, but I was without a rescue can, since I had already left the truck and was halfway to the tower (when the water was this high and fierce we had to park the truck back in the lot behind the pier and use a makeshift ladder to climb into the tower). If I ran back to the truck to get a can, I would be too late to get to the victim.

My associate took a can from the high tower and flung it in the air at least twenty yards and it landed a few feet from where I stood. I dove and grabbed the can and then the victim and was able to pull us both out of the current before we hit the surf. Thus I became the only lifeguard I know to have made a water rescue behind his tower. Teamwork like this is usually the result of solid training, good communication, and an intense need.

What impresses me about this story (besides the eyes in the back of my associate's head) is the way a rescue can was passed from one person to another so simply and quickly in a desperate circumstance.

The Life Transformation Group system is also a simple tool that can easily be passed from one rescuer to another. It is a grassroots tool for growth. Through this simple system the most essential elements of vital spiritual ministry are released to ordinary Christians without the need for specialized training. It taps the disciple's internal motivation and provides the support needed to grow in the essentials of a spiritual life. The LTG empowers the ordinary Christian to do the uncommon work of reproductive discipling.

LTGs can work in any ministry environment and are not bound to a single model of church. They are working well in megachurches and in microchurches and everything in between. They are not a threat to Sunday school, cell groups, or any other kind of ministry structure. It is hard to imagine any godly leader being opposed to LTGs. If a pastor doesn't want you reading the Bible, confessing your sins to a trusted friend, and praying for lost friends and associates, it is probably time to find another church.

An LTG is made up of two to three people, all of the same gender, who meet weekly for personal accountability in the areas of their spiritual growth and development. A group should not grow beyond three but multiply into two groups of two rather than remain a single group of four. If a fourth person is added to the group, it is recommended that the group consider itself pregnant and ready to give birth to a second group. Once the fourth person has demonstrated sufficient faithfulness (two to three weeks), the group should multiply into two groups of two. I have found that the values and objectives that are the core of an LTG will intrinsically keep the group size down to two or three. This is the natural size for such a group with these intended objectives. Once the group grows beyond this, the group will lose what is most important about it, and my experience is that it will naturally return to its smaller size.

There is no curriculum or training needed for the LTG. The Bible and a simple card, which stays in the participant's Bible, is all that is needed.

The LTG consists of three essential disciplines for personal spiritual growth—confession of sin, a steady diet of Scripture, and prayer for others who need Christ.

Confession of Sin

The first thing the members of the LTG do when they meet is ask one another the eleven Character Conversation Questions found on one side of the LTG card. (These cards can be found at www.cmaresources.org.) The meetings should always begin with this because it is easy to get lost in conversation and run out of time for the questions. Beginning each meeting with confession of sin tends to sanctify the rest of the time together. The questions are straightforward. Each person in the group takes a turn answering each question honestly. The group must be a safe place where the participants feel they can be honest and vulnerable. This is the reason coed groups do not work well.

Here are the eleven questions:

1. Have you been a testimony this week to the greatness of Jesus Christ with both your words and your actions?
2. Have you been exposed to sexually alluring material or allowed your mind to entertain inappropriate sexual thoughts about another this week?
3. Have you lacked integrity in your financial dealings or coveted something that does not belong to you?
4. Have you been honoring, understanding, and generous in your important relationships this week?
5. Have you damaged another person by your words, either behind their back or face-to-face?
6. Have you given in to an addictive behavior this week? Explain.
7. Have you continued to remain angry toward another?

8. Have you secretly wished for another's misfortune?
9. A blank to fill in your own accountability question. (For example, Have you kept to your diet? Have you worked out three times this week? Have you finished your homework on time?)
10. Did you finish the reading and hear from God? What are you going to do about it?
11. Have you been completely honest with me?

These Character Conversation Questions are designed to bring to remembrance any sin that may need to be confessed. The system is meant to be simple and transferable so that anyone can apply it. We have worked through many drafts of questions to find a simple list that can cover a broad scope of behavior that needs regular confession.

There is, however, a potential danger inherent with the questions that I want to make clear. It is important for those who are involved with an LTG to submit to the spirit of the system more than the letter of the law. These eleven questions are meant to stimulate open sharing and discussion, but they are not an exhaustive list of all that sin is, nor do they define what true righteousness is. Simply adhering to the behavior promoted in these questions does not necessarily constitute righteousness.

Certainly obedience and the confession of sin can lead to righteousness, but we dare not believe that this list of questions is the standard of all that is righteousness. Jesus is the standard of righteousness (Matt. 5:17–20; John 5:39–47). We must follow Jesus, not a list of eleven questions, if we want to pursue righteousness. The questions we have given as samples are only tools to help you in your pursuit of Jesus.

Another reason these questions alone are insufficient to establish righteousness in our lives is that most of us have enough creativity to sin between the lines.

These questions have proven very helpful in uncovering sinful patterns that need to be openly confessed in a safe and healing community. The LTG provides a wonderful place for accountability that leads to overcoming patterns of sinful behavior. There are, however, other questions that can do the same thing. I have always said that people should feel free to adjust the questions to be of the most personal benefit. Some use questions that are more open-ended and less specific. For example, one pastor I know uses questions similar to the following in his LTGs:

1. How has God made his presence known to you this week?
2. What is God teaching you?

3. How are you responding to his prompting?
4. Is there someone you need to share Christ with this next week?
5. Do you have a need to confess any sin?

These questions are simple and transferable, yet they allow for a much broader application and openness to the leading of the Spirit in a person's life. (An LTG card with these questions is also available at www.cmaresources .org.) The advantage of the eleven Character Conversation Questions listed above is that they bring to light more specific behaviors that may need to be confessed but which may be forgotten otherwise. Both types of question have advantages and disadvantages, and either list will accomplish the goal if applied in the proper spirit.

See appendix 1 for a variety of questions used for accountability. Adopt whatever works best for you. I have only three suggestions in this regard. First, somehow include in your list of questions one that holds the group members accountable for openly sharing with others a testimony of Christ's goodness. It should be something that goes beyond living as an example and include a verbal witness. I also suggest that you have at least one question that asks the group members if they are listening to the Lord and being responsive. Finally, I suggest confession of sin as a part of the accountability process.

The goal of having accountability is not sin management. That would be a useless and feeble goal that we could never accomplish. God calls us to so much more than sin management; he wants us to foster an honest relationship that is transparent, caring, and cleansing.

A Regular Diet of Scripture

The confessing of sin cleanses and prepares the soul for every good work God has for a person. While confession cleanses us from all unrighteousness (1 John 1:9), it alone does not produce righteousness in us. That is why the second discipline of the LTG is so important—the intake of God's Word.

The power of the LTG system is in the unleashing of God's Word into the lives of people. The Lord made it clear that the Word of God is the seed of new life. He said, "Now the parable is this: the seed is the word of God. . . . But the seed in the good soil, these are the ones who have heard the word in an honest and good heart, and hold it fast, and bear fruit with perseverance" (Luke 8:11, 15).

Each group agrees on a book of the Bible to read. Sometimes an introductory reading schedule is used to help get things started. The goal is to have the people reading large amounts of Scripture repetitively and in a whole context, from start to finish.

For a steady diet, I *strongly* recommend reading twenty-five to thirty chapters each week. If the book agreed on is a short book, such as Ephesians or Jonah, it is read five to seven times in a week. If the book is a moderate size, such as 1 Corinthians or Romans, it is read twice in a week. If the book is longer than that, such as Proverbs, Revelation or Acts, the book is read once during the week.

Books that are even longer, such as Genesis, Psalms, or Isaiah can be broken up. Use natural breaks if possible. Each section can be read as you would the shorter books mentioned above. For example, Genesis can be broken into three sections: chapters 1–12, chapters 13–35, and chapters 36–50. Each section can be read twice in a week. Or you can break Genesis into two groups of twenty-five chapters and read each section once in a week. There is no set pattern, only a goal of reading twenty to thirty chapters of Scripture per week. Some books have shorter chapters, which can mean an increased number read in a week. For example, Psalms can be read in two parts of seventy-five chapters in a week.

Sometimes sections of books can be read repetitively. Many have read Matthew 5–7 (the Sermon on the Mount) seven times in a week and found it to be very powerful. Psalm 119 can be approached that way, as can Jesus's letters to the seven churches of Asia Minor in Revelation 2 and 3. The key is to choose a section that forms a natural unit and read it enough that you are reading approximately thirty chapters in a week.

When the LTG meets the following week, the members ask one another if the entire reading was completed in time (number 10 of the accountability questions). If anyone in the group was unable to complete the reading portion, the same reading assignment is to be taken up again. The LTG will continue reading the same portion of Scripture repeatedly until the group finishes it together in the same week. Once all group members finish the reading in the same week, a new book is agreed on for the next week. Group members can rotate the privilege of choosing the next book to read if so desired.

It is not the goal of this system that each person finish the reading every week. I repeat: *It is not the goal to finish the reading every week.* One of the powerful values of this method is the repetition in the reading. It helps people truly grasp the meaning of the message of the book they are reading. If everyone is finishing twenty to thirty chapters each week, then you need to increase the reading to thirty to forty chapters, until you find that it takes three to four weeks before you all finish.

It is important to note that a person who has been unable to complete the reading in a given week is not a failure. Rather, as I explained above, it is advantageous if that happens. It is best if it takes a few weeks to get through a book because the repetition helps in the understanding and application of the truth. For this reason, we suggest that the amount of Scripture chosen to read be a stretch for the group to finish. Ideally, it should average about three to four weeks for the group to complete the assignment.

In my own experience, in those weeks when any one of us failed to complete the reading, we felt that the Lord was not done teaching us something in that particular book. So we went into the next week with anticipation, believing that the Holy Spirit had a special lesson in store for us. We were never disappointed.

This form of accountability is a breath of fresh air in this highly segregated and individualistic society we live in. A major weakness of the Western church is the independent and individualistic approach to spiritual development. In the Eastern world, ideas of family and community are stronger. It is interesting to note how cell-based ministry and multiplication are occurring more easily in cultures that understand community naturally as opposed to the Western world that prizes the individual over community. This affects all areas of the church.

The LTGs, in biblical fashion, operate naturally in community. We stay together. We learn together. We move forward together. Our spiritual growth is tied to others in a natural bond (Eph. 4:11–16). We care about one another's progress. In a sense, we learn to love one another as ourselves. My progress is tied to my brother's, and vice versa. This sanctified peer pressure works to stimulate growth in one another. Like a team, as each player improves, the ability of the entire team is raised to another level, far beyond any individual effort alone.

God has always intended for his people to work as a team. He wrote in Hebrews 10:24–25: "And let us consider how to stimulate one another to love and good deeds, not forsaking our own assembling together, as is the habit of some, but encouraging one another; and all the more, as you see the day drawing near."

The LTG can be a first step for the Westerner to learn what community really is. Then groups can be built on transformed lives that have discovered the true value of community in an LTG.

Prayer for Souls

On the reverse side of the LTG card is printed the Strategic Prayer Focus. This is designed to be a reminder to pray strategically for lost people every time the Bible is opened (which is frequently in this system).

Each member of the LTG is to identify the two or three people who are the highest evangelistic priorities that God has laid on their hearts. They share the names of these people at a group meeting and each writes the names down on the card in the spaces provided. Each person should have listed all the names represented in the group, totaling six names. Each time we do our Bible reading, we select one of the names and pray for that person, using the suggested prayer guide. With this system, the person who is targeted for strategic prayer is prayed for two to three times by two or three different people every week. The prayers (listed below) that are offered are specific, progressive, and extensive. They are also in accordance with biblical principles of prayer and the salvation of lost souls.

1. I pray, Lord, that you draw ____ to yourself (John 6:44).
2. I pray that ____ will seek to know you (Acts 17:27).
3. I pray that ____ will hear and believe the Word of God (1 Thess. 2:13).
4. I ask you to prevent Satan from blinding ____ to the truth (2 Cor. 4:4; 2 Tim. 2:25–26).
5. Holy Spirit, I ask you to convict ____ of his/her sin and his/her need for Christ's redemption (John 16:7–11).
6. I ask you to send someone who will share the gospel with ____ (Matt. 9:37–38).
7. I also ask that you give me (and/or my fellow disciple) the opportunity, the courage, and the right words to share the truth with ____ (Eph. 6:19–20; Col. 4:3–6).
8. Lord, I pray that ____ will turn from his/her sin (Acts 17:30–31; 1 Thess. 1:9–10).
9. Lord, I pray that ____ would put all of his/her trust in Christ (John 1:12; 5:24).
10. Lord, I pray that ____ will confess Christ as Lord of his/her life, that his/her faith would take root and grow, and that he/she would bear much fruit for your glory (Luke 8:15; Rom. 10:9–10; Col. 2:6–7).

It is a group effort to bring these souls before the throne of grace. When we see a new soul born into the kingdom, we all rejoice, because we played a significant role in the process. Jesus said, "If two of you agree on earth about anything that they may ask, it shall be done for them by My Father who is in heaven" (Matt. 18:19). Those who come to faith in Christ as a result of these prayers can form the next group, and multiplication can occur naturally, spontaneously, and in a manner over which the whole group rejoices.

I remember clearly a holy moment in my life when the potent power of simply praying daily for people's souls struck me in a new way. I was a year into my first church plant in the urban part of Long Beach, California. Unlike so many church plants these days that draw Christians from other churches to form a new one, Awakening Chapels was born out of the harvest.

It was a warm Saturday afternoon, and I had gathered the new emerging leaders together for a day of training. We all sat around four rectangular tables put together to form a square so that we could all be at tables but communicate easily with one another. There were about fifteen people around the tables; almost all were not Christians a year earlier. I was explaining to them the ideas behind the Life Transformation Groups, similar to the way I have described them in this book. They all knew how to do LTGs because they had all been involved in them from the moment they found Christ, but I was giving them the whys of LTGs not just the hows.

When I got to the explanation of why we pray for those who are not yet in the kingdom, I felt goose bumps all over. I had my LTG card in my hand and as I looked down at it, there was Mick's name checked off, and she was sitting on my left. There was Scott's name and he was sitting on my right. Anne Marie's name was checked off as was Josh's. I had real faces smiling at me, each one representing one of the names on my card that I had once prayed for. Answered prayers were sitting across the table from me.

Each of these people had the same card in their Bibles, with names on them that are now checked off. Josh's card has Elsa's name on it, checked off. Elsa has a card with other names checked off. The Lord was smiling at me at that moment while he was saying to me, "See, I want to see them transformed even more than you do!" His words, "Ask, and it will be given to you" (Matt. 7:7) are clearly true. I fear that the other words: "You do not have because you do not ask" (James 4:2), are equally true.

I was struck, not with how powerful an LTG is, but with how powerful the simple idea of prayer is. I was reminded that Jesus told us to beg the Lord of the harvest for workers for the harvest (Luke 10:2). The people around the tables did not really need much convincing of the power of these simple prayers.

I have had at least six LTG cards in my Bible over the past ten years and there is not one of them that doesn't have names checked off as having come to Christ. Of course we are not praying for souls so that we can check off names on our list and feel good about ourselves. But there is no greater joy than to watch a life be born again into the kingdom of God. To that end we pray, God answers, and we rejoice.

Summary of the System

The LTG system is simple yet powerful. It incorporates the values of community, life transformation, and reproduction of disciples. At our church there is a place for anyone who wants to grow in Christ. There is no need for a new Christian to wait for a class to open. There is no ceiling to the care we can offer because the groups can multiply quickly and easily to accommodate any number the Lord grants us. The usual barriers do not limit us. Truly we have a sense that we can provide help to anyone who has a need, whenever he or she has a need. If the Lord chose to bless us with a large number of new conversions, we would be able to be responsible for their spiritual growth and development.

Let's summarize:

- LTGs meet once a week for approximately an hour.
- LTGs are groups of two or three (a fourth person is the beginning of the second group; multiplication is imminent).
- The groups are not coed.
- There is no curriculum, workbook, or training involved.
- There is no leader needed in the group.
- Only three tasks are to be accomplished:
  1. Sin is confessed to one another in mutual accountability.
  2. Scripture is read repetitively, in entire context and in community.
  3. Souls are prayed for strategically, specifically, and continuously.

A simple tool is often very profound. When you are struggling to stay afloat in deep waters, a complicated machine is not what you want. You don't have time to read an operational manual or fumble with batteries. Something that floats is all you want.

However, knowing that the seat cushion you are planted on at thirty-six thousand feet over the earth is a floatation device doesn't really bring you any comfort. But when you are in deep water with no land in sight, a floatation device is highly valued. Simple tools in the right context are of utmost value.

Context is important. I repeat throughout this book (and really, in all my teaching) that we must start with desperate people who will cling to the Good News as if they are about to go under for the third count.

We need to get back to the simple yet profound basics when it comes to disciple making. When we attempt to teach all the theologies, disciplines, and methods to a brand-new Christian from the very beginning, we slow down his or her obedience. The church is suffering from a bottleneck of teaching without obedience. In essence, we are educated beyond our obedience, which is not to say that we know a lot, but that we do not practice the elementary things we do know. We should simplify the process so that all Christians can be involved in disciple making and multiplying. Then we will be able to build on a solid foundation of spiritual growth.

Something similar to LTGs has been at the grassroots of some of the greatest revivals. The early church saw some of the most expansive growth of any time in church history. Eventually, the Roman Empire, the most dominant world power of human history, succumbed to Christianity's growth. Early on, many false rumors had been spread about this strange sect called Christians. Many thought Christians were cannibals who ate a person's flesh and drank his blood. A letter was written from Pliny the Younger to the Emperor Trajan some fifty years after the New Testament books were completed to explain what he discovered about this group. In this letter he described their regular practice this way: "They were accustomed to meet on a fixed day of the week before dawn and sing responsively a hymn to Christ as to a god, and to bind themselves by oath, not to some crime, but not to commit fraud, theft, or adultery, nor falsify their trust, nor to refuse to return a trust when called upon to do so."

The disciples, who were turning the world upside down, had a weekly accountability group where they devoted themselves to honestly deal with the temptations of life. What we have here is a description of these radical followers of Christ in action as seen from a non-Christian who is actually looking for something evil and suspicious. The letter went on to say, "When that was over, it was their custom to depart and to assemble again to partake of food."[1] It appears that there were two small group meetings practiced by the early church, a small, weekly accountability group and a spiritual family where they would share a meal together.

As I have already alluded, at the heart of the Methodist revival of the late 1700s and early 1800s was a simple weekly meeting called the Class Meeting, in which ordinary Christians would all answer a list of accountability questions (see appendix 1 for a few samples).

An LTG is so simple, yet it is profound in what it can do. It is something simple enough that even a drowning soul can get hold of it and float. But a person can also hand it off to others who are treading water in desperation or toss it to a rescuer who needs something to help save someone in a crisis.

Now that we've described an LTG, in the next chapter I will delineate many of the advantages of this method.

14

Instant Access to the Almighty

Advantages of the LTG System

Every lifeguard tower on the Los Angeles County beaches is equipped with a phone. It isn't an ordinary phone that you can dial a number and call anyone you like. This phone is directly linked to the headquarters switchboard operator. As soon as you pick up the phone, you are instantly connected to the operator.

Why is it set up this way? It is the best way to communicate directly with the headquarters in cases of emergency. The lifeguard doesn't need to remember an extension and take the time to dial. All he or she has to do is pick up the phone and the lifeguard is instantly connected to the people who can send out the emergency vehicles in response.

In a dire emergency the lifeguard is simply supposed to knock the phone off the hook, and when headquarters hears no response from the guard, they will know that an emergency is occurring and they will take immediate action. First they will call the towers on either side of the one tower to see if they can spot the emergency; then they will scramble the nearest emergency vehicle in response to the potential crisis.

One time I accidentally nudged the phone. The receiver appeared to be still on the cradle but was in fact not holding down the cutoff button. All of a sudden people started showing up with concerned looks on their faces, asking me if everything was okay. I kept assuring them things were fine. Eventually we realized what had happened, and I put the receiver back down on the cradle.

Imagine how fouled up everything would be if each tower could connect only with the tower on either side. To get a message to the headquarters would take a massive effort of connecting one tower at a time. If even a single lifeguard were unavailable and any link in the chain was broken, the whole system would crash. In such a state, even if every link was intact, the message would have to be perfectly relayed every single time and the chances of having a corrupted message would be extremely high.

The system works because every lifeguard knows that with a simple and swift move of the hand, he or she is immediately in connection with the people that can make a difference in a crisis.

Similarly, God is always just a thought away. We don't even have to dial to get through, and there are no busy signals, call waiting, or annoying message systems.

In our spiritual lives we must realize that every one of us has immediate and direct access to Jesus Christ. We do not need to route our communication though a middleman. In a dire situation, help is only a request away.

In this chapter I want to describe the advantages of using LTGs as a simple and reproducible system of disciple making that connects each disciple to God himself without any middleman.

Not a Seed Substitute

LTGs plant the seed; they are not a seed substitute. The simple and yet significant ingredients found in the LTG system can bring health and vitality back to the follower of Christ, but the LTG system itself is not a solution for all that ails a church, nor is it the agent of transformation for lives, ministries, and churches. The Holy Spirit and the Word of God bring transformation to a life that is cleansed and open to obey.

A catalyst is not the ingredient that hardens the varnish or glue, but it accelerates the properties that are already inherent in the other ingredients. Similarly, the LTG system is really just a catalyst that brings together the properties that cause spiritual change in a relational context that is conducive to growth via multiplication.

As I mentioned in the previous chapter, Jesus made it clear that the seed is the Word of God. In the parable of the sower, Jesus tells us, "The sower went out to sow his seed; and . . . [some] seed fell into the good soil, and grew up, and produced a crop a hundred times as great. . . . Now the parable is this: the seed is the word of God" (Luke 8:5, 8, 11).

Peter adds: "For you have been born again not of seed which is perishable but imperishable, that is, through the living and enduring word of God" (1 Peter 1:23).

We are the most biblically privileged generation in all of human history. We have more Bible translations, helpful study tools, and mountains of scholarly information than any previous generation. Nevertheless, we are now seeing the emergence of the most biblically illiterate generation this nation has ever seen. In other parts of the world and in other times, people gave their lives willingly for free access to God's Word, yet here in the Western world many of us have several unread volumes in a variety of translations collecting dust on the shelf.

We have forgotten the power of God's word. It was by his word that the created world was formed. God spoke, and the world was! His word holds the created universe together. And he is still speaking. We can hear his voice in our intimate relationship with him. We can also hear his voice in the Scriptures, which are alive and powerful. When we think of the Bible as simply an ancient book written by long-dead men in other languages and cultures, we diffuse its potential to have an impact in our lives simply because we expect so little of it. When God speaks, things change, if we would but listen.

In reading the book of Acts, it becomes clear that the Word of God fueled the growth and expansion of the church.

To gain a perspective of the power of the Word in spontaneous church expansion, let's start in Luke's account of the church multiplication movement in Asia Minor and take a brief walk backwards through the book to track the spread of the church to that point. You will see how the Word of God is the fire that ignites a new life and passion and which spreads that new life in Christ like a wildfire until ultimately an entire empire is overcome.

Acts 19:20: "So *the word* of the Lord was growing mightily and prevailing" (in Asia Minor).

Acts 19:10: "This took place for two years, so that all who lived in Asia heard *the word* of the Lord, both Jews and Greeks."

Acts 18:11: "And he settled there [Corinth] a year and six months, teaching *the word* of God among them."

Acts 13:49: "And *the word* of the Lord was being spread through the whole region" (Pisidian Antioch).

Acts 12:24: "But *the word* of the Lord continued to grow and to be multiplied."

Acts 8:4: "Therefore, those who had been scattered went about preaching *the word.*"

Acts 6:7: "*The word* of God kept on spreading; and the number of the disciples continued to increase greatly in Jerusalem, and a great many of the priests were becoming obedient to the faith."

Given this view of the expansion of the church and the power of God's Word, we can certainly understand why the apostles would conclude, "It is not desirable for us to neglect *the word* of God" (6:2). Instead of being distracted from the essential ministry of spreading God's Word among the growing disciples, they determined, "But we will devote ourselves to prayer and to the ministry of *the word*" (v. 4).[1]

Unfortunately, today's Western church has allowed herself to be distracted from this vital ministry. It's time for Christian leaders in the Western church to make the same determination that these apostles made. Not that we need to lock ourselves up for an even longer time in our study, preparing for our sermons, but we need to be fed by a steady and voluminous intake of Scripture with no purpose other than to hear from God and obey his voice.

The two contributions Martin Luther wanted to make most to Christendom were a Bible that all could read and understand and a hymnal from which they could sing. He said, "Let them loose. The flame will spread on its own." The flame spread in the early history of the church and has done so through much of history. It can do so once again if we will trust it and let it loose.

To see revival spread through our churches and touch our society, we need to trust God's Word *more* than all our "helpful" study tools and great growth ideas. In a sense we need to get out of the way and let God do what he does best, which is the next advantage of the LTG.

Remove the Middleman

The ordinary Christian has become totally dependent on clergy to tell him or her what the Bible says and what it means. Many Christians in this country feel they are unable to read the Bible without some professional help. For most, the only time they receive any of the Word at all is in sermons at church services.

If you doubt this claim, simply examine the facts. According to George Barna's research, three out of four American adults cannot read the Bible they have at home.[2] What is the most published Bible in America today? It's the King James Version (KJV). What is the most read Bible in America today? Again it's the KJV by a landslide. The problem is that, according to the U.S. Department of Education, only 51 percent of Americans are functionally literate. That means that about half of the people in the United States do not have the literacy levels to comprehend the KJV. No wonder they are dependent on the clergy for understanding God's Word.

Human Interpreters

I used to get a little offended by some study Bibles that have a famous teacher's name on the cover, as if that author wrote the book. Then one day I opened one and realized the author did write at least half of it. It used to be that when you opened a Bible in the middle, you would be in Psalms or Proverbs; today you are in Leviticus! There are so many notes explaining everything that in some of these study Bibles half of every page is Scripture and the other half is some scholar's explanation of what it all means. What ends up happening is that the scholar's words become as important as the Scriptures for the Christian's growth and understanding of God's voice. I am sure the scholar would object to this idea, but the subtle reality of the situation is that Christians are trained to think that the Bible is too difficult to understand without help. As a result, many would not venture to try to read it without a theologian's notes.

I am all in favor of study helps and study Bibles, but we have unintentionally separated people from a simple approach to God's Word. We have placed so many filters between God's voice and God's flock that they can no longer simply hear and obey. They need others to supply definition, application, and illustration. We need to make sure that the Scriptures stand alone. All the helps are indeed useful but only after people have spent time in God's Word without anyone aiding their understanding. It seems that Christians are no longer able to listen to God's Word without help. They need others to take in the nourishment, digest the meal, and regurgitate the understanding for them in simple language.

Imagine a marriage in which the husband and wife each needed to speak through an interpreter with a lexicon of both masculine and feminine vocabulary to define each word. Granted, there are times when an objective third party may actually help with the communication between spouses, and I wouldn't mind getting a copy of the feminine lexicon, but if there were a need for such an interpreter all the time, it would sap all intimacy and immediacy from the relationship.

A Proper Hermeneutic

Pastors also contribute to the gap between Christians and God's Word. Without meaning to, pastors can communicate the importance of the clergy's help in understanding Scripture. When they speak about the Greek or Hebrew meaning of the text, they separate their flock a little farther from God's Word. After all, how can ordinary Christians understand the Scriptures without help if they don't know the original languages? When a pastor publicly ridicules someone's misinterpretation of Scripture, he scares the congregation into thinking that they had better not risk trying to understand it themselves without "professional" help. This implication that the average Christian can't understand the Scriptures has actually erected a "false priesthood" between the Christian and God's Word.

Once a young pastor challenged me regarding the LTG system. He didn't feel I was being responsible, allowing people to read the Bible without first giving them a sound hermeneutic. *Hermeneutic* is a ten-dollar theological term that has to do with the ability to rightly interpret the Bible. He thought it dangerous to actually put the Bible into the hands of ordinary Christians without first training them in how to study it. To do otherwise, he felt, was to allow wrong interpretations that would spur heresy in the church.

I was tempted to suggest that what he really meant was that it allowed interpretations that differed from his own point of view, but restraint got the better of me. I said, "Our hermeneutic is actually a man-made system we have developed to help us understand the Word of God, correct?"

He said, "Yes, we need it because we are all sinful, depraved, and incapable of understanding the truth of God's Word without help."

I agreed and emphasized, "We do need help, but we disagree on the best help. You believe that we need help from our hermeneutical systems, and I believe we need help from the author and illuminator of the book—the Holy Spirit." Then I asked, "Do you mean to tell me that given a choice of trusting a man-made system or trusting the Holy Spirit, the pure, resident-author of the Scripture, to interpret the Bible, you would choose the system made by corrupt and depraved man? You would choose to trust the corrupt man and his system rather than the divine Author?"

He paused a long time before he responded. In fact he didn't really answer my question, he simply said, "You know, I hate to admit it, and I'll deny it if you ask me later, but you're actually a more pure biblicist than I am."

That was one of the greatest compliments I've ever received. And by the way, he did deny it later when he labeled me a heretic.

Am I saying that we don't need a proper hermeneutic to understand Scriptures? Do I mean to say that to use one is to lack faith? No, absolutely not. I strive to apply proper principles of interpretation when I am studying the Bible, and I do teach them to those I train in ministry. The key is in the timing of such training. I train proper interpretation techniques to those who are responsible for teaching others. However, before they ever get to that point in leadership training, they have already been reading and hearing from God through his Scripture for a long time through LTGs. It is when we are responsible for teaching the Bible to others that our hermeneutic becomes most important. I have found that teaching principles of hermeneutics to people who have already learned to read Scripture and to understand the Holy Spirit's illumination in their personal lives becomes very easy. Most find they have already used the principles in their study because they reflect common sense, and the Holy Spirit has already helped them along in the process.

One very liberating idea is that we don't have to be responsible for accurately interpreting every line and every word to gain appropriate truth for life application. I confess that there have been many times that I have read portions of the Bible and come up with more questions than answers, but that doesn't make the Bible wrong or me irresponsible. It simply means that I still have many levels of the riches of his Word to explore. But I also want to point out that many of those times where I came away with questions, I still found relevant truth that spoke to me personally. I have also found, years later, when I have pored over copies of my worn-out Bibles, that now many of the questions have answers. Still, I have a whole new set of questions. All this shows me that I am a learner, and I want to be a learner for the rest of my life.

Jerome, an early church father, once claimed that the Bible was shallow enough for a babe to wade in without fear of drowning yet deep enough for theologians to dive into without ever touching the bottom. Who can actually claim that whenever they read the Bible, they have full understanding of all that is in it? Who has a monopoly on what real truth and doctrine are? This kind of attitude leads to an arrogant mockery of real Christianity.

Removing the Barriers

As it is, however, we have placed a middleman between the Christian and God's Word at every front. For instance, often we hear the gospel first through a tract. After we receive Christ, we are given a fill-in-the-blank booklet to tell us what the Bible says about our new life. We buy a study Bible to interpret for us what the Bible is trying to tell us. Even in the theological training of our leaders and teachers, often we read more books about the Bible than we do the Bible itself. Instead of digesting God's pure Word, we end up taking in predigested spiritual food coming through another's mind and mouth. Predigested food may still have nutrients in it and may be necessary at times, but it isn't much fun to eat. I believe that one of the reasons more people don't read the Bible is that they don't think they will enjoy it. They think of the predigested stuff they've had and expect the Bible to taste the same, but it doesn't. There is nothing in the world like hearing the God of the universe speak to you about your own life and circumstances.

In Hebrews the writer says the readers ought to be eating solid food but could only handle milk like a baby (Heb. 5:11–14). There are a variety of explanations as to what the author meant by "milk" and "solid food." While he may have had deeper teachings in mind, you can make a case that he was referring to eating the Word directly rather than being dependent on others' teachings. After all, what is milk but predigested food from another? The mother ingests the food, and it is processed and finally delivered to babes who are absolutely dependent on their parent for sustenance. The exhortation given is that they ought to have become teachers by now (milk distributors) but are still receiving milk from others. All the tools and helps are good, but we also need to hear from God directly without a middleman.

Please don't misunderstand me. I am not advocating ignorance in the church. I am suggesting the opposite. The problem is that in spite of our efforts to educate Christians with all the tools and teachings at our disposal, we have failed. The people of God do not know the Word of God. In seminary I had a professor who once told me, "Where the Word of God is not known the work of God is not seen."

I believe the problem is that pastors and theologians have been teaching the people *what* to think instead of *how* to think. We must remove the barriers between God's Word and God's people and see what happens when the two mix.

There was a time when Scripture was available only to the elite clergy who were literate in the sacred languages. We call that time the Dark Ages! It is time for a new reformation in the church. The people must be enlightened with the truth of God's Word.

By introducing a middleman to the disciple-making process, we have introduced a seed substitute, which harms all the succeeding generations.

The seed substitute looks like the real thing, boasts of being the real thing, but ends up confusing the disciples. A synthetic seed is not the same as the real thing and this is most evident when examining the fruit that grows out of the seed.

A Healthy Spiritual Life and Spiritual Formation

LTGs integrate the DNA of a healthy spiritual life into spiritual formation. Spiritual formation is a process of life, and as such it has a needed DNA—a code that keeps it all together, healthy and growing. In *Organic Church* I discuss at length the DNA of the kingdom of God.[3] Suffice it to say here that the DNA for the healthy growth of disciples, leaders, churches, and movements is:

1. *Divine truth.* The reading of Scripture introduces divine truth into the heart of the disciples and sets a foundation on which to build.
2. *Nurturing relationships.* The confession of sins in a vulnerable yet safe relationship establishes the foundation of nurturing relationships.
3. *Apostolic mission.* Begging God for the souls of lost friends and family members on a daily basis is the foundation of a heart set on apostolic mission.

All three are needed, and they must be integrated to have health and life. Do not supplement, subtract from, or separate the DNA into component parts. Only when divine truth, nurturing relationships, and apostolic mission are intact and feeding off one another do they make the DNA alive and powerful.

The LTG integrates the entire DNA in the smallest possible grouping of the church—two or three. When the DNA is intact in each disciple, then it is present in each gathering of disciples as well.

An integrated DNA with disciples who are in close relationship with one or two others brings health to the disciples and to the entire church. Ultimately, each church will be evaluated by only one thing—its disciples. Your church is only as good as her disciples. It does not matter how good your praise, preaching, programs, or property are; if your disciples are passive, needy, consumeristic, and not radically obedient, your church is not good.

There is a strong need in the kingdom of God for more intimate relationships. It is in community that life change can happen.

Wesley's Class Meetings

John Wesley used to preach to crowds of up to twenty thousand people outdoors in a day when the only public address system was vocal cords and a good set of lungs. He would preach the gospel with great effectiveness. People would weep and wail over their sin and need of salvation. Wesley, however, did not rely on these crusades as the means for lost people to be saved. Rather, he considered the public preaching ministry as a means to partially awaken people to their need of salvation, but then he would gather the people into small groups where they experienced the sanctification process in relational accountability. Here, in the *class meetings*, Wesley believed that souls were justified before God. He believed this so strongly, in fact, that he thought preaching the gospel without forming class meetings was actually detrimental.

Wesley said, "Preach in as many places as you can. Start as many classes as you can. Do not preach without starting new classes."[4] In his book *To Spread the Power: Church Growth in the Wesleyan Spirit*, George Hunter says:

> [Wesley] observed that awakening people without folding them into redemptive cells does more harm than good! In a journal entry of 1743 he declares, "The devil himself desires nothing more than this, that the people of any place should be half-awakened and then left to themselves to fall asleep again. Therefore, I determine by the grace of God not to strike one stroke in any place where I cannot follow the blow."[5]

We may not all share Wesley's doctrine of justification, but he is on to something when we look at the subject of changing lives. Wesley brought together the key ingredients of life transformation and close relationships of accountability, which were not dependent on highly trained leaders. The class meetings multiplied and kept pace with his large evangelistic preaching ministry. The system was so effective that more people came to Christ and joined the church and more churches were started after his death than while he was alive. His influence lived well beyond his life span and still exists today.

Perhaps we do damage by awakening people to their sin only to leave them unaccounted for in relationships with other redeemed followers. They go back to their lives as they were, only a little more hardened to the gospel, having "tried it once" and found it ineffective. Is it possible that all our services and preaching have simply inoculated our culture to God's vital communication because the message was presented without being tied to relationships?

Because we have cheapened the salvation process, and thus the gospel, we see pitiful results to our own evangelistic efforts. According to Barna, the majority of people who make a decision for Christ are no longer in the church just eight weeks later.[6] This is partly because we have not understood what salvation truly is, and thus we short sell the meaning and power of the gospel. If people see the gospel's relevance and power in our lives, they will want it too. They must see the power in us before they will be willing to hear the message from us. The late Donald Soper, a Methodist leader and social activist, once said, "Christianity must mean everything to us before it will mean anything to others."[7]

Relational Evangelism

The LTG system incorporates the digestion of truth and the closeness of an intimate relationship with evangelism in the disciple's spiritual formation. A subtle yet effective strategy is inherent within the system itself. Being a real testimony to the greatness of Jesus is a part of one's character formation and is included in the accountability questions. LTG participants do not have to explain the way of salvation to others each week. This is not as vital as being a living (through our actions) and verbal (through our conversation) testimony of love and appreciation for Jesus. We have found that when people do this, seeds are scattered in relationships, and they will often sprout into fuller and deeper discussions, often at a later time. This kind of interaction produces a more natural, relational evangelism that flows out of one's personal experience of salvation. It is not forced but not subdued either; it is a spontaneous expression of love that comes from the joy of salvation itself.

Often Christian leaders have thought that if we train our people in methods of evangelism, they will automatically have more courage to share their faith with others. We assumed that it is training that is needed, but we have found that training does not overcome the barriers that keep Christians from sharing the gospel. Offering more and better training is a good thing, but we have found that it does not necessarily produce more evangelists in the church or the world. It does help people once they are in the world but doesn't always motivate them to go.

I have found that with the LTG system people share the gospel because it is a part of spiritual growth—a natural expression of a soul that God is touching. When people become connected to God by the Holy Spirit, they become witnesses (Acts 1:8). I have had some people, after they have grown in faith, come and ask me for training in evangelism so that they can be more effective with the contacts they have already made just by being a living testimony. People who ask for training in evangelism, because they have a friend whom they love and are praying for and who is asking them good questions, make the best students. They are eager learners, motivated to receive and apply all that is taught.

Add to the process daily intercession for the souls of lost people, and the burden for sharing the gospel becomes a natural product of a growing disciple. It is interesting that the very men Jesus instructed to pray for the harvest (Matt. 9:37–38) are the ones he sent into the fields in the next chapter (10:5). Praying for lost people cultivates an authentic compassion for them.

The gospel flies best on the internal motivation of a life that God has touched, rather than as a result of any external pressure from methodology or persuasive tactics.

Some people in my LTGs don't even realize that others are embarrassed about bringing Christ up in conversation. They see their witness as a part of their spiritual life and growth rather than an obligation they grudgingly accept. The gospel means so much to them that they can't help but share the good news with others. Can it be that a big part of our hesitancy to witness is a learned behavior? Can it be that a Spirit-filled life will naturally produce a bold witness in a Christian (Acts 1:8)? I have to admit that I was quite surprised by how easily people responded to the challenge to be a testimony of Christ in their world. In fact it is not rare for a group to go for several weeks with unanimous affirmation to the question, "Have you been a testimony this week to the greatness of Jesus Christ with both your words and actions?" All through the book of Acts, one thing is clear—being filled with the Spirit resulted in bold witnessing.

The LTG is not intended as an evangelistic methodology. It is intended to produce disciples who are actively following Jesus; as they do so, evangelism will come naturally.

Lifelong Spiritual Disciplines

LTGs form lifelong spiritual disciplines. The disciplines introduced in an LTG—reading Scripture, confession of sin, and praying for lost people—are sadly lacking in the Western church today. These can become the foundation on which other spiritual disciplines are built.

As a rule, Americans are not very good at patience and perseverance. We have come to expect instant gratification. The ideas of discipline and delayed gratification are not valued much. An LTG can introduce a new disciple to the value of discipline, and thus they will be more receptive to trying other spiritual disciplines once they recognize their benefits.

The Holy Spirit's Place in Spiritual Formation

Kevin, who was part owner in a plumbing business, was a good man. He was an elder in our church. He was faithful and available—an example of what an elder should be. I never really considered having Kevin in an LTG because in my mind he was already walking with God. After seeing so many lives changed through the LTG system, curiosity was aroused in some of the elders in my church, including Kevin. I began meeting with two of these men. Kevin took quickly to the disciplines and began to grow immediately.

We were reading the book of Revelation at the time, and I was teaching a series on the role of the Holy Spirit in the Christian's life when something new began to happen in Kevin. It was Good Friday and Kevin had been fasting when he was called to a job site on the other side of town. On the way there he felt the conviction of the Holy Spirit. He turned off the radio, and the Lord laid on his heart that Jesus died on the cross for his sin. This was not any new idea for Kevin, but that day the Spirit made it clear to him what price Jesus had to pay for his salvation. Kevin could barely contain the emotional outpouring that came on him.

That Sunday was Easter, and Kevin was giving our announcements in church. Kevin was not a tremendous speaker by any means, but he had a warm and friendly personality, so we often had him greet the congregation on Sundays with announcements. This particular Sunday it seemed as though a different man stood up to speak. He said, "Any important announcements can be found in your bulletins, but turn in your Bibles to Revelation chapter 4." Kevin went on to share some thoughts on the glory of heaven and the worship of Jesus. When he was finished, there was hardly a dry eye in the auditorium. We concluded that there were two possibilities, either God had done a new work in his heart, or he had been secretly abducted by aliens and replaced by this imposter.

I began to encourage Kevin's newfound giftedness with more opportunities, and he began to grow in his abilities. A short time later, while in transit to another job site, Kevin heard clearly from the Lord a call to preach and teach God's Word. In just a little over a year, Kevin was given his first pastorate—he took the lead of our church as I was called to start a new work. Our church had made Kevin an elder, but the Holy Spirit made him a pastor.

From plumber to pastor in a little over a year, Kevin is evidence of what the Holy Spirit can do in a life that is empowered with the Word and a relationship of accountability. It is important to note that the Holy Spirit is by no means finished with Kevin. He continues to grow and still has much to learn. It is not how much stuff Kevin has learned that qualifies him, but that he is called, learning, and is still listening to the Lord.

The Holy Spirit is a surprisingly good teacher. The LTGs allow the Spirit of God and the Word of God to take their rightful place in leading the Christian into all truth. Most segments of the Christian faith believe in the illumination ministry of the Holy Spirit. However, many do not trust in it. When it comes to understanding the Bible, we tend to trust more in our interpretive systems and apologetic reasoning than we do in the Author himself. Many churches have been going on for far too long without the help of their most powerful and influential member: the Holy Spirit. There's no doubt that he is the best convincer of sin (John 16:8–11), witness for Jesus (15:26–27), glorifier of Christ (16:14), and teacher of Scripture (14:26; 16:13–15) in your church. He is the one called alongside to help (14:16–17). We can all use his help.

We're reminded of this in the book *Pastors at Risk*, where Jerry Bridges of the Navigators is quoted as saying, "One way to gauge ministry is to ask yourself, 'If the Holy Spirit were to back out of this effort, would it collapse?' Many ministries would continue because they are humanly produced programs."[8]

When Paul was giving his farewell address to the elders in Ephesus, he acknowledged that it is the Holy Spirit who calls out his leaders for the work he desires of them. He said, "Be on guard for yourselves and for all the flock, among which the Holy Spirit has made you overseers, to shepherd the church of God which He purchased with His own blood" (Acts 20:29). It was the Holy Spirit that called out Paul and Barnabas to take the gospel to the Gentiles (13:1–3).

Because the LTG system is not leader dependent and uses only the Word of God rather than a man-made curriculum, the Holy Spirit is given greater opportunity to lead, guide, and call out the disciples into the ministries he has for them.

Tangible Evidence of an Emerging Leader

The crying need of the church today is leadership. From workers in the nursery to missionaries sent overseas, the church is lacking leaders. The need is for more and better leaders. As we have seen, Jesus identified the need for workers as the one limiting factor in reaching the harvest (Matt. 9:37). His solution was to pray and ask the Lord of the harvest to raise up workers from the harvest for the harvest.

Ministries that make disciples from the harvest never seem to lack leaders, while those that recruit leaders to fill leadership roles never seem to have enough leaders.

While the LTG system does not actually produce leaders, it does provide a deep well in which to discover emerging leaders. The groups provide the perfect initial testing ground for emerging leadership. If a person can't influence and multiply a group of two, why should we entrust him or her with fifteen, fifty, or a church of two hundred or more?

When anyone approaches me desiring to lead a ministry, I always challenge him or her to first initiate and multiply an LTG. This helps in several ways:

1. It tests the real fortitude of the potential leader. I can see whether he or she can be obedient to the most basic of commands.
2. I can have confidence that people in leadership are in vital relationships of accountability and are reading the Word of God regularly. Yet I don't have to be the one looking over their shoulders to make sure they are taking care of business in their personal lives.
3. This also provides me with an opportunity to see if leadership candidates can be faithful before I entrust them with weightier responsibilities.
4. Another advantage to starting the process of leadership development at the disciple-making level is that I am assured that those who actually emerge as leaders do indeed know how to make and multiply disciples. This is a skill that, unfortunately, has been sadly lacking in Christian leadership of recent years. Most of us have heard stories of people who have gone through years of seminary training, raised prayer and financial support, arranged for passports and visas, learned another language, and relocated their family to another part of the globe to live in another culture, only to discover that they do not know how to make and multiply disciples—*in any language!* There is no other word for this but *foolishness.* This has to stop. Paul wrote to Timothy regarding the appointment of deacons, "These men must also first be tested; then let them serve as deacons" (1 Tim. 3:10). This is a warning to us as well.
5. As leaders reproduce themselves, a natural benefit is more leaders. Like produces like. We tend to reproduce after our own kind. Of course, as I reinvest those new leaders right back into the Great Commission, the payoff promises to be great.

Spontaneous Multiplication

LTGs release spontaneous multiplication into the church at the grassroots level. Early in the development of this system, I was teaching that the groups needed to multiply. I believed that I needed to stress this point, or the groups would not reproduce. I applied a lot of external pressure and persuasion to try to get this to happen.

At the same time I had been studying spontaneous multiplication principles from the Word of God and some other books.[9] Some ladies in my church challenged me one evening by saying, "Don't talk to us about multiplication. We don't want to hear it. We like our group and don't want to split up." I considered this a good opportunity to test the natural function of planting seeds in good soil, so I told them that if they didn't want to multiply, they didn't have to. I stopped pushing reproduction to test the truth of natural and spontaneous multiplication. Within about four months, that same group of women became three groups without any help from me.

In the past I found that I needed to sweat and bleed to see even the most modest multiplication occur in discipleship. Today I have seen the kind of spontaneous multiplication that I have always longed for but doubted I would ever experience. We need to remember that reproduction is a natural function of the church and that it's part of God's design and plan. The power to produce multiplication is already inherent in the body of Christ; we need only to tap that power. If we plant the seed—rather than a seed substitute— into soil that is prepared, we will see multiplication.

The very fact that it takes so much personal effort to see the most measly results in reproduction of disciples is strong evidence that we are doing something wrong, something that is not natural to the process.

Jesus described, through parables, a kingdom that didn't have any trouble expanding and multiplying. Luke documents a movement that gained such momentum through spontaneous multiplication of disciples and churches that its opponents accused Paul of turning the world upside down. We may have read of such a thing happening in church history or on foreign mission fields, but most of us must confess that we have never experienced such spontaneous multiplication in the Western church.

If we focus on making disciples, and keep the system simple and solid, multiplication becomes easy and natural. The thought of multiplication becomes more palatable in the disciples. They are not forced to split up their groups; rather, they can reach out to friends. Once the disciples experience a taste of reproduction, it is embraced more readily in other levels of church ministry. Multiplication of cells, ministries, and even churches will be a more natural function because multiplication is in the genetic code of the base unit of the church—the disciples.

As was mentioned before, there is not a single command in Scripture to plant a church or to multiply small groups. There is a lot of church planting and multiplying of groups going on in the New Testament, but not because the church was instructed to do so. The reason that groups and churches multiplied is because the first generation of Christians was obeying Christ's very specific and simple command to make disciples. When Christians are obedient to this single command, it results in the multiplying of groups and churches. To attempt to multiply groups and churches without multiplying disciples is not only disobedient, it is downright impossible.

Many leaders are very intentional about multiplying groups and churches, assuming that disciple making will result, but usually the results are less than effective. This is backwards, according to the Bible. The truth is that only when we become intentional about making and multiplying disciples can we be assured that groups and churches will multiply.

I have seen groups multiply through conversion growth in as little as three months with the LTG system. In fact I was not prepared for how fast and easily multiplication could occur.

Dramatic Multiplication

The most dramatic example of multiplication I have seen occurred in the beginning of my new ministry of planting a church in the greater Long Beach area that reaches young people with a postmodern view of life. I began an LTG on the campus of Long Beach City College with two students. One day, after one month of meeting together, we were sitting in the school cafeteria having coffee and going over the Character Conversation Questions. We were on about the second question when another student came by, recognized his friend, who was in the group, and took an interest in the questions and what we were doing. His friend asked if he wanted to join us, but he couldn't meet at that same time, so they set up a time to get together, and he went on his way as we moved to question number three.

By the time we got to the fifth question, another student happened to come by, saw what we were doing, and asked if he could be a part of a group as well. The other student in the group set up a time and place to begin meeting with him.

We went back to the questions and got as far as the sixth question, when one of our guys saw someone he hadn't seen in a while so he excused himself for a moment and went to talk with her. When he returned, he told us that his friend needed a group and wanted to know whom she could meet with. We discussed the possibilities and settled on a woman we thought would be the best person to ask to meet with her. By the time we got to the last question, the very woman came up to us to see what we were doing. After explaining the other woman's need, she agreed to try to get together with her.

In one hour a single group multiplied into three other groups, and as usual, yours truly was the one lagging behind. By the next day, though, I also had a new group. Within two weeks we had ten groups going on two college campuses and in the community.

These groups spread like wildfire because God is with his obedient disciples. The system is simple enough to pass on with one easy description, so the flame spreads unhindered. Ordinary Christians are empowered to do the most important work any of us can do. This was borne out in a study of churches in Texas. It was discovered that the churches that were most vital, alive, and fertile for church planting used a method the report labeled "microchurch," another term for Life Transformation Group.[10]

Simple Multiplication

Early in the discovery process of LTGs, I would send new ideas to Paul Kaak, my good friend and my counterpart at another church, to try each idea out in an entirely different context and make sure what we were doing was transferable. When I gave him the simple idea of an LTG, he quickly found reason to try it. He led a young man to Christ and used the concept to disciple him. They decided to meet on Sunday mornings at a local McDonald's. At their first meeting, the young man brought a friend who was not a Christian. Paul explained that they would be reading the Bible and asked if that was okay with him, and he said sure, it sounded interesting. Paul then showed him the LTG card and shared that they would each be answering the questions to confess sins and asked if he was cool with that. He said, "Sure, as long as you don't mind that I answer 'yes' a lot." Paul chose the book of John to read as a starting place.

When they got together the next week, the non-Christian had a pad of paper full of notes from the reading. When they started to discuss the reading, he chimed in and said, "I don't know if any of you noticed this or not, but in my reading I noticed something. I think Jesus thinks he's God!"

Paul is an outstanding teacher and knows a teachable moment when he sees one. So he asked the young man, "Really? Where did you see that?" and the man started to bring up all the passages where Jesus claimed deity.

They read the book again the next week. The man came again with more notes, and this time he commented, "I think everyone else thinks he's God."

Within a couple weeks, this young man came to believe that Jesus is indeed God. Paul had his friend, the new Christian, lead the non-Christian to the Lord right there at McDonald's.

Paul mentioned a week or two later that he was going on vacation and wouldn't be able to meet with them for a couple of weeks. Both said that he should let them know as soon as he got back because they really liked the meetings and wanted to start back up as soon as Paul returned. Paul responded, "You don't have to stop meeting just because I am not here. You can do this without me." They both realized he was right. It is simple enough. They really didn't need Paul, so they continued meeting in his absence. When Paul returned a couple of weeks later, there were four other guys meeting. They started to try to fill McDonald's with groups of two or three each Sunday.

This is a great example of how people can hear from the Holy Spirit when they read the Bible, even when they do not have the help of others or a strong doctrinal background. When people have a hunger for change and they connect with the Scriptures (with only the Holy Spirit as a teacher) in an accountable but not religious system that is simple enough for anyone to do, multiplication can and often does occur.

In spite of all these advantages, there are still many objectives raised about LTGs. In the next chapter I will address the most common.

15

The Security of a Trustworthy System

Answering Common Objections to the LTG System

One rule that we had to enforce on the beaches of LA County that may seem strange is that we would not allow people to take rafts and inner tubes into the water. The reason for this is that these floatation devices are often unsafe in the ocean, because people who ordinarily would not venture into the deep feel a false sense of security floating on a raft.

A raft filled with air on the warm beach loses much of its buoyancy when the air inside cools in the water, with the result that the raft becomes less stable and secure. People find themselves out in the waves putting their trust in something that is not reliable. A simple puncture or a mistaken release of the cap holding the air in the raft is all it takes to go from a pleasant and relaxing float on the sea to drowning. Boogie boards and surfboards are not as dangerous because their buoyancy doesn't rely on hot air that can cool or escape.

Many Christians have found themselves in deep water, putting all their trust in faulty systems full of hot air that cannot bear their weight. One small tear in the fabric of the system and the whole thing quickly loses all its strength and leaves victims in deep water.

These systems appear to be sound but prove to be unable to get the job done. Undeserved trust is always the problem with faulty systems. The typical fill-in-the-blank curriculum for disciple making usually requires more trust in the workbook than in God's Word. Most of these processes also require a lot of trust in the leader of the group to guide the members into truth and fulfillment of a godly life. These systems create a dependency on the course and/or the trainer more than on Christ and his Word, and very little trust is placed in the strength of committed relationships. For a more complete analysis of some of the pitfalls of discipleship curricula, see pp. 150–51.

The ABCs of Sound Discipleship Methods

Lifeguards are trained extensively on what to do when we first come on the scene of an emergency. When we encounter a victim, we must be able to quickly evaluate the situation so that we can treat the worst problems first. Otherwise we may be putting a Band-Aid on a scratch while the victim is not breathing. To make it easier to remember what to do in such a crisis, the trainers have come up with a simple acronym to make sure we cover the most life-threatening problems first—the ABCs of emergency treatment. First, we are to check to see whether the victim is able to breathe, whether the victim is breathing, and whether the victim has a heartbeat. These are the ABCs: *airway, breathing, circulation.*

I have come up with an ABC evaluation to determine if a disciple-making tool or method is a healthy or a faulty system. Here are three questions I use to decide if a system is worth using:

- *Access*: Does the tool continue to release the disciple to tap into his or her own access to God for guidance, power, and values rather than create an unhealthy dependence on others?
- *Bible*: Does the authority come directly from the Scripture or does the method simply use the Scripture to borrow undue authority for the system itself?
- *Compassion*: Does the tool catalyze the compassion of Christ for others from the heart rather than from obligation or duty?

Objections to LTGs

When I introduce LTGs to people who are already trying to get sinking systems to float their ministry, I usually run into the same objections. These objections reveal that those who are voicing them have been trained to trust in faulty equipment.

In the few years that we have been applying these principles and seeing fruit, I have had a chance to consider some objections to what I've shared. In this chapter I will share the most common objections and respond to each.

Out of Control

The first objection to LTGs is that they can't be controlled. Because the groups give birth, multiply, and die spontaneously, it is very difficult to keep track of them.

The temptation is to try to control them, but this would stifle their potential. Allow LTGs to be controlled by the Holy Spirit and none other.

A good question to ask is, "Who was in control of the expansion of the church in the book of Acts?" It is clear from chapter 1 to chapter 28 that there was not a single human leader in charge of the expansion of the early church. The Holy Spirit was in charge. He is mentioned some fifty-seven times in twenty-eight chapters.

Control is often a big concern in our churches. We are careful to control all the activities for fear that all hell will break loose if we don't. I don't think hell is our greatest threat right now. Jesus already dealt with the power of hell, and he has declared that hell's gates pose no barrier to the church's advance.

The real question we need to ask is, "What will we do when all heaven breaks loose in our churches?" Would we be prepared if revival really came? Can we handle the lack of control? Can our egos manage not having the answers? Could we be comfortable with the chaos? Our church structures, our doctrinal statements, and our denominational polities and distinctives are insufficient to contain the wealth and the power of heaven. Heaven is beyond our grasp, beyond our comprehension, and beyond our control. Perhaps we should count the cost before we pray, "Thy kingdom come, thy will be done on earth as it is in heaven."

In the classic book written ahead of its time, *The Spontaneous Expansion of the Church*, Roland Allen describes the advantage of losing control in a release of spontaneous multiplication.

> By spontaneous expansion I mean something which we cannot control. And if we cannot control it, we ought . . . to rejoice that we cannot control it. For if we cannot control it, it is because it is too great, not because it is too small for us. The great things of God are beyond our control. Therein lies a vast hope. Spontaneous expansion could fill the continents with the knowledge of Christ: our control cannot reach as far as that. We constantly bewail our limitations: open doors unentered;

doors closed to us as foreign missionaries; fields white to the harvest which we cannot reap. Spontaneous expansion could enter open doors, force closed ones, and reap those white fields. Our control cannot: it can only appeal pitifully for more men to maintain control.[1]

If we are willing to relinquish control and allow for spontaneous multiplication in our churches, we will see the gospel go further than we ever dreamed possible. When it does, we should rejoice.

Personal Questions

Another objection I hear is that the Character Conversation Questions are too personal to expect new believers to answer.

My observation is that when people are ready to change, they are ready to address the personal problem areas in their lives. Even in the world today, those who don't believe in Jesus are willing to stand before a crowd and confess to being an alcoholic, drug addict, or some other form of compulsive sin behavior dealt with by a twelve-step program. They are willing to do so because they know that it's the only way to be free of the behavior. How much more should we who have the truth and know God personally and have the Holy Spirit within be willing to confess our sins openly to one another in a safe place?

In my experience new believers and even pre-Christians are more receptive to this system than older Christians who have been able to keep people at arm's length over the years by wearing a mask of spirituality. New believers don't really think that the questions are too personal. They don't even know to think such because they are only just forming their opinion of what this "Christianity stuff" is all about. The questions are too personal for staid Christians who are content with the status quo and threatened by opening up the closet and exposing what is inside. The truth is that we have been part of a Christendom that is quite comfortable with smiling masks and pleasant greetings but that is very uncomfortable with delving into the real issues that people face.

It is true that the LTG system requires a high commitment level for those just entering the church. Today many, if not most, church growth philosophies try to lower the level of commitment up front to attract more people and hopefully woo them into Christianity gradually. They treat the salvation of people as a step-by-step process, which it is. But we can sometimes sabotage our message by cheapening the strength of the truth we embrace. If it is true, then it should be true at every level and have strength at every level, even the entry point.

I think that the lost of the world will respond well to truth that we embrace wholeheartedly and do not compromise in any way. We are in a day when it is important to call sin, sin, and truth, truth. I have found that lost people who want to be saved respond well to authentic lives willing to admit their need for forgiveness and grace. Those who need their lives changed thrive in a safe place where others are willing to confess openly their deficiencies. In fact it is when we hide this authenticity from the world, and pretend to be better than we are, that the world takes offense at our hypocrisy and rejects our message.

When Jesus spoke of an entry point into salvation and the kingdom of God, he didn't attempt to lower the standard so that more could enter in. He did the very opposite. He said, "If anyone wishes to come after Me, he must deny himself, and take up his cross and follow Me. For whoever wishes to save his life will lose it; but whoever loses his life for My sake will find it."

This is hardly a "seeker sensitive" approach to winning the unchurched. It doesn't allow for anonymity. It doesn't allow people to come out of the world slowly. It calls for a strong and uncompromising commitment right up front, at the entry level. The LTG challenges people to deny themselves and follow the Savior, and people have responded. At the same time, however, it provides the support needed to carry on with the commitment.

Too Much Bible Reading

A third objection is that the amount of reading suggested is too much for a busy person to do. LTGs make the Bible a chore to read.

If an average reader will give half an hour every day to reading the Scripture, he or she will be able to keep up with the required amount. Most of us give at least that much time to getting ready each morning for the day ahead. If we can devote that much time to our physical readiness, why not our spiritual readiness? Many people can't get through the day without reading the sports page of the newspaper, yet we can go a whole week or month without reading God's Word.

I have found that the busier I get, the more I need to read the Scripture. I have recently reached a point in my life where if I don't read the Scripture, I cannot effectively juggle the demands of my life and maintain a level of sanity or composure needed to remain fruitful.

I remember reading that Martin Luther said, "I am so busy that I must spend the first three hours of every day in prayer." I used to admire him for this and thought that he was an example well beyond my reach. But in recent days I have personally come to understand what he meant. To be able to deal with the external pressures of leadership, he needed to have an internal strength to balance the demands of life and ministry, keeping him healthy enough to go the distance. That internal strength comes from extended times in devotional prayer and meditation on the Scripture. If an aircraft flies at thirty-five thousand feet, the air pressure in the cabin must be equalized to make people comfortable—and to survive. In the same way, the more we read the Scripture and pray, the better prepared we will be to handle life's external pressures. If you think you are effective now, and are not reading much Scripture, try spending a half hour a day reading Scripture and see what happens.

As I have been practicing and teaching these things more and more across the country, I have made an interesting observation. It's not the new Christians who object to reading so much of the Bible; it's the older Christians who do. And the people who complain the loudest tend to be pastors.

I suggest thirty chapters of reading a week because I have realized that it shouldn't be easy to finish the reading. It should take a few weeks before the group is able to finish with one book and move on to another. The system doesn't fail if people aren't able to finish the reading. Rather, it succeeds. That may sound strange, but I want you to understand that the goal is not to check off a reading chart dutifully, but to learn to develop an appetite for Scripture and to listen repeatedly to the message of a whole book of the Bible.

Therefore I do not recommend that you decrease the suggested amount of reading. In our own field-testing we have discovered that when the reading is reduced, the disciple's growth and the LTG's multiplication is dramatically stunted. In contrast, however, when a group chooses to increase the reading to the amount we have suggested, spiritual growth is much more evident in the disciples' lives.

THE BENEFIT OF A CHALLENGE

David, one of the youth pastors I used to work with, shared with me one day that the guys in his group were not getting their reading done every week. He was frustrated because they would be reading the same book over and over again and not make any progress. I asked him how much they were reading each week and he looked a little embarrassed and said, "We're only reading about seven to ten chapters a week, and they still can't get the reading done!"

I suggested they increase the reading to thirty chapters a week.

"What?" he said in disbelief. "If they can't get ten chapters done in a week, what would make you think that they can do thirty?"

I said, "Just try it."

About a month later we were meeting for another mentoring appointment and I asked David how his LTG was doing.

"Oh," he said, "you'd be amazed! Since I increased the reading assignment, they have all finished the reading each week. I don't understand it, but it worked."

I told David, "They weren't getting enough of a taste of the Word to really enjoy it. They weren't taking the Bible reading that seriously because they weren't being challenged."

There is value in stretching a Christian's capacity for reading. If a group is able to complete the assigned reading every week, they will not get all that they could from the reading, because the value of repetition will be removed from the process. We have found that often a group will stay in a specific book long enough for one or more of the members to discover something especially significant. For this reason, when someone has not finished the reading for any given week, we go into the next week expecting to discover what the Holy Spirit has intended for us—something that we may have missed in the previous week(s). To find a good balance with the amount of reading, we suggest that you experiment until you find an amount that keeps the group in the same book for about four weeks before moving on. For most, that is about twenty-five to thirty chapters per week.

Remember: *The goal is not to finish the reading every week.*

An Appetite for the Scriptures

The sad truth is that many people already consider Bible reading a chore. How tragic! I believe the reason people consider it a chore is because they haven't fallen in love with it yet. They haven't developed an appetite for it. There is a real sense in which the Scriptures are an acquired taste. Those who love the Word of God have found that the more they read it, the more they love it.

When people don't appreciate the Word of God, it's because they haven't tasted enough of it. Most people take the Bible in small doses of a chapter here and a verse there and find that it doesn't speak to their lives. We take our Bibles like medicine, believing that a little bit is good for us and will keep us healthier, even though we don't like the way it tastes. It's as though we think that a verse a day keeps the devil away.

Those who read the Scripture in large amounts, in context, and repetitively, quickly develop an appetite for it. I have yet to find someone who has been faithful in an LTG who doesn't learn to appreciate the Word of God and develop a true hunger for it.

Jesus said, "Man shall not live on bread alone, but on every word that proceeds out of the mouth of God" (Matt. 4:4). We need to develop a hunger for God's Word.

Sure, there are mornings when you open the Bible out of duty rather than desire, but most of those mornings soon become a lively spiritual time because you read enough of the Word to overcome your complacency and you find God speaking to your life situation. If you are reading only a chapter a day, that would not be as likely to happen. Once you have heard God speak directly into your life from his Word, you soon want more. Eventually you can develop a godly addiction, much as a dedicated runner does for the endorphins released in a good workout.

The first time I saw this appetite for God's Word in another's heart was when Kenny and I were just beginning our LTG. We were reading Romans twice in a week. Kenny read Romans all the way through once and then read it a second time up to chapter 16, verse 24, and intentionally stopped short of reading the last paragraph. When we met together that week, I asked him if he had finished the reading, and he looked at me with a smile and said, "Nope, we get to read it again this week." He didn't finish the reading intentionally just so that he could read it again at least a couple more times (in fact he did this more than once). Imagine what the church would look like if even 20 percent of our people had this kind of appetite for the Word of God.

I was amazed when my fellow disciple, Kevin, finished reading a whole gospel or Acts in our LTG and read Hebrews on the side during the week. Thirty-plus chapters wasn't enough to satisfy his hunger. This is what can happen to people who are willing to invest a half hour each day in reading God's Word. People fall in love with the Word, and even better, they fall in love with its Author as he speaks to them personally and powerfully.

A Love Letter or an Owner's Manual?

Unfortunately, in most of our churches today, we have made the Bible something to be *studied* or *interpreted* rather than something to be simply read, admired, and obeyed. We treat the Bible like an owner's manual. We do not open it up until there is a problem, and when we do open it, we turn to the "troubleshooting" section in the back and find the page that deals directly with our specific problem. Then we shut the book.

It is so bad for some of us that God can't speak to us through his Word without a commentary, a study Bible, an exhaustive concordance, and a Bible encyclopedia. For some the Bible is not a love letter anymore but a legal document in which every word and punctuation demand careful research.

Imagine what your sweetheart would think if you treated his or her love letter with that kind of scrutiny.

Many ask me if they need to stop their more reflective meditation on a single verse or shorter passage of Scripture. Of course not. The repetitive reading can serve as a foundation, and the meditative reading should be added on top of it.

The fact is that you cannot know how much of an impact this type of Bible reading can have until you try it. In *The Matrix*, Morpheus says to Neo, "Unfortunately, no one can be told what the matrix is. You have to experience it yourself to understand it." I have found that doing this sort of Bible reading is similar; unless you have tried it, you cannot understand the benefit of reading entire books of Scripture repetitively. The only way for you to understand is to try it.

In my experience it is not unusual to hear people complain in the first week or two of an LTG that they don't get to really study the Scriptures because they are too busy reading them. This complaint comes only from those who have been Christians for a long time, and it comes only in the first few weeks. Once they have actually done the level of reading that the LTG suggests, in just a few weeks they realize how much they are receiving. The repetition and the sheer volume of Scripture begin to awaken the reader to truth and he or she begins to become acquainted again with the voice of God. I have found that reading the Scripture in this way actually stimulates further study rather than reducing it. Questions naturally arise from the reading that motivate the reader to find out more. It is not uncommon to have people in an LTG still studying passages from a book in the Bible that was read weeks earlier, even though the group has already moved on to another book in its weekly reading.

And remember: *The goal is not to finish the reading every week.*

Opening the Church to Heresy

Often I hear that LTGs will allow heresy to run rampant in the church.
Heresies develop when:

- The congregation is ignorant of truth, not feeding on the Word of God.
- The Scriptures are taken out of context.
- Controlling individuals want to influence large numbers of naive people.

All three of these factors are eliminated with this strategy. Because believers are reading entire books of the Bible in context, natural checks and balances are inherent within each group. People in the group are less likely to be led astray because all are reading the same Scripture. Of course there is no way to eliminate the threat of heresy, but this is a very effective way to reduce it.

At our website we have a section dedicated to the latest thinking about organic church multiplication movements. There is a deep archive of free articles available to all. One article deals exclusively with the threat of heresy in an organic church multiplication movement that has no controls. Go to www.cmaresources.org/articles/keeping_heresy_out.asp.

Sin Management

The final common objection I hear is that the Character Conversation Questions are an attempt at sin management.

There is a difference between an LTG and a typical accountability group. While accountability groups may be helpful, they usually do not reproduce, because they are inward focused and lack the apostolic mission component. LTGs are more than a human attempt to manage personal sin using a ministry tool. As was mentioned before, the Character Conversation Questions do not reflect an inflexible definition of sin or righteousness; they are a starting place for a conversation about what is going on in a person's soul. It is easier to start from the questions than to simply launch into a deep, spiritual conversation.

We encourage adjusting the Character Conversation Questions in any way that is useful. We even offer more than one list of questions on our website.[2] There are also sample questions in appendix 1 of this book.

Even with all these tools available, there are people who have tried LTGs and found that they do not work as well as I have described. Granted, there is no perfect system or magic wand for fruitful ministry, but there are reasons that LTGs have not worked. In the next chapter I will address the most common of those reasons.

16

When Groups Go Wrong

Troubleshooting Unproductive Groups

Some lessons of life are best learned through experience. I will never forget my first rescue as a rookie lifeguard. It taught me a lesson so deeply that to this day, whenever I go to the beach, I check and double-check to make sure I am practicing this lesson.

It was the time of the day when the overcast skies from the morning marine layer could no longer hold sway over the beach. The determined sun was breaking through, and sunbathers were starting to fill the sand and pay homage to Apollo.

I was stationed at Rose Avenue in Venice Beach. It was called a "hot" tower, known for making many rescues because of the surf and rip currents that were caused by submerged debris from a former pier. It was my third day of lifeguarding but my first time in a tower alone without a more experienced lifeguard to show me the tricks of the job.

I saw a rescue about to happen at the tower to the south of me where the lieutenant's emergency truck pulled up, so I started to head out to back them up when something else caught my attention. A strong riptide started sucking just to the north of me, and a patron was struggling hard against the pull. Even as a rookie, I could tell this was the real deal. His wet hair was down over his face, almost covering the panic in his eyes, but there was no doubt that this guy was about to drown.

Immediately I took off running up the beach. I tore off my jacket and flung my sunglasses aside. I strapped the rescue can over my shoulders. By the time I got to the water, a small crowd of bystanders had gathered to watch this heroic moment in my life. The man was literally yelling for help in between gasps and gurgles as he struggled to climb a nonexistent ladder.

With a long stretch I leaped over the first wave, took two long strides and then dove under the next wave. It was at that very moment, in the midst of an urgent crisis with a crowd watching, that I learned a very valuable lesson that every lifeguard needs to learn. Always tie the drawstring on your bathing suit! Yes, what should have been a heroic moment in my life turned quickly into a comical one. When I should have been swimming with both arms, I found myself barely catching the last stitch of cloth around my feet and started pulling it up as fast as I could at the same time as I was trying desperately to get to a drowning victim.

A few moments earlier I heard gasps on the beach as people were pointing to a drowning man calling out desperately for someone to help him. Now I was hearing chuckles as they were pointing to something completely different. I managed to rescue the victim but not my dignity. I pulled the man to shore and the suit to its proper place all in the course of a couple of intense minutes.

I have also learned through experience some things about making disciples that I want to share. These lessons have come through the crucible of trial and error (and more from the latter than the former), so this chapter is worth reading more than once.

Since Life Transformation Groups have been at work around the world, I have had a chance to dialogue with many new practitioners. Often when I am told that the groups are ineffective, I find that there are a few ways in which the principles shared in this book have been compromised in some way. Typically there are four errors that slow down the process. You will find that some of the information in this chapter repeats some of what I have already shared, but if you are having less than productive results with an LTG, chances are you need to pay attention to these principles.

Four Reasons for Failure of LTGs

Reduced Scripture Intake Syndrome

When someone tells me the LTGs just aren't working, usually the first question I ask is, "How much Bible reading are you doing each week?" Often the reading has been cut down, usually to about five to fifteen chapters each week. The Word of God is what changes people's hearts (Heb. 4:12). When we cut back on its intake, we slow down the transformation process. It's that simple. More Word, more transformation. Less Word, less transformation. If you want to see the kind of spontaneous multiplication I have described in this book, you can't compromise on the intake of God's Word (see "Too Much Bible Reading" on pp. 200–204).

Poor Disciple Selection Syndrome

The second area I often find that has been compromised is in the selection of disciples. It is very important to find desperate sinners if we want to make disciples. The more desperate they are, the more their lives will change. If you start with pious Christians, you shouldn't be surprised if you don't see much change in their lives because there isn't much there to change. Jesus didn't start with the good religious people. He started with the common sinners who had a rough edge to them. Later, after his disciples started blossoming into leaders, religious leaders started coming—first, Nicodemus; later, Joseph of Arimathea; last of all, "to one untimely born" (1 Cor. 15:8)—Saul of Tarsus. Eventually many religious people came into the movement (Acts 6:7), but these men were both a blessing and a problem (15:5).

There is an interesting portion of Luke's Gospel when Jesus has determined to go to Jerusalem, where he knows he will be killed. With a resolute face he presses forward up the path to the city and ultimately the cross.

While on the journey, Luke tells us of various people he encounters along the way. A healed leprous Samaritan returns to follow Christ (Luke 17:11–19). Jesus rebukes the disciples for trying to keep the children from coming to him and gladly accepts them (18:15–17). He meets a poor blind beggar who is healed and becomes one of his followers (vv. 35–43). He stops to chat with a short and despised tax collector in a sycamore tree, and he too follows Christ (19:1–10). In each of these examples most of the people in Christ's entourage were caught not believing that these sick, immature, cursed, and corrupt people should have access to Jesus. More than once Jesus had to sternly tell his disciples to let them come to him.

Of all the encounters Jesus had with people, there was only one person to whom Jesus was not receptive, and I suspect that this was the only person the disciples felt good about introducing to Christ. It was the rich, young ruler (18:18–27). This man comes to Jesus and asks how he can be saved. Jesus never really shares the gospel with this man. He points him to the law to humble him to the point where he could receive the gospel. The rich man walks away dejected and does not become a follower of Christ (at least at that time). One of the other Gospel accounts mentions how much Jesus loved this man, but he let him walk away, nevertheless, without chasing after him with a message of grace, in case he changed his mind later.

Salvation came to the leprous Samaritan, the blind beggar, the small children, and the corrupt tax swindler, none of whom asked to be saved. The one who did ask left without the gift of salvation.

These stories are very insightful for us today. Most of us would be quick to assimilate into our church the wealthy, young leader who wants to be saved. Jesus does the very opposite. He turns the rich ruler away but accepts the sick, the outcast, the cursed, the children, and the hated into his kingdom. We should learn from Jesus when it comes to selecting those we want to disciple.

I have intentionally left the criteria for selecting candidates for the kingdom very simple so that it is easy to remember (it is also very biblical). The question is often asked, "Should I start with Christians or non-Christians?" That is not the right question to ask. As I said in chapter 3, there are really only two questions to consider when choosing who will be in an LTG:

1. Do they have a desperate need for Jesus in their lives?
2. Are they faithful to the process?

Whether or not the person is a Christian is not an issue. If he or she is desperate enough to read the Scriptures and confess sin and pray for others, he or she will be a Christian soon.

I understand the desire to implement accountability among leaders and the temptation to influence the entire church by starting with leaders. You will probably be able to do just that if you start with desperate sinners first and let the leaders see it working in others. Let a godly jealousy emerge in the heart of your leaders as they watch lost causes become men and women consumed with a cause. They will notice and *some* may desire the same transformation. Then you can work with them as well, but I don't recommend you do so before they sense the need in their own lives.

If you simply must implement this with your leaders initially, I suggest that you also start a second group with a couple of desperate sinners as well. This may give you a chance to test the substance of your leaders and also test the truth of what I am expounding in this book. The comparison of the two groups may teach you a lot. If I am right, you've only gained, and if you are right you have still gained.

Leadership Intrusion Syndrome

A third area where the system is often compromised is in the addition of supplemental material or a more defined leadership role. As bad as it sounds, often pastors don't trust the Holy Spirit and the Word of God to do what they do best. Instead, they tend to get in the way with "better stuff" and then find that the whole process is lacking. They would never admit this, even to themselves, but their actions betray their misplaced belief. This is a natural temptation, but it should be resisted.

Faith in God and his Word will never end in disappointment (Rom. 10:11). Leadership will emerge in groups naturally, but when it invades a group unnaturally, it tends to hijack the natural processes that these groups can create. I can't tell you how many stories I have heard of healthy groups being hijacked by people who are supposed to be mature Christian leaders that end up leaving behind lifeless groups. I am not against leadership at all, but Life Transformation Groups do not benefit from dependency on leadership.

Programmatic Implementation Syndrome

A fourth reason LTGs may not succeed in some churches is because they are implemented as a program instead of a grassroots system. Pastors, eager to find a solution to ministry demands, sometimes will apply this system as a blanket program for everyone, often assigning accountability partners. This approach goes directly against many of the values and principles shared in this book. You may find that this works in some cases, but it is not the recommended method of implementation. The system works much better if natural relationships are formed and the influence of LTGs is allowed to develop organically.

If you must implement it as a program, my suggestion is that you also initiate a group or groups in a more organic fashion. These other groups, begun more naturally, will likely become a basis for real change in your church. The danger with approaching the LTGs as a blanket program for the whole church is that if the first attempt doesn't bring immediate results (which is likely, given the amount of compromise to the principles), the system is thrown out. Then the church can say, "We've tried that before and it didn't work," when in fact they did not truly give it a fair trial.

Many leaders have taught the principles in this book and have created a vision for LTGs in their congregation. But nothing should take the place of simply making disciples naturally, organically, and relationally.

Review the Principles

If you find that people involved in LTGs are not experiencing the kind of transformation described in this book, go back over the principles and see if there is a place where you have compromised one or more of them. Before you write off the LTG concept, examine what you're doing and see if it indeed matches what I have explained. You may choose to adapt and change some of the methodology because you don't buy into all my values or have some others that you need to take into account. That is fine, just realize that these principles work and the more you diminish them, the more you diminish the results.

If the methodology that I have explained doesn't fit you or your context, I encourage you to take the principles that I have expounded and see if you can develop a method that embraces them and works for you. The method is not what changes lives, it is the Spirit of God and his biblical principles that transform people.

Recently I sat across the table from a young leader who said the groups hadn't seen the results he'd expected after listening to one of my audiotapes on the subject. I asked him the usual questions and found that he hadn't compromised any of the principles and seemed to understand and value them. Finally, I asked him how long they had been meeting. He said with a degree of exasperation, "Over a month now!" I must say, I was challenged by his faith. I told him to be patient and keep plugging on.

Don't expect to change the world in a month—a generation, maybe, but not a month. The saying is true: "We tend to overestimate what we can do in a year and underestimate what we can do in five." Remember that multiplication begins slowly and gains momentum as it goes.

Keep in mind, as well, that not every group will have the same results. Some will never multiply, while others may multiply countless times in a short period. Jesus told us that there were four kinds of soil and only one was good soil and produced fruit (Mark 4:3–20). Expect to lose some of your seed in less than fertile soil. Remember as well that there were three different capacities of good soil: those that produced thirtyfold, those that produced sixtyfold, and those that produced one hundredfold fruit (v. 8). All fruitfulness is good; not all is the same.

Common Questions about LTGs

1. *How do I get these groups started in my church?* We recommend that you initiate these groups more organically than organizationally. In other words,

don't just start with your elder/deacon board and hope the strategy will trickle its way down to the masses. The place to start is at the grassroots—you and a new believer, a seeker, or a Christian who desperately needs help. Then you can increase the number of groups in two ways: multiplying your own groups, and adding new groups by giving people copies of this book and telling others how they work.

Whenever a person who needs spiritual growth comes along, introduce him or her to another Christian and recommend that they help one another using this simple system. Follow up with them in three to four weeks and inquire as to how they are implementing the system.

It is not hard to find people who need Christ and desire his help. The LTGs provide a natural connection for those who seek counseling, those who need to transition from a twelve-step group, or even those who return from a Promise Keepers rally full of energy and zeal. It is also a natural follow-up for new believers. LTGs can provide the needed balance and substance for those who come to Christ at large crusades or "seeker services."

Once the groups start to grow and multiply, they can incite a godly jealousy in a congregation, when people see the new life in other members and hunger for a transformation of their own.

The LTGs can also be a great means for winning new souls to Christ. Friends, neighbors, co-workers, or family members who want help can come to meet the Savior in a context of hearing directly from God through the Scriptures and coming to terms with their own sin in a confidential relationship of accountability. It is very refreshing for seekers to find Christians who aren't perfect and know it. The LTGs are a quest for righteousness in a context of mutual love and support. There is hardly a better place to introduce new babes into the kingdom.

2. *How long will a group last?* LTGs are living things that have their own life span. Some have lasted as long as three years; others have multiplied in as short a time as one month, and it is common to see multiplication occur sooner rather than later. If you do find, however, that you have a group that is not multiplying after a year of faithful participation, we recommend that you look to start another group quickly and initiate multiplication yourself. Don't just blame the other participants for not multiplying. The group is *you* as much as it is *them*.

Because these groups implant the true seed, rather than a seed substitute, multiplication rarely needs to be forced, coerced, or manipulated. Our experience has shown that it doesn't usually need to be mentioned at all. It is good to cast vision for multiplication, but the real impetus for it comes from the seed itself, germinated in good soil.

A group will end in one of two ways: it will give birth to one or two other groups, or it will die. Both will happen; both are to be expected. Read the parable of the sower again (Mark 4:3–20). You will see that there are four kinds of soil, which have four different responses to the gospel, only one of which was fruitful. If you are in a group, and it dies, don't be too discouraged. Try again. The fruit you will see in the end will far outweigh any discouragement.

3. *Can I have more than one group, and how do I manage the amount of reading if I am in multiple groups?* Yes, it is possible to be in more than one group at a time, though it is not necessary. For six years of fruitful organic church planting, I only ever had one group. But if for some reason you do find yourself in more than one group, here are some options to keep in mind:

- You can read sixty chapters of Scripture each week.
- You can select the books you read and read the same book in both groups.
- You can buy the Bible on CD and play the audio recording of the book one group is reading and read the book that the other group is reading.

4. *What about doing LTGs with people who have literacy problems?* This is a simple solution: get them the Bible recorded (on cassette tape, CD, or Mp3) so that they can listen to the reading. I also suggest that they read as much as they possibly can while listening to it, and they may improve their literacy levels.

The lessons learned in the crucible of experience are learned in a deeper and more profound way than those we learn from a book. Don't just take my word for it, go and experience this stuff yourself. Try doing an LTG and learn from your mistakes and successes. Refine your approach and try again. Oh, and tie your drawstring before you dive into the water!

As we come to the end of the book, we could ask, "So what? What difference could all of this make in the world?" In the next chapter I will address that very subject.

The Kingdom Come

The Results of a Life Changed for God

Often when speaking about making disciples, I tell the stories of my lifeguarding days. Usually I start off by saying, "I once worked as a beach lifeguard for the LA County Beaches just like *Baywatch* . . . but not really." People usually laugh when I say that. Then I joke that the real lifeguard women are not nearly as gorgeous as those on the TV show, and the men are actually much better looking. They always laugh even more at that last comment, and I can't understand why that is.

The TV show *Baywatch* was one of the most successful shows ever on TV. It was not one of the best shows on TV; it didn't make it on any regular network but found its home in an upstart network. Internationally the show became a huge hit. Often I joke that the reason the show was such an international hit was so that I can share my own lifeguard stories while I travel around the world and everyone will be able to relate. But actually I do not think it was the reality of the show that captivated viewers; it was the unreal. It was the plastic and silicone that drew viewers, which is why it became known for its nickname: "Babewatch."

The few times I could get myself to sit through an episode, I was always amazed by a stark contrast. There were some minor things that were very realistic set in a context that was anything but realistic. One of the executive producers of the show was a lifeguard who worked on the beach at the same time I did. But the reality is that watching a guy sit in a tower for eight hours staring off into the surf is anything but exciting, so they spiced up the show, and it became unreal. I don't know any lifeguards who solved murders, beat away sharks, had their pier explode, or diffused ticking bombs.

Baywatch is a false caricature of true lifeguarding. In a similar way, Christendom has been seduced by an alternate story of what it is supposed to be about, and this seduction has global implications. Our reputation around the world is based on a false sense of what a true expression of Christianity is supposed to be.

Thy Kingdom Come

If aliens came and abducted all of the truck drivers at once in our country, our whole economy would soon unravel. You probably give little thought on a daily basis to truck drivers, except for the annoyance of having to get around a slow moving semi on the highway. But if they were suddenly gone, stores would close due to a lack of merchandise. People would lose jobs. Prices for the goods that are in stock would triple. Families would soon go hungry because stores would not be able to stock their shelves. The influence of truck drivers on our life every day is very real, even if we don't give it much thought.

If suddenly all the garbage collection trucks broke down, everyone in town would soon know about it. If all waiters and waitresses were suddenly sick and unable to work, many of us would go hungry. If teachers couldn't work, we would have a crisis on our hands.

But if all the churches in your community suddenly disappeared, would the average person in your town even notice? If just your church closed its doors for good, would the people who live within a fifteen-mile radius even know about it?

I suspect that somewhere along the line we lost the game plan, and consequently we lost our influence. It is time to awaken again to what it means to bring the kingdom of God to the world around us. What does that look like? What happens when Jesus comes and does what only he can do? What does he do for people? Does he give us something besides the gift of life eternal? I suspect he also gives something very present and real in the here and now.

In the Bible the announcement of God's kingdom had a common response: repentance and belief. This was the response John called for (Matt. 3:2), and it was also what Jesus compelled people to do when the kingdom had arrived (4:17). Like two sides of the same coin, repent and believe go together and cannot be separated. To repent is to turn away from the path that we were following. To believe is to turn to the new path of Jesus's kingdom. It is one move, away from the old and to the new.

All kingdom life begins with this same response of faith. When the only response is to accept intellectually two or three facts about the historic person of Jesus without any change in direction, we end up with "Christians" who are self-absorbed rather than kingdom agents. When we start with the foundation of what is best for "me," we end up self-centered. But when the foundation is about surrendering to the King of Kings, we end up with an entirely different result.

There are two great examples in the New Testament of what sort of things happen when the gospel of the kingdom is preached, and people respond well.

John the Baptist came preaching a baptism of repentance and the forgiveness of sins (Luke 3:3). His message was, "Repent, for the kingdom of heaven is at hand" (Matt. 3:2). When some came who would only listen to what he said without any intention of changing, he said boldly, "Bear fruits in keeping with repentance" (Luke 3:8). This inspired the people to ask him for specific examples of what it means to respond to the kingdom of heaven. John's answer was, "The man who has two tunics is to share with him who has none; and he who has food is to do likewise" (v. 11). To some tax collectors he elaborated, "Collect no more than what you have been ordered to" (v. 13). To some soldiers he said, "Do not take money from anyone by force, or accuse anyone falsely, and be content with your wages" (v. 14). Luke concludes this summary with the words, "So with many other exhortations he preached the gospel to the people" (v. 18). At another place the impact of the kingdom coming through the ministry of John resulted in the hearts of the fathers being turned back to their children. This is not just a nice Christian thought that results in warmer family reunions. If this sort of effect could come again to America, do you realize what consequences there would be?

Society is filled with problems, but trying to fix society one problem at a time is daunting and suffocating. But it doesn't have to be that way. There are some problems that are root causes of others. If we can identify and bring kingdom healing and restoration to those areas, scores of other problems will be resolved.

One such problem is the irresponsibility of men in our society, especially fathers. If the hearts of the fathers returned to their children, and if fathers were faithful to their children's mothers, street violence would subside, drug and sexual abuse would decrease, theft would drop, schools would improve, illiteracy would decrease, and dependency on the state's welfare system would diminish—releasing more tax revenue to address other problems. Sexually transmitted diseases would die down quickly. Unwanted teen pregnancy rates would drop significantly. The AIDS crisis would end. The abortion issue, one of the most divisive issues of our day, would be resolved, not because of political lobbying and picket signs, but because the hearts of fathers would be turned back to their children.

You may think that this is a grand oversimplification, and perhaps to an extent it is, but I am thoroughly convinced that if men's hearts were changed and men were challenged to live bold and authentic lives for Jesus—as heroes—our whole society would be changed in a short time. These are but a fraction of the benefits to our society if only the men would stand up and take responsibility for their lives. And this is what happens when the kingdom of God comes to a place. This is one of the main reasons I am writing this book.

The issue of slavery provides us with an interesting comparison between England and the United States. On this side of the Atlantic, we attempted to settle the issue with a war, and it was the bloodiest war in all our history, especially considering every casualty was one of our own. It is called the Civil War, but there was little civil about it. Eventually the war won the freedom of black people in our country, but don't be deceived, we are still battling this war in our nation. The "civil war" has ended, but the battle over "civil rights" continues.

England, however, did not shed a drop of blood to overcome slavery, and they have not had nearly as much difficulty getting along after freedom was acquired. Why? Because slavery was overcome in England by the revival of God's people. Their hearts were changed from within rather than being ruled from legislation and the barrel of a musket. The Wesleyan revival, the Quakers, an emerging evangelical Anglican movement, and a widespread spiritual renewal accomplished what seemed impossible.

Granted, it wasn't easy. It took much effort from godly men such as William Wilberforce, but eventually the laws were changed because the hearts were changed, and the hearts were changed because the kingdom of God came to England in a revival.

When this sort of revival comes to a nation, all of society changes. Redemption touches all parts of life. Bars would close down. Crime would come to a halt. Police would be laid off because there would be nothing for them to do. With the decrease in crime, prison populations would begin to shrink, releasing more state revenue to address other needs. Manufacturing would improve because the work ethic of people would improve. When the products improve, sales and exports improve, and the entire economy is raised to higher levels. Then unemployment would drop to negligible rates. There is evidence in many places around the world that nature itself would be healed. Droughts would end and crops would be restored. I have heard that with the coming of revival, the reefs in Fiji were reborn and fish returned, thus restoring the nation's lost natural resource.

John is telling us that the good news of the kingdom will change the way we behave in all the little details of our lives. We will respond justly, with grace and kindness. We will not seek our own benefit but the benefit of others. This is what it means when the kingdom of God seizes the lives of a people.

According to John, the good news of the kingdom must bear appropriate fruit if it is received with repentance and belief. How can it be good news if it doesn't change things for the better?

The ancient prophet Isaiah described in poetic language what would happen when the Messiah would come. When we go out into the world and bring Jesus with us, we can expect our Lord to do his thing. These are the things that happen when Jesus shows up:

> Jesus brings good news and restoration to those who are poor and oppressed.
>
> He will set captives free.
>
> He will announce the coming of a year of favor and a day of the Lord's justice, which is to comfort all who mourn (Isa. 61:1–2).

Jesus used this passage to identify himself as the Messiah who was to come (Luke 4:16–21). When the King comes and rules, those who are poor and oppressed are set free. Justice prevails. Hope returns. Healing and restoration reign.

When John was in a dark night of the soul, filled with doubt and despair about the significance of his life—the greatest life lived next to that of Jesus (Luke 7:28)—Jesus sent word to encourage him (vv. 18–23). He reported, or rather described, what happens when Jesus shows up:

> The blind see.
>
> The lame walk.
>
> The lepers are cleansed.
>
> The deaf hear.
>
> The dead are raised.
>
> The poor hear a message of hope.

Jesus does not just overcome the bondage of sinful behavior or darkened understanding. He does not just instruct us in a better way of life. He overcomes the curse. He heals the sick, reigns with justice, rights the wrongs, and brings hope back to any people who have been afflicted and oppressed. The very fabric of society itself is set back in order.

This is more than filling the seats and offering plates of our churches. He brings more than a Christian education or set of conservative political agendas. When the kingdom of God comes in power, everything changes from the inside out. Nothing shy of transformation from an individual basis to a translocal and even global basis will occur. We must not become content with lesser things. Perhaps this is the greatest sin of our generation: we are happy with so little.

Too Small a Thing

Another messianic passage from Isaiah speaks to our shortsightedness regarding Jesus's good news. In Isaiah 49:6 God the Father says to the Son: "It is too small a thing that You should be My Servant to raise up the tribes of Jacob and to restore the preserved ones of Israel; I will also make You a light of the nations so that My salvation may reach to the end of the earth."

Sometimes I sit on the hill surrounded by the city in which I live thinking of the gangs, the fatherless homes, the dominance of immorality and I think, *It's all just too much.* Jesus always whispers back to me words from that messianic prophecy in Isaiah: "No, it is too small a thing."

When I think of the challenges of the United States—a crumbling justice system, a deteriorating education system, greed, poverty, bigotry, evil being called good and good being called wrong—I think, *Lord, it is too much for us to fix. It is too big a mess!* Jesus always speaks back to me, "No, my son, it is too small a thing."

The global AIDS crisis, oppressive dictators holding their people in bondage to poverty, genocide of entire people groups, the religious fanatics holding the world hostage with terror, the ugliness of rampant immorality, destruction of our environment, these things and more on a global scale are only part of what Jesus wants to address in our age through his servants—you and me. We are too often content with too small a thing. We are shortsighted and suffer from small-mindedness. The kingdom of God is bigger than your church, your denomination, or your nation. It is bigger than all the churches, all the denominations, and all the missions agencies.

We must understand that Jesus's death and resurrection are too important to affect only small places and few peoples. His sacrifice deserves nothing less than a holistic global change, impacting every nation and every culture. Anything shy of this is selfish, lacking in faith, and an insult to the King and his sacrifice.

We should be ashamed of the fact that software business moguls, movie stars, and rock musicians are doing more to overturn poverty, AIDS, and injustice than the majority of God's people. Sure, Bill Gates has lots of money, and fame can influence people, but there is nothing more powerful or influential than Jesus. Nothing! You may not have lots of money or fame, but if you have Jesus, you have all you need.

We have all it takes to overturn the giants that are oppressing our world and keeping people in darkness. All we have to do is realize God's heart for the world and step out and bring his transforming kingdom to the lost. Our global impact will start small; the kingdom of God always does. It is like a little leaven or a mustard seed. It starts with a single life under the rule of the King, and it grows one life at a time. But if each impacted life impacts another, we can affect the entire planet with his kingdom in this lifetime.

Do you think I am naive? Is my idea simplistic? Am I overstating this? Perhaps. But why not try it? What can we lose? There is evidence in history that this sort of transformation can have enormous effect. Why shouldn't such a revival start with a single changed life? Why not start with your life? Become a hero, an agent of God's incredible kingdom. If truck drivers can have a big impact on our society, how much more someone who loves Jesus with his or her whole life? Shouldn't we at least try?

If we all begin to live a more heroic life within God's kingdom, we can spark change. Perhaps one day we can present a more real picture of the kingdom of God in this world, rather than the caricature that we have been displaying. Changing the world does not start with hundreds of people, it starts with a few. In fact it may start with just one life—yours. Be the change that you want to bring to others.

Sample Character Conversation Questions for Life Transformation Groups

The use of questions for accountability is not a new idea. I have been collecting examples of such questions for a few years and have included these samples to give you more ideas of how you can keep accountable for a godly life.

Some Concerns

There are advantages and disadvantages with any system. I will briefly address a few very common concerns when applying accountability questions of any type.

Legalism

Legalism is a very severe threat to the church and is not treated lightly in the Scriptures. There is no other sin in the New Testament that receives a more severe condemnation. Think about that a moment—*no other sin!* It is not unusual for people to use a man-made system of accountability as a measure for righteousness. This has tragic results that should *always* be avoided. The intent of questions is not to define what sin and righteousness are but to be a platform for opening up discussion about what is going on in one's character development. Some of the questions below do a better job than others at being cautious not to overstep into providing a man-made standard of behavior.

Open-ended versus Close-ended Questions

Some have found that the published questions that this book suggests are close ended and less conducive to stimulate conversation, so they have developed more open-ended questions. Experience has shown that only one question on the list has solicited a curt yes or no answer: "Have you given in to an addictive behavior this past week?" For that reason we added the simple statement: "Explain," which seems to have helped. It is probably true that having more open-ended questions will promote more elaboration and discussion. The balance here is that most LTG meetings are pressed to keep to an hour as it is. Again, your preference should prevail.

Evangelism Incorporated in Spiritual Formation

We have found that including a question that brings up the subject of being a testimony of Christ in word and in deed does much for the growth and reproduction of any group. When the spread of the Good News of Christ is included in character formation, spiritual growth is accelerated and re-production is often the result. This has been proven over and over again in the course of using accountability questions. It can be argued that simply turning the focus of the group inside out—to the needs and concerns of the lost—rather than remaining internally directed is what separates LTGs from other accountability groups. There is definitely a difference between an accountability group, which strives to manage sinful behavior, and a Life Transformation Group, which capitalizes on new life and produces growth and the reproduction of disciples.

The idea that one can grow in character and not fulfill the Great Commission is a curious concept to say the least. I do believe we have fallen under a delusion that character is separate from obedience to the basic command of Scripture in this regard. For those who live under the constant threat of real persecution, being a testimony for Christ is a significant part of their Christian character. For them, though their life is on the line, they will not compromise their character or their obedience. This shames those of us in the Western church who do not live under such a threat and yet are fearful of speaking up in the marketplace or neighborhood.

Listening to God's Voice

Personal connection to the Lord is a very real concern behind many of the sample questions below, and rightfully so. When questions are addressing less specific behavioral issues, they need to include some question that prompts the participant to listen to the guiding presence of the Holy Spirit. Such questions will affect the participant's behavior because they cause them to hear from God rather than just reading a list of questions on a card. I commend those who have thought this through and revised the questions to better reflect the guidance of the Holy Spirit.

Perhaps there is a balance to be found in this regard. It is suggested that newer believers and pre-Christians use the more specific questions and that after some growth and maturity is evident, the less specific questions may enhance the confession of sin. The difficulty with this is that I do find it very healthy and important for mature believers to be in groups with seekers and newer believers. The key is to understand that the questions are to help us start listening to the Lord and to share the struggles each is going through in his or her own walk with the Savior.

As you read through the variety of Character Conversation Questions listed below, keep these observations in mind. Look for the strengths and weaknesses of each set of questions and you will be better prepared to choose or create questions that best fit your own needs.

Sample Accountability Questions

John Wesley's Small Group Questions: A Popularized Version of Wesley's Holy Club Questions

1. Am I consciously or unconsciously creating the impression that I am better than I am? In other words, am I a hypocrite?
2. Am I honest in all my acts and words, or do I exaggerate?
3. Do I confidentially pass on to another what was told me in confidence?
4. Am I a slave to dress, friends, work, or habits?
5. Am I self-conscious, self-pitying, or self-justifying?
6. Did the Bible live in me today?
7. Do I give it time to speak to me every day?
8. Am I enjoying prayer?
9. When did I last speak to someone about my faith?
10. Do I pray about the money I spend?
11. Do I get to bed on time and get up on time?

12. Do I disobey God in anything?
13. Do I insist on doing something about which my conscience is uneasy?
14. Am I defeated in any part of my life?
15. Am I jealous, impure, critical, irritable, touchy, or distrustful?
16. How do I spend my spare time?
17. Am I proud?
18. Do I thank God that I am not as other people, especially as the Pharisee who despised the publican?
19. Is there anyone whom I fear, dislike, disown, criticize, hold a resentment toward, or disregard? If so, what am I going to do about it?
20. Do I grumble and complain constantly?
21. Is Christ real to me?

Wesley's Band Meeting Questions

1. What known sins have you committed since our last meeting?
2. What temptations have you met with?
3. How were you delivered?
4. What have you thought, said, or done, of which you doubt whether it be sin or not?
5. Have you nothing you desire to keep secret?[1]

Chuck Swindoll's Pastoral Accountability Questions

In his book *The Body*, Chuck Colson lists seven questions used by Chuck Swindoll and a small group of pastors.[2]

1. Have you been with a woman anywhere this past week that might be seen as compromising?
2. Have any of your financial dealings lacked integrity?
3. Have you exposed yourself to any sexually explicit material?
4. Have you spent adequate time in Bible study and prayer?
5. Have you given priority time to your family?
6. Have you fulfilled the mandates of your calling?
7. Have you just lied to me?

Renovare Questions

James Bryan Smith and Lynda Graybeal, along with Richard Foster, have compiled a list of questions for accountability to spiritual disciplines, which is a part of the Renovare resources.[3]

1. In what ways did God make his presence known to you since our last meeting? What experiences of prayer, meditation, and spiritual reading has God given you? What difficulties or frustrations did you encounter? What joys or delights?
2. What temptations did you face since our last meeting? How did you respond? Which spiritual disciplines did God use to lead you further into holiness of heart and life?
3. Have you sensed any influence or work of the Holy Spirit since our last meeting? What spiritual gifts did the Spirit enable you to exercise? What was the outcome? What fruit of the Spirit would you like to see increase in your life? Which disciplines might be useful in this effort?
4. What opportunities did God give you to serve others since our last meeting? How did you respond? Did you encounter injustice to or oppression of others? Were you able to work for justice and shalom?
5. In what ways did you encounter Christ in your reading of the Scripture since our last meeting? How has the Bible shaped the way you think and live? Did God provide an opportunity for you to share your faith with someone? How did you respond?

Sample Adapted LTG Questions

Phil Helfer, pastor of Los Altos Brethren Church in Long Beach, California, has simplified the LTG questions into five open-ended questions:

1. How have you experienced God in your life this week?
2. What is God teaching you?
3. How are you responding to his prompting?
4. What sin do you need to confess?
5. How did you do with your reading this week?

A church in Palo Alto, California, called The Highway Community, has adapted the questions in the following way:

1. Did I invest the proper quality/quantity of time in my most important relationships?
2. Did my life reflect verbal integrity?
3. Did I express a forgiving attitude toward others?
4. Did I practice undisciplined or addictive behavior?
5. Was I honorable in my financial dealings?

6. Was I sexually pure?
7. Did I spend time with the Lord this week, completing the Bible reading for the week?
8. Did I pray for my pre-Christian friends? Did I talk with someone about Christ?

In an attempt to bring the authority of Scripture into personal obedience and growth, Florent Varak, a French pastor in Lyon, has developed these questions:

1. What have Scriptures revealed in your life this week:
    In terms of specific sinful behavior?
    In terms of specific sinful thoughts?
    In terms of specific sinful words?
2. What errors or lies that you once believed have now been corrected by your reading of the Scriptures?
3. What encouragement have the Scriptures given you in your daily walk?
4. What do you need to ask the Spirit of God to reveal to you that you have not yet understood?

Recently some children have asked if they could be a part of the Life Transformation Groups. I challenged Lori Dillman, a mom in our church, to help me write a set of questions appropriate for preadolescent kids. These are the questions we have come up with:

1. How have your actions and words shown others that you love Jesus?
2. How have you been respectful to your parents and the adults around you this week?
3. How have you loved others even when you didn't feel like it?
4. How have you seen God answer your prayers this past week?
5. In what ways have you been angry or frustrated this week because you didn't get something that you wanted or didn't get your way?
6. In what ways have you taken anything that does not belong to you this week?
7. In what ways have you not told the truth this week?
8. In what ways have you been mean to others this week?
9. In what ways have you not completed the responsibilities you have been given?
10. Have you finished your Bible reading? What did you learn?

Working on a list of questions that are less specific, I came up with these:

1. What is the condition of your soul?
2. What sin do you need to confess?
3. What have you held back from God that you need to surrender?
4. Is there anything that has dampened your zeal for Christ?
5. With whom have you talked about Christ this week?

As a church planting missionary in Buenos Aires, Argentina, Dave Guiles (currently the director of Grace Brethren International Missions) developed these questions based loosely on the tests of a true believer found in 1 John:

1. How have you sensed God's presence in your life during this past week?
2. Have you received a specific answer to your prayers? What was it?
3. Have you spoken with a nonbeliever about your faith in Jesus Christ? With whom?
4. To whom have you shown God's love during this past week?
5. What have you learned about God in your personal Bible reading this past week?
6. As a result of your Bible reading this past week, how have you determined to better obey God?
7. Specifically, what area of your life do you feel that God most wants to change? Have you taken specific steps to make those changes?
8. What good habit do you feel God wants to form in your life? Have you taken specific steps to develop that habit?

Paul Klawitter, a church-planting missionary in France, has developed the following questions:

1. What worries or other issues are you currently facing?
2. Is there an area that God is working on in your life or any sin that you would like to pray about?
3. For what non-Christian friends can we pray?
4. In your reading of the Bible: Who is God? What does he expect of you? What do you think he is saying to you? How do you think you should respond?

The most simplified and basic questions I have found to date are the following:

1. What is God telling you to do?
2. What are you going to do about it?

Names for LTGs Worldwide

There are a variety of names that churches and movements use for LTGs around the world. I have delighted in making a collection of the various names used for this simple method. Here are some that I have found so far:

Bible Impact Groups (BIG)
Life Transformation Groups (LTG)
Growth Groups
Spiritual Triads
Commitment to Grow Groups (CTG)
Anchor Groups
Greenhouse Growth Groups (G³)
Life Groups
Link Groups
Missional Living Groups
Fitness Teams
Mutual Accountability and Discipleship (MAD) Groups
Kingdom Come Groups (KCG)
CPR (Confess sin, Plant Scripture, and Reach out) Groups

APPENDIX 3

How LTGs Can Help Start Organic Churches

Below are a number of approaches for starting organic churches.

1. A team of two evangelizes a pocket of people while also being committed to being in an LTG. They continue this until the LTG multiplies via relational contacts with lost people. As these groups multiply through the transformed lives of lost people, a church (or churches) comes into being in a home or other place.
2. The church planter(s) reach a single person of peace (someone God providentially placed among a group of non-Christians who will be the first to follow Christ and start a chain reaction to Christ among his or her peers in the group), who seemingly overnight brings together their whole *oikos* (the Greek word for household, often means social network of relationships) to hear the gospel. Over some time, they respond to it, sometimes as an entire group. The group is then encouraged to carry on as a church and join one another in LTGs. Note: these concepts are discussed in great detail, with multiple examples in my book *Organic Church*.
3. A church-planting team decides to start a church in a pocket of people, and they begin inviting acquaintances and new contacts to come to a

gathering. The gospel is shared regularly and some are saved, baptized, and brought into existing LTG relationships. As the new believers assimilate into the gathering, they are also encouraged to reach their own *oikos*.

4. Believers in the cells of a cell-based church decide they can be a church, independent of the larger celebration gathering. Their pastor has an equip-and-release orientation and is enthusiastic about releasing this new church to the fields. Using LTGs, their relationships are healthy even as the faith community steps out from under her "mother's" wings as a group committed to organic growth and reproduction.

5. The church-planting team encounters numerous Christians who are hungry for real authentic expressions of faith and desire to be witnesses among the lost. These folks join the church planter(s) with renewed enthusiasm and energy directed outward toward the harvest fields. Moving into LTGs with one another and/or people in their *oikos* is an important first step.

6. A person comes to faith in Christ—independent of intentional church-planting effort—and shares that faith with his or her friends. They start meeting and soon several become Christians. Somehow they discover LTGs and start using them among themselves.

7. A group of unchurched Christians in an area find each other and begin meeting regularly, sharing their lives together. Similar to above, they somehow come to understand what an LTG is and begin using this method.[1]

Notes

Preface

1. Neil Cole, *Organic Church: Growing Faith Where Life Happens* (San Francisco: Jossey-Bass, 2005), 216–17.

Between a Rock and a Hard Place

1. It is also called Peter's prison because, well, this is Rome. It is possible that Peter was also in this same prison just prior to his own execution, though he did not write his epistles from there.

2. Neil Cole, *Cultivating a Life for God* (Carol Stream, IL: ChurchSmart Resources, 1999).

Chapter 1 Revealing a Secret Identity

1. Go to http://en.wikipedia.org/wiki/Hero.

2. See Beth Nimmo and Darrell Scott, *Rachel's Tears* (Nashville: Thomas Nelson, 2000), 91–92.

3. When my son, Zach, was fourteen, over a weekend camping together, I taught him five core qualities of becoming a man: initiative, influence, intentionality, integrity, and identity. On a diagram of a hand, each finger represented one of the five qualities.

4. It is a responsible interpretation of the passage to understand that Titus and Crescens have done the same thing, because the verb for each of them is the same one used of Demas. I do not mean that Paul used the same *language* but actually did not use another verb in the sentence. The names Crescens and Titus are dependent on the same verb. In the English sentence, the verb is repeated with Crescens for clarity. Is it possible that even Titus, the recipient of a New Testament letter, has fallen away and deserted his own call? Yes it is. Though some would disagree with my unpopular interpretation, I believe I stand on solid ground. Paul includes Crescens and Titus in his disparaging words about Demas and does not bring them up a few verses later when he is describing in a positive tone those who are sent out to do good things in fulfillment of their call.

5. See Cole, *Organic Church*, xvii–xx.

Chapter 2 Good News Worth Sharing

1. I want to affirm that "Four Spiritual Laws" (a booklet produced by Campus Crusade for Christ and written by Bill Bright in 1965, explaining the need for salvation) is a good tool that has been used across the globe. In fact I accepted Christ after reading through the booklet. But the point of this chapter is that the gospel is more than just the four laws.

2. See, for example, Dallas Willard, *The Divine Conspiracy: Rediscovering Our Hidden Life in God* (New York: HarperCollins, 1998); John Eldredge, *Waking the Dead* (Nashville: Thomas Nelson, 2006); E. Stanley Jones, *Mastery* (Nashville: Abingdon Press, 1955).

3. For more information, see Cole, *Organic Church*.

4. For much more elaboration of what is taking place on university campuses and especially this story of transformation at UCLA, I recommend Jaeson Ma's book *The Blueprint* (Ventura, CA: Regal, 2007).

Chapter 3 Scuba-la Happens

1. Cole, *Cultivating a Life for God*, 41.

2. Charles Colson, *Loving God* (Grand Rapids: Zondervan, 1983), 24–25.

3. Ibid., 25.

Chapter 4 This Is a Job for . . . Me?

1. Charles H. Spurgeon, "Our Omnipotent Leader," *Metropolitan Tabernacle Pulpit* 42 (1896): 229.

Chapter 5 More Powerful Than a Locomotive

1. Walter A. Henrichsen, *Disciples Are Made—Not Born: Making Disciples Out of Christians* (Wheaton, IL: Victor, 1985), 143.

2. Christian A. Schwarz and Christoph Schalk, *Implementation Guide to Natural Church Development* (Carol Stream: ChurchSmart Resources, 2001), 136.

3. Henrichsen, *Disciples Are Made—Not Born*, 142.

4. Ibid.

5. Schwarz and Schalk, *Implementation Guide to Natural Church Development*, 136.

6. Ibid.

7. This was originally a book by Catherine Ryan Hyde (New York: Simon & Schuster, 1999).

8. See www.payitforwardmovement.org.

Chapter 6 The Heart of a Healthy Hero

1. Cole, *Organic Church*, 151–54.

2. James Hudson Taylor, *A Retrospect* (London: Religious Tract Society, 1900).

Chapter 7 Who Needs a Utility Belt?

1. I have found that certain Eastern, shame-based cultures have a tremendously challenging time confessing their sins to one another. Every culture, just as every person, has good qualities reflecting the image of God and ugly qualities reflecting the refuse of sin. The gospel is to redeem the good qualities and transform the bad. It is countercultural by nature. We must not bend to the pressures of an ungodly culture. We can never transform neighborhoods or nations unless we bring change. The very people that the New Testament was written to were mostly an Eastern, shame-based culture. This is hard for some, but still a necessary part of transformative spiritual growth. Many, in a desire to be culturally relevant and sensitive, have lost the countercultural nature of God's kingdom and the gospel itself. We must not bow to the dark strongholds found in every culture.

2. Fritz Rienecker and Cleon Rogers, *Linguistic Key to the Greek New Testament* (Grand Rapids: Zondervan, 1980), 647.

3. Cole, *Organic Church*, 159–69.

4. Ibid., 181–84.

5. You can see a more in-depth explanation of the Universal Disciple Pattern from Thom Wolf at www.universal-disciple.com.

6. Cole, *Organic Church*, 109–21; chapter 8 has a detailed discussion of the New Testament discipleship pattern.

7. The other two parts of the universal pattern are to be filled with the Spirit and Word, which results in loving submission in all our relationships, and then to do battle against spiritual forces with the gospel.

Chapter 9 The Boy Scouts Have It Right

1. The NASB says, "do the work of an evangelist," but I think this translation is not sufficient. I believe that the word *evangelist* should be translated more fully as "one who tells others the Good News," which is what the term *evangelist* literally means. The NASB, KJV, and NIV all seem to make the verse too specific to an office that Timothy is to fulfill, and I think that is stretching the verse too far away from the ordinary Christian and is reading too much of our own professional Christian culture into the verse. The Jerusalem Bible translates this verse as "make the preaching of the Good News your life's work." I like that better.

2. Charles R. Swindoll, *Dropping Your Guard* (Dallas: Word, 1983), 121.

3. Ibid.

Chapter 10 More Than a Catchphrase

1. In reality there are a few false dichotomies that we have accepted in the church to our misfortune. The separation between secular and sacred is one. "To the pure," Paul writes, "all things are pure" (Titus 1:15). The dichotomy between clergy and laity is also a false separation. These paradigms are unhealthy and lead to whole sets of false patterns of thinking and actions that are based on illegitimate beliefs.

2. Jack Canfield and Mark Victor Hansen, *Chicken Soup for the Soul* (Deerfield Beach, FL: Health-Com.Inc, 1991), 27–28.

Part 2 A System for Making and Multiplying Disciples

1. This section contains updated and expanded chapters from a book previously published under the title *Cultivating a Life for God*. All the chapters have been changed to flow with the themes of this book and have also been updated. Two additional chapters have been included that were not previously published. Even if you have read *Cultivating a Life for God*, you will still find this section worth reading.

Chapter 11 Falling into a Powerful Current

1. Much of my story is told in my book *Organic Church*, especially chapters 2 and 13.

2. Robert J. Logan and Neil Cole, *Raising Leaders for the Harvest* (Carol Stream, IL: ChurchSmart Resources, 1995). This resource was a workbook that included tapes (now CDs).

3. All of the resources mentioned in this chapter can be found at www.cmaresource.org under the "resources" page.

Chapter 12 The Value of Simplicity

1. Malcolm Gladwell, *The Tipping Point: How Little Things Can Make a Big Difference* (Boston: Back Bay Books, 2002).

2. Church Multiplication Associates is an association of like-minded churches and church leaders who value starting reproductive churches. Our mission is to produce simple systems that are catalysts in reproducing healthy disciples, leaders, churches, and movements. You can learn more about us at www.cmaresources.org.

3. Thom Wolf, "The Universal Disciple," www.universal-disciple.com.

4. See chapter 7 of Cole, *Organic Church*, 91–105.

Chapter 13 A Tool Easily Passed to Others

1. Pliny, *Letters* 10.96–97, paragraph four of letter 96.

Chapter 14 Instant Access to the Almighty

1. "The word" in this context was not strictly the written Scriptures, though it would certainly include the Old Testament and not at all be contrary to what we have in the New Testament. Obviously, at the time of Luke's writing, the New Testament had not been completed. Perhaps we should understand it as the "message" of God. Today we are privileged to have the Old and New Testaments. In fact we have multiple translations of them ready at our disposal. The message has not changed, and now the Word of God is complete and available to us.

2. George Barna, *Trends That Are Changing Your Ministry World: Current Trends in Culture and Religion*, (Ventura, CA: Gospel Light, 1996).

3. See chapters 8 and 9 of Cole, *Organic Church*, 109–40.

4. John Wesley, quoted in George Hunter, *To Spread the Power: Church Growth in the Wesleyan Spirit* (Nashville: Abingdon, 1987) 56.

5. Hunter, *To Spread the Power*, 58.

6. Barna, *Trends That Are Changing*.

7. Donald Soper, quoted in Robert E. Logan and Thomas Clegg, *Releasing Your Church's Potential* (Carol Stream, IL: ChurchSmart Resources, 1998), 4–10.

8. H. B. London and Neil B. Wiseman, *Pastors at Risk* (Wheaton, IL: Victor, 1993), 120.

9. If you are interested in this subject, here are some great books to read: Roland Allen, *The Spontaneous Expansion of the Church* (Wipf & Stock, 1997) and *Missionary Methods: St. Paul's or Ours* (Eerdmans, 1962); David Garrison, *Church Planting Movements* (Wigtake, 2004); Alan Hirsch, *The Forgotten Ways* (Brazos, 2006); Rad Zdero, ed., *Nexus: The World House Church Movement Reader* (William Carey Library, 2007); Neil Cole, *Organic Church*.

10. Go to http://www.dplnet.com/texasdawnproject/public-downloads/TEXAS_DAWN_PROJ ECT_May_04.pdf.

Chapter 15 The Security of a Trustworthy System

1. Allen, *Spontaneous Expansion of the Church*, 13.

2. Go to www.cmaresources.org/resources/allproducts.asp.

Appendix 1 Sample Character Conversation Questions for Life Transformation Groups

1. D. Michael Henderson, *John Wesley's Class Meetings: A Model for Making Disciples* (Nappanee, IN: Evangel Publishing House, 1997), 118–19.

2. Chuck Colson, *The Body* (Dallas: Word, 1992), 131.

3. James Bryan Smith with Lynda Graybeal, *A Spiritual Formation Workbook: Small Group Resources for Nurturing Christian Growth* (New York: Harper Collins, 1999).

Appendix 3 How LTGs Can Help Start Organic Churches

1. Neil Cole and Paul Kaak, *The Organic Church Planter's Greenhouse Intensive Participant's Workbook* (Signal Hill, CA: CMAResources, 2005), 4-8, 4-9. Paul and I discovered and developed these approaches to starting organic churches with LTGs, and they are part of our Greenhouse trainings, which are offered throughout the year in a variety of settings. You can find upcoming training dates on our website, www.cmaresources.org/greenhouse/happenings.asp.

Illustration Credits

Between a Rock and a Hard Place

Neil on the rocks: Photo courtesy of Erin Cole.
Rocks in big surf: Photo courtesy of Vladi Sytnik. Used by permission.
Mamertine prison: Photos courtesy of Kenneth Fairfax and Rob Wheeler. All rights reserved.

Chapter 1 Revealing a Secret Identity

Wesley, Syshe, and Shuqui Autrey: Source: AP. Used by permission.
Dr. Liviu Librescu: Source: AP. Used by permission.

Chapter 2 Good News Worth Sharing

Surf at Venice pier: Photo courtesy of Rachel Rhodes. All rights reserved.
Lifeguard with rescue can: Photo by David Brittan. Used by permission.

Chapter 6 The Heart of a Healthy Hero

Lenny Skutnik: Photo courtesy of Frank Johnston, the *Washington Post*. Used by permission.
Hole in Kimberley: Photo courtesy of Mo Louw. Used by permission.

Chapter 11 Falling into a Powerful Current

Rip current: Image courtesy of NASA. Used by permission. All rights reserved.

Chapter 12 The Value of Simplicity

Lifeguard on a rescue: Photo courtesy of Dr. James Garza. Used by permission.

Page 238

Current photo of Neil: Photo courtesy of Erin Cole.

Neil Cole is executive director of Church Multiplication Associates. He is also a church planter in Southern California. He is the author of *Organic Church: Growing Faith Where Life Happens, TruthQuest,* and *Cultivating a Life for God.* Neil also coauthored *Beyond Church Planting* and *Raising Leaders for the Harvest* with Robert E. Logan, as well as *The Organic Church Planters' Greenhouse* with Paul Kaak.

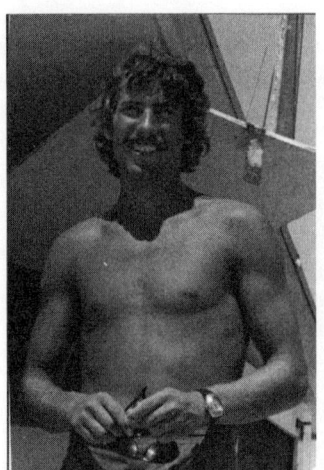

Neil then (left) and now (right).

CMAResources seeks to identify missional principles and reproducible methods that can propagate in a variety of cultures and contexts. We aim to empower ordinary Christians to accomplish extraordinary works with the powerful gifts given by Jesus. All of our resources are focused to that end. We also want to provide a voice to the artists, authors, and pioneers of this new movement.

We believe that any resource worth producing meets the test of the following criteria.

It can be received personally.
It has a profound effect in what it sets out to accomplish.

It can be repeated easily.
It is simple enough that it can easily be passed on in a short encounter.

It can be reproduced strategically.
It can be applied in a variety of cultures and contexts globally.

Our highly scrutinized list of resources helps contribute to seeing church multiplication movements internationally. Resources such as *Cultivating a Life for God*, *Organic Church*, TruthQuest: A Community-Based Doctrinal Discovery System, Life Transformation Group cards, and Organic Church Planters' Greenhouse are all available at CMAResources.

We also offer Greenhouse, which involves practical training, all over the world. Visit our website to find out more about Greenhouse events, where they are being offered, or hosting the training in your own area.

You can also visit our website to order resources, to find information on our training events, or to sign up for our weekly e-newsletter. And don't forget to read newly posted articles dealing with organic church planting.

Please contact us at:

CMAResources
1965 E. 21st Street
Signal Hill, CA 90755

phone: (562) 961-1962
fax: (562) 961-1982
website: www.cmaresources.org

THE FORGOTTEN WAYS:
Reactivating the Missional Church

"When I first read *The Shaping of Things to Come* there was one thing I didn't like about the book—I didn't write it. Now, with *The Forgotten Ways*, Alan has brought us closer to the reality of seeing a true apostolic church-planting movement in the West. This is a seminal work that will change our thinking, our vocabulary, and hopefully our way of being the church in this new century. I have already read the book twice and will probably devour it again."—Neil Cole, author of *Organic Church: Growing Faith Where Life Happens* and *Cultivating a Life for God*

"Among the welter of 'how-to' books calling the church to this new strategy or that, *The Forgotten Ways* is a full-blooded and comprehensive call for the complete reorientation of the church around mission. Nothing less than the rediscovery of a revolutionary missional ecclesiology will do for Alan Hirsch. His book makes an irrefutable case for its establishment and offers the exciting, though frightening, DNA necessary for it to flourish. A master work."—Michael Frost, coauthor of *The Shaping of Things to Come* and author of *Exiles*

Alan Hirsch is the founding director of Forge Mission Training Network. His experience includes mission and church planting to the marginalized as well as leading at the denominational level. He is coauthor of *The Shaping of Things to Come: Innovation and Mission for the 21st-Century Church.*

 BrazosPress

a division of Baker Publishing Group
www.brazospress.com